THIS IS PHOTOGRAPHY

This is

Photography

ITS MEANS AND ENDS

BY

THOMAS H. MILLER

Manager, Photographic Training Department
Eastman Kodak Company

AND

WYATT BRUMMITT

Writer and Editor
Eastman Kodak Company

Published by The Case-Hoyt Corporation for
GARDEN CITY BOOKS, GARDEN CITY, NEW YORK

TO BEGIN WITH..

PHOTOGRAPHY seems so simple. In fact, it is completely simple if you require nothing more of it than casual pleasure and snapshots.

Many of us, naturally, aren't content to stop there. We want to know *why* and *how*.

The moment we become curious, we become vulnerable. We ask questions. And the answers may floor us with their complexity, their strange language, and—above all—their implications of a vast and hitherto unsuspected world of photographic technicalities. Some of us hurriedly retire from photography at this point. But others of us pull ourselves together, breathe deep, and ask, "Now let's have that again, please, and slowly this time."

"This Is Photography" is not a primer. It assumes that you know enough about photography to know that it is not utterly simple. On the other hand, it does not pretend to be a technical encyclopedia.

The *means* of photography are in themselves so absorbing that the *ends* —the pictures we want to produce—are sometimes overshadowed. Naturally, any such book as this must talk about processes and equipment; but the *ends* of photography are our primary concern—in short, better photographs.

With many of the chapters there are experiments. You'll get something out of the mere reading of them, more out of performing them, and still more out of doing them with variations which your own interests may suggest.

Whether used for study or simply read for the enjoyment there may be in it, the ultimate aim of "This Is Photography" is to make you feel at home in photography.

You can be sure of this: Out of your increasing photographic understanding and skill will come a lot of deep personal satisfactions—satisfactions far beyond any you might know were you content to accept photography as the simple thing it seems to be.

T. H. M.

W. B.

CONTENTS

prints can be made from almost any reasonably fair negative. It takes only the "know how."

Because it deals in bigness, because it is an extremely flexible, controllable process, enlarging is the favorite darkroom operation. Enlargers differ—and for very good reasons.

The science of photography is based on the remarkable achievements of workers to whom the jargon of sensitometry is the mother tongue.

If you can alter, under control, the character of the light reaching a film, you can achieve some remarkable and useful results.

Light and color are inseparable, yet color photography has not been easily achieved. Two basic procedures have been developed.

To make the most of color photography you need, first, to understand the nature and the language of color; after that, it's a matter of applying what you know.

Some depend on them entirely; others scorn them. And both groups are missing something.

It's a picture if it makes sense—and if it makes sense it's almost certain to be the result of a little attention to what the artists call "composition."

With all outdoors to picture, the photographer is sometimes embarrassed by the richness of his opportunities.

With a nod to Mr. Einstein, it is suggested that relativity applies to the fine art of picturing action.

Artificial lighting for photography, it appears, is also something of a science. It can be applied to your picture making, however, without recourse to slide rule or log tables.

People are popular with practically all photographers, but not all photographers are popular with people. How to be a popular photographer.

There's more than meets the eye in the production of many a picture.

It's when photography casts off its smock and rolls up its sleeves that it becomes not only interesting, but important.

Dedicated to the proposition that if pictures are worth making they are worth using—and in more than one way.

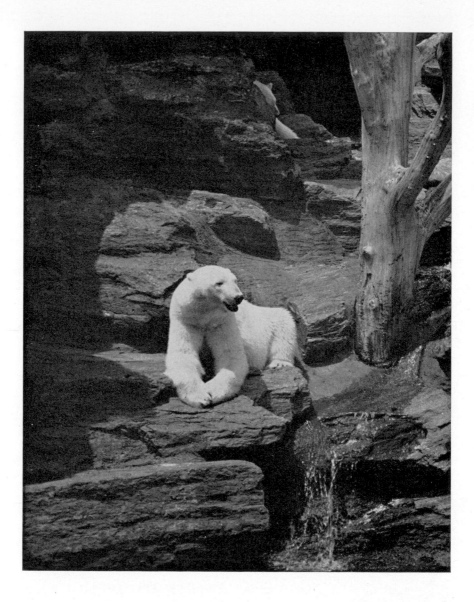

. . . as Johnny saw it

CHAPTER 1

You and Your Camera

STARTING right now, practically every word within these covers concerns *pictures* and the photographic means of producing them. Under the circumstances, it seems fairly reasonable that we decide, at the start, what a picture is.

Well, the cavemen drew pictures on the walls of their caves. Michelangelo painted pictures in the Sistine Chapel, Griffith lined up a million or so snapshots on a movie film to picture *The Birth of a Nation*, and Johnny Whoozis made a Brownie snap of a polar bear at the zoo last Saturday.

In each case, the picture served as a more or less vivid form of communication. With his wall-scrawlings the caveman told his friends and descendants something of contemporary natural history as he saw it; with his frescoes Michelangelo told the world something of his religion; and with his snapshot Johnny tells all who will pause and behold that he saw a bear at the zoo the other day.

But there's more than mere communication involved. Even Johnny's polar bear snapshot is more than a mere factual record. It is not the same as a printed sign saying, "Bear:" It is the bear *as Johnny saw it*. And its success as a picture depends on the point of view Johnny selected, on the kind of light there was, on the angle of the light, and on the degree to which the finished print puts the emphasis on the bear.

But of all those factors, none is as vital as the personal factor summed up in the phrase, "*as Johnny saw it*." Putting it more directly, you are the most important part of any camera you will ever use. Despite the fact that photography is a scientific affair based on a fascinating lot of physics, chemistry, and mechanics, the real satisfactions of photography depend on your eyes, your imagination, and your mastery of photographic processes.

Photography is an intimate, intensely personal thing. Your use of it expresses you, characterizes you as certainly as does your handwriting, your manner of speech, or the friends you choose.

That's why millions find such deep pleasure in photography; we are all at our best when we are responding to an inner hunch to create, to build. Some people satisfy this urge by writing, some by cabinet work, some by making music, some by painting, some by tinkering with the car, and so on. In photography many different creative skills are involved, from a discerning, picture-wise way of looking at things to a mastery of the tricks of enlarging. And it's fun all the way.

But, no matter how involved you may become with the technique of photography, keep in mind the central fact that every bit of technique has only one real function—to give you, ultimately, a photograph which will be a permanent record of something you saw, something you looked at and enjoyed in your own, individual way.

In other words, don't mistake *means* for *ends*. That is the fatal mistake of the misguided gadgeteer who is always sure he'll make a picture *someday*—when he gets another gadget. Someday never comes.

YOUR EYE AND YOUR CAMERA

In most respects, a camera is a pretty good imitation of the human eye. Your camera may be a battered veteran, a survival from earlier, more reckless days; or it may be a shiny new creation, equipped with the latest and best in lens, shutter, and all the gadgets so dear to the hearts of many. But, old or new, simple or complex, it is still a mechanical approximation of an eye.

Here are simple diagrams of an eye and camera. The eye is, essentially, a little enclosed chamber with a lens at one end and a light-sensitive area at the other. The lens gathers rays of light from the scene at which the eye is looking, and transmits those rays, nicely organized, back to the sensitive area. By a complex system of nerve reactions the image, formed by the rays of light on the retina of the eye, is wire-photoed to the brain.

In a camera, much the same business goes on. The glass lens is like the eye's lens. Instead of the retina, there's a light-sensitive film or plate, on which the image is recorded. When the film is developed—a fascinating bit of chemical sleight-of-hand—the image is there for you to see and to use in making one or thousands of prints.

Naturally, this is a sketchy outline of the photographic miracle, but it should suffice to stress the point that an eye and a camera are very similar.

But there are extremely important *dis*similarities. And an appreciation of them is the beginning of wisdom, as far as photography is concerned.

First, never forget that the camera is, after all, only a mechanism—devoid of sense or imagination. It may cost a thousand dollars, but it is just as dumb as a fistfull of mud. It is more dependent on you than a brand new baby on its doting mother. Your camera can "see" only as you allow it to see; it cannot take matters into its own hands and balk at attempting something that's inane or impossible. It is your unquestioning, totally submissive slave. So the responsibility is entirely yours.

Second, there's the fact that, in seeing, you use a kind of visual shorthand, whereas your patient camera takes everything within its ken in laborious, literal longhand. For example, you see a friend on the street. On the basis of a quick glance which possibly includes a scanning of his face, his expression, and the way he walks, your mind completes the picture. "Good old George," your mind says, "George, who has a nose he busted playing tackle for dear old Siwash; George, who still owes me five

The camera "sees" indiscriminately . . . the eye sees selectively.

11

bucks; George, who has a dancer tattooed on his right arm; George, who drives a Buick . . ." and so on.

But your camera, being dumb, goes at George in a strictly impersonal, objective way. It pays as much attention to the wrinkle at the hem of George's coat as it does to George's amiable eyes.

You can sense something of the camera's point of view when you find yourself, overnight, in a totally strange place. You see details you never bother to observe at home; at home, things are so familiar that you take them for granted, merely checking now and then on some particular detail. The camera is always a stranger; it takes nothing for granted.

It appears, then, that the most important thing about your camera is not its similarity to your eye, but its dependence on you, on your appreciation of the visible world, on your ability to pick out scenes which your camera can convert into good pictures. It's trite but, in the manner of most trite things, true that a box camera in the hands of a good photographer will produce pictures far superior to those made with the best camera in the world operated by someone with neither imagination nor skill.

So, develop your own sense of seeing. Look at things. A casual glance isn't enough. Get the habit of scanning a scene, appreciating its qualities. For, unless you do enjoy what you see, unless you get an honest bounce out of the beauties, the ironies, the design of the visible world, you can't expect your camera to give you any but lack-lustre pictures. If you delight in seeing, there's a grand chance that you'll make really fine pictures.

Then, backing up your ability really to *see* with a sound appreciation of the technique of photography, you will make the fine pictures which, today, may seem beyond your reach.

Look about you. You'll find pictures where you least expect them.

CHAPTER 2

Which Camera?

"I AM ABOUT to buy a camera. Which one do you advise?"

This question is Old Faithful. It never fails. In letters to camera makers, in conversations with camera counter clerks, and with anyone else suspected of harboring photographic information, it is bound to emerge, sooner or later. And the askers ask in good faith; for there are hundreds of cameras on the market, and to select one from the many may be bewildering.

But, as it stands, it's a question that cannot be specifically answered. Before an answer can even be approximated, a number of counter-questions must be asked. To wit:

> What do you want to do with photography?
> What do you expect photography to do for you?
> Do you want snapshots for an album? Or do you plan to go in for exhibition prints?
> Is color your first interest? Color in transparencies for screen projection? Color in prints and enlargements?
> Do you plan to do your own developing, etc?
> Do you require a pocket-sized camera?
> Do you want to be able to make extreme close-ups?
> Architectural subjects?
> Do you want a lot of adjustments and controls, or few of them?
> And, ahem, how much money do you plan to spend?

In basic principle all cameras are much alike, whether they cost five or five hundred dollars. Then why the "spread" in prices?

There are three prime points on which cameras differ. The first is the lens, which is usually the most costly single component of any camera.

A "simple" and a complex lens; one costs little, the other much.

A good small lens made of a single piece of glass, ground and polished to conform to a simple formula, can be turned out easily and in quantity. But a fine lens is an achievement, involving many carefully made and assembled elements. It may, alone, cost hundreds of dollars.

Then There's the Shutter

In the average inexpensive camera the shutter is a simple flap, swung back and forth across the aperture by a wire spring. It has only one speed. A second general type of shutter, is the complex spring-winding shutter, with a precision gear train capable of giving a series of reasonably exact different timings, including, in some cases, a fascinating one-second exposure, a seemingly long second full of gentle whirring noises. This type is usually mounted between the elements of the lens; if the workmanship is good, it is worthy of the finest camera. The third type is that of the focal plane shutter—a shutter located in the back of the camera, as close as possible to the focal plane where the film is. Focal plane shutters work in a manner similar to window blinds. For the exposure, a slitted curtain is drawn across the focal plane. By varying the width of the slit and the tension of the spring mechanism, a wide variety of exposure times can be obtained.

High shutter speeds are not essential unless your first concern is stopping rapid action. However, high speeds do overcome the hazard of camera motion during the exposure. The more you wish to enlarge your picture, the more important this becomes.

Third among the major points on which cameras differ is the view finder. On inexpensive cameras it may not be absolutely accurate; but it does show you a view which conforms approximately with the actual field embraced by the camera. Usually, there's no harm done by this slight discrepancy. But for precise work an accurate view finder is essential, and an accurate view finder is an optical instrument. It runs into money. There are direct-vision view finders, with and without lenses; there are wire frame finders for fast, not-too-exact work; there are reflex finders using either the camera lens itself or a similar lens to project an image of the view, periscope fashion, up to a hooded ground glass. Then there is the straight lens-to-ground-glass arrangement, where the image is seen directly as focused by the lens.

Now, let's look at the different general kinds of cameras to see what they have to offer. First, and dearest to the hearts of our childhood is:

The Box Camera

And we'll tolerate no condescension, if you please. For the box camera, in its simplicity, in its remarkable capability, achieves greatness. It minimizes picture-making technicalities by operating in terms of averages—average shutter speed, average lens aperture, average focus, and so on. It is not meant for specialized work. Offhand, it is impossible to think of any everyday parallel to the box camera; no other single bit of equipment combines so much creative zest with so little fuss.

The box camera is basic, and it is complete, as far as it goes. It consists of a small light-tight box with a lens and shutter at one end, and film at the other. Controls are reduced to the perfect minimum. The one shutter speed is usually something between 1/25 and 1/50 second. There is one lens aperture. There is no focus to bother with. You merely load, aim, fire.

Box cameras make remarkably good pictures. Being fixed-aperture, fixed focus, fixed-speed cameras, however, they cannot be expected to master every photographic situation. Extreme close-ups, action shots, precision shots requiring maximum lens corrections, shots in bad light—all such work is beyond the proper sphere of box cameras.

The lenses in box cameras aren't intended for making pictures under adverse lighting conditions or for extreme enlargement. They are simple little affairs, made of good quality glass and finished to considerable precision. Still, when you consider that the retail sale price of the average box camera is somewhere in the neighborhood of five dollars, it's hardly reasonable to expect the lens to be a masterpiece.

Some accessories, such as close-up lens attachments and provision for photoflash, expand the box camera's usefulness. And variations in the basic idea—a better lens with variable aperture and focus—so enlarge the box's

15

scope that it becomes a remarkably versatile camera, a box camera *plus*. The Kodar Lens model of the Kodak Duaflex II is such a camera.

The box camera is ideal for youngsters and for other photographic beginners, no matter what their age. Since it keeps the emphasis on photographic ends rather than means, it is valuable to those who are tentatively feeling their way toward the mastery of photography. Indeed, it is a good thing even for experts to revert to box cameras once in a while. The experience tends to restore their sense of proportion—the sense which comes closest to that other invaluable but indefinable sense, the sense of humor.

So, do not underrate the box camera. Use it. Enjoy it. And, outgrow it!

The Folding Camera

Because there are so many different cameras within this category, we could wish for a more specific type name. But, outside of trade names, there is none available.

The simplest, most inexpensive folding camera is nothing in the world but a box camera with an accordion-pleated bellows replacing the box. It costs somewhat more because the construction is trickier, but lens, shutter, and view finder are quite the same. Picture sizes vary from about $1\frac{5}{8}$ x $2\frac{1}{4}$ inches to $3\frac{1}{4}$ x $5\frac{1}{2}$ inches.

From there on up the price scale, the folding camera involves increasingly elaborate variations on the basic theme. Lenses get better, focusing adjustments appear, shutters increase in complexity and precision but remain in the camera front, and view finders become more accurate.

At the top of the folding camera bracket are those with fast, well-corrected lenses which permit both black-and-white and color snapshots even under adverse light conditions. Their shutter speeds of 1/800 can stop most action. Practically any modern folding camera can be equipped with an accessory flash outfit; indeed flash is an assumed accessory in all present-day picture making.

The Miniature (35-mm.) Camera

Back in the '30's there appeared a new type of camera, the miniature. Originally, its claims to fame were based on the facts that (1) it used short lengths of 35-mm. motion picture film, (2) it usually had a fast, short-focus lens that permitted picture making under the most unlikely conditions, and (3) it was a precisely engineered mechanism. Too, because many and fascinating accessories were provided for it, it became the

A modern box camera

Simple reflex-type camera

Classic folding camera

"Economy" miniature

Miniature with high quality

Continental style miniature

favorite of gadgeteers.

But the miniature's appeal changed and broadened vastly when Koda-chrome film was made available for 35-mm. cameras. The whole plan, which involved the color processing and return of the customer's film in little slides suitable for projection, ushered in a new kind of personal photography.

Picture making was, to the miniaturist, no darkroom matter, for the color film manufacturer took care of the delicate processes involved. The camera owner was left to concentrate on the use of a fine, precise piece of mechanism. With it he recorded any colorful scene that delighted or interested his eyes. And later, when his processed films were returned, he could project them on a screen, big as life and just about as brilliant.

Thus the miniature came to have special appeal to travelers, to teachers and lecturers, to business people, to specialists in any of the professions and arts.

The first miniatures came out of Europe, and some are still produced there. But today America is making more miniatures than is Europe. And the quality of many of our cameras is unbeatable. In lenses, particularly, the old idea that real quality was to be found only in imports has been cancelled out.

In an effort to retain high quality but at a reasonable price, designers have used new kinds of plastics—and in precise mechanisms that aren't at all in the cheap toy class.

The modern miniature camera, in the 35-mm. format, usually loads with magazines or cassettes of film sufficient for 20 or 36 exposures. Each frame measures 24x36-mm., or about $1 \times 1\frac{7}{16}$ inches. Lens equipment is rarely slower than $f/4.5$; $f/3.5$ is fairly general and even $f/2$ is encountered once in a while. Happily enough, the short focal length of these lenses assures great depth of field even at wide apertures. Many present-day miniatures have provision for precise range finding, with lens focus coupled to the range finder. A miniature has to be really good, for the pictures it produces must be capable of great enlargement, either on a projection screen or as color enlargements.

Very similar to the 35-mm. miniature is the so-called "Pony 828," a specialty of the Kodak Company. This is a true miniature in every respect, the only difference being in the fact that each film loading gives eight exposures, and each frame measures 28×40-mm., roughly $1\frac{1}{8} \times 1\frac{5}{8}$ inches.

The 828 format has another asset: Kodacolor film is spooled for use in such cameras, and with Kodacolor your end product is a print, not a transparency. And, despite the small size of the Kodacolor negative, your print is full album size, on the order of $3 \times 4\frac{1}{2}$ inches.

Of course color film is not the only film used in miniatures, but the number of miniaturists who stick to black-and-white—except for the most workaday jobs—is decreasing rapidly. Color is really the miniature's *raison d'être*, even if it did come along some years after the little cameras came into being.

With color film, and especially the little color transparencies, there has come a great assortment of accessories. Projectors for screen presentations, table and hand viewers for close-up enjoyment, screens, files, special lenses and lens attachments—these and many more products are available to increase the miniaturist's pleasure in his camera.

Incidentally, the miniature has produced a brilliant flashback to the days of the parlor stereoscope. With either a special miniature camera, or an attachment, you can produce stereoscopic pictures for viewing in a small transparency holder. Obviously, such a system is, at least for the present, limited to one-person-at-a-time viewing.

To sum up, the miniature camera is today predominantly a color camera and its use is no longer limited to advanced and fanatical photographers. It repays careful and intelligent use, but does not demand great skill.

Camera Capabilities

It is impossible—or inadvisable, at any rate—to establish arbitrary limits for the capability of any camera, no matter how simple. But here is a highly condensed classification of camera capabilities in terms of standard lens and shutter equipment. No accessories are assumed. Naturally, the finer cameras embrace all the abilities of humbler equipment.

Simple, fixed-focus cameras for average snapshots.

f/6.3 lens, 1/200 shutter—snaps by Photofloods, moderate action.

f/4.5 lens and 1/400 shutter—many stage shots, most sports.

"Ultra" lens and shutter—poorly lighted or high speed shots.

Twin Lens Reflex Cameras

Among the most popular modern cameras is the twin lens reflex, which embodies a viewing lens and a taking lens, geared together so that an object *viewed* in focus is in focus for the picture making, too. Such cameras have become almost standard equipment for press and illustration work, partly because of their easy adaptability to varied jobs and partly because they are relatively compact and rugged.

As a rule, the twin lens reflex is strictly a quality camera, with superior optical and mechanical equipment. Picture format is usually 2¼ inches square, to give 12 exposures per roll of film. And such film, color or black-and-white, usually coded as 620 or 120, is available wherever film is sold.

Single Lens Reflex Cameras

The classic example in this field is, of course, the Graflex—a formidable but wonderful camera lugged around for a whole generation of press photographers. Generally they referred to it, with deep affection, as "the ole doghouse."

In the Graflex, as in all single lens reflexes, the trick, as the saying goes, is done with mirrors. For focus and view-finding, the photographer inspects a hooded ground glass on which appears the image as forward passed from the lens by a mirror, set at 45° within the camera.

When the instant for exposure arrives, the release *first* whips the mirror up out of the way and *then* operates the shutter. Obviously, best viewing is done with the lens at full aperture; just as obviously the best pictures are seldom so made. So either the operator or an integral mechanism has to shift the lens diaphragm to the desired aperture just prior to the exposure. Or, you can view-find with the aperture pre-set for the right exposure; veterans do it, and skillfully, too.

Because viewing is done through the taking lens, the shutter must be back of the mirror. The usual solution is a focal plane shutter, a type with which high speed is readily attained.

In general, single lens reflex cameras produce negatives 2¼ x 3¼, 3¼ x 4¼, 4 x 5, or 5 x 7 inches in size, using film pack or sheet film. Some are designed for 620 or 120 roll film; a very few are miniatures. Provision for synchronized flash is, of course, a modern necessity, and is incorporated in most reflexes.

Press Cameras

As has been indicated, the Graflex was for a long time *the* press camera. In recent years, however, the field has broadened materially. Photojournalism itself has changed. The advent and universal use of photoflash has shifted the burden of obtaining speedy exposures from the camera to the flash lamp, with the duration of light as the determining factor.

A true, twin-lens reflex   A reflex camera, the Graflex

The Speed Graphic   A versatile view camera

So, today, photojournalists will be found using several kinds of cameras.

The Speed Graphic, a brother of the Graflex, is as nearly a trade standard as any. It is usually seen in its 4 x 5 format, complete with flash synchronizer and, very often, with flash extension or "slave" unit to afford side as well as frontal lighting. The Graphic has two shutters, one between the lens elements and the other at the focal plane. When the front shutter is used the other must, of course, be in open position, and vice versa. With the Graphic and similar cameras it is possible, if time permits, to do critical viewing in a ground glass; otherwise an optical range finder is used or, in emergencies, a sports finder, which is simply a combination of a peephole and a wire frame.

A press camera without a good lens would be an anachronism, a Rolls-Royce with a scooter motor. Hence, you'll find press camera lenses are generally top quality, coated, and rated at $f/4.5$ or better. Graphics are usually equipped to take film packs or sheet film.

Many press men and magazine illustrators favor twin-lens reflexes, a few cling to miniatures. The increasing use of color in magazine articles puts a premium on films and processes from which good four-color engravings can be made. Hence a professional photographer selects camera and accessories which will work best with the kind of process a specific publication prefers.

View and Studio Cameras

The time-honored spectacle of a bulky camera on a tripod, with a man behind it, half hidden under a black cloth, is the trade mark of all view and studio cameras. They are intended for serious, deliberate work, and, as such, are often recommended for students in photography.

The view camera differs from other cameras in that it can be adapted easily for use with a wide variety of lenses, in its great bellows extension, in the fact that the ground glass is its only view finder, and in its adjustments which permit correction or distortion of perspective. Usually, the lens is stopped way down for maximum depth and detail, and the shutter time often runs into several seconds or even minutes. It loads with either sheet film or plates.

Once you have a reasonably good camera, concentrate on it. Study it. Read all that its makers have written about it. If your camera is a really good one, it can serve you faithfully for many years and, in its potential capability, continue to inspire and lead you on.

CHAPTER 3

Lenses

No LIGHT—NO PICTURE. This is a photographic fundamental which we sometimes forget. We tend to become preoccupied with new processes, new fast films, and new, faster lenses. Very naturally, we feel that light doesn't matter and that the day will soon come when we can make pictures in complete darkness. That day is infinitely remote, however, for without light of some sort (light which may even be invisible, as far as our eyes are concerned) there can be no photograph.

Since light, then, is the basis, the without-which-nothing of photography, it seems reasonable to consider the nature of it, and the way it behaves.

Light is one of a large group of energy-types, all of which travel radially from their points of origin, in waves. For the simplest form of radial wave action, consult your nearest swimming pool. Drop a pebble into the middle of it, and watch the waves spread, in expanding circles, until they reach the edge of the pool. But waves of this type are slow and clumsy compared to waves on which, for example, sound is carried through the air. And sound waves are slow compared to the waves on which radio impulses are carried. Light waves travel at the same speed as those of radio impulses, but they have a different wave-length classification.

It is in this difference of wave length that light achieves its personality, its visibility. Radio wave lengths, for example, are long, measured from the crest of one wave to the crest of the next. The ordinary broadcast wave lengths run from 545 meters to about 187 meters long, with special short wave transmissions traveling on waves as short as 10 centimeters, or about 4 inches.

But light waves are vastly shorter, beginning at .00008 cm. with the deepest visible red light and winding up at .00004 cm. for the point where violet merges into ultraviolet. Of even shorter lengths than ultraviolet waves are the X-rays, the Gamma Rays, and radiation associated with Cosmic Rays.

SHORT WAVELENGTHS				1 CM.	LONG WAVELENGTHS

| COSMIC RAYS | GAMMA RAYS | X-RAYS | ULTRA-VIOLET RAYS | INFRA RED OR HEAT RAYS | HERTZIAN WAVES | WAVES USED IN RADIO BROADCASTING |

VISIBLE LIGHT

In the whole spectrum of radiation, visible light occupies a very thin section. And it will undoubtedly become relatively thinner as we learn more and more about ultra-long and ultra-short waves. But thin as that slice is, it is all-important.

Because light and radio waves have a family resemblance, you can think of your camera as a kind of receiver—an optical radio set designed to capture and reproduce light rays. But there's no need to complicate photography by elaborating on this parallelism; it is in the special qualities of light, in its own peculiar behavior, that photographers are interested.

Here Are Five Basic Generalities About Light:

1. Light waves travel in straight lines; they travel in an infinite number of straight lines radiating out from any specific point of origin.

2. Light can be deflected or reflected, as by a mirror. And the rule of Physics I, that "the angle of reflection equals the angle of incidence," holds comfortingly true.

3. Light can be bent (refracted) and sent off on a new path by a prism, a fact relied on in designing lenses.

4. Light can be absorbed. A piece of black felt, for example, absorbs most and reflects a minimum of light, whereas a shiny white surface reflects a maximum, absorbing only a little light.

5. Light can be systematically filtered, so that some of its component qualities are absorbed and the rest passed on, unaltered.

Photography makes use of all of these characteristics. For example, photography is concerned—just as our eyes are concerned—primarily with light which has been reflected (No. 2 in the list) and absorbed in varying degrees (No. 4). We are seldom interested either in looking

24

at or picturing a light *source* such as the sun or an arc-lamp; our concern is with the light from that source which has been reflected by an object or a scene. On the degree to which an object reflects and absorbs light depends its visibility. In complete darkness you cannot see a sheet of white paper held in your hands. It's invisible, for there is no light for it to reflect. Turn on a light, and the paper instantly becomes visible, reflecting light generously, with just enough absorption to give you a good idea of its texture. Photography, like the sense of sight, is almost exclusively concerned with light which has been reflected, refracted, absorbed and otherwise affected.

Nowhere, however, is the application of these fundamentals more interesting than in the lens—the lens which is the most important single component of your camera.

It's important but not, oddly enough, wholly indispensable. We *could* struggle along without lenses, but it would be a fearful struggle and photography as we know it today simply would not exist.

Pictures Through a Pinhole

Ever hear of a pinhole camera? It's a little box, very much like a Brownie camera in shape, but it has no lens in the front of it. Instead, there's a fine, clean pinhole. With such a camera it is entirely possible to make pictures. Here's how. With a piece of film in place inside the back of the camera, the little box is placed on a tripod, aimed at any subject which will stand still for a while, and the pinhole uncovered. An exposure of several minutes is usually required. During those moments this is what goes on.

Waves of light "broadcast" from, for example, a pair of automobile headlights, enter that pinhole and, continuing in straight lines, go on back to the light-sensitive film. Almost an infinite number of rays from these lamps strike the front of the camera, but all are excluded except one from each point in the source. These admitted rays cross one another while passing through the pinhole. Thus, rays from the right are imaged on the left side of the film and vice versa, and the image is inverted.

At the end of a fairly long exposure, possibly several minutes, the camera is closed and the film developed. You'll have an image—a pretty good image, too. It won't be as sharp as a good snapshot, but it won't be too bad.

The trouble, of course, is that you need to let more light into the

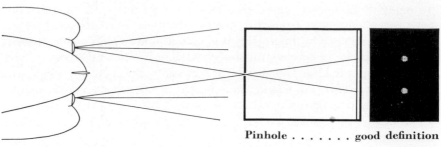

Pinhole . . . . good definition

AUTOMOBILE

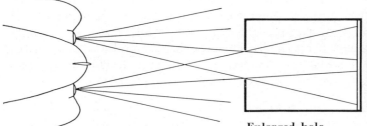

Enlarged hole . . . . no definition

camera and thereby cut down the exposure time. If, however, you enlarge the pinhole to permit more light to enter, you further decrease your sharpness because you get a little cone of light from every point in the scene. The cones from neighboring points overlap, and you get a really first-class blur. The illustrations above compare the possible and impossible of pinhole photography.

The pinhole camera is a pleasant little scientific novelty, but it simply will not suffice for modern photography. A lens is needed to admit more light and to control it.

The specific characteristic relied on in designing a lens is that light is bent or *refracted* as it passes from air to glass, or glass to air. An extreme close-up view of refraction may serve to clarify its significance.

Here an enlarged light ray traveling in air approaches glass, where it is destined to be slowed down because glass is more dense than air. Because the ray is approaching the glass at an angle, one side of it will strike sooner than the other, hence will be slowed down while the other side continues unimpeded for a while. This uneven "pull" on the ray changes its direction. It's much like an automobile with faulty brakes. When the brakes grab hold on one side before the other, the car swerves to the side first slowed down.

Now, once the light ray is wholly in the glass, it continues on a new straight line course through the new medium. When the light emerges from the other side, when, as it were, the brakes are released, light automatically speeds up to its usual rate of air travel, 186,000 miles per second. One side of the wave front, because it is released first, gets ahead and pulls the whole ray around into the new direction.

By changing the slants of the glass surfaces, the side of the ray emerging first, the side exerting "pull" on the ray, may be controlled. Light passing through a prism, then, would run as indicated below.

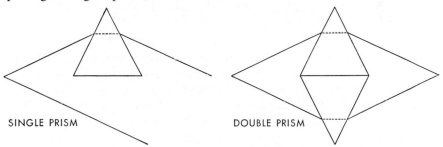

SINGLE PRISM   DOUBLE PRISM

But now take two prisms and put them base to base. And look what happens. Along comes a second ray of light from the same point entering the lower prism. The bending action of the prism sends those light rays on so that they again come together.

Now, having gone that far, take the next obvious step. Get a lens maker to make, in a single piece of glass, a complete circle of prisms, all base to base. And the combination of a practically infinite number of prisms, all ground to a scientific nicety, gives a vastly greater convergence of light rays from any one point. If there's a film at that meeting place, we gain by the impact of much more light than we had in the pinhole camera, which could accommodate only one ray from any one point. Obviously, then, we need no long exposure, as with the pinhole camera; for we are blessed with vastly more light falling onto our film.

27

That's a tremendous step ahead, but it doesn't quite solve the whole problem.

The very fact that a lens is accurately made so that it bends light in a very definite, predetermined way introduces a new problem—the problem of focus. As long as the subject being photographed is at a certain, specific distance, and so long as the lens-to-film distance coincides with the plane in which the lens brings light rays together, all is well. But when either of those distances is changed, trouble arises.

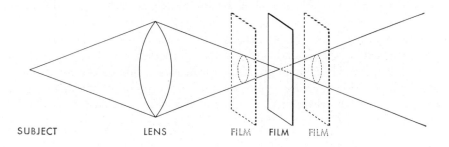

SUBJECT   LENS   FILM   FILM   FILM

Here's what happens when the lens-to-film distance is changed. Light rays from any point in the pictured scene are converged, by the action of the lens, so that they approach the film in a cone-shaped formation. Obviously, if the rays encounter the film in front of or beyond the place where they all come to a point, the resulting image will be a circle—a cross-section of the cone-shaped formation. This circle is called, in photography, the *circle of confusion*, and a better, more down-to-earth name would be hard to find. For, when the rays from millions of points in a pictured scene are imaged on the film not as points but as little over-lapping circles, confusion is what you get.

Much the same situation arises when the lens-to-subject distance is changed while the lens-film distance remains unaltered. For the angle between the paths of a ray of light as it enters and leaves a lens is prac-tically the same, no matter what the distance may be between the source of that ray and the lens.

The lens, in a physical sense, acts as a sort of pivot or fulcrum for the complete, subject-to-focal-point travel of the ray. Therefore, the closer the subject, the farther back the point of convergence; and the farther the subject, the nearer the converging point.

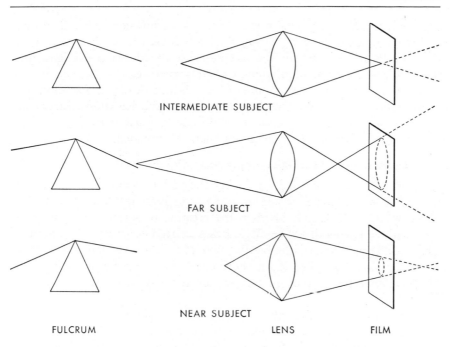

INTERMEDIATE SUBJECT

FAR SUBJECT

NEAR SUBJECT

FULCRUM   LENS   FILM

Obviously, then, if the film is placed at the converging point for rays from one subject distance, as in the top sketch, objects at considerably greater or shorter distances will be imaged as circles of confusion instead of points.

Box cameras have small lenses and produce their best results when used to picture objects about 15 feet away. In manufacture, the lens-to-film distance in the box is adjusted for pictures at this distance. Obviously, points imaged on the film from other distances should appear as circles of confusion. And they do, but the circles are so tiny that the average user of this type of camera doesn't mind. They are tiny because the lens is so small that there is very little difference in the angles of light striking the lens from points 15, 25, 50, or 100 feet from the camera.

With large-lens cameras, this fixed adjustment is impossible. If a camera with a large lens were focused for pictures at 15 feet, attempts to picture objects at 50 feet would be utter failures.

Therefore some means has had to be devised to make the lens-to-film distance variable, so light rays from any specific distance can be con-

29

verged on the film as points, not as circles of confusion. This, in short, is what is meant by *focusing a camera*. On a track or screw threads, you move the lens in or out for the sole purpose of adjusting the lens-film relationship to meet the requirements of your picture.

For close-ups you need maximum lens-to-film distance; for shots of distant objects, beyond a hundred feet or so, the lens-film distance is considerably less. Thus, by mounting the lens so that it can be moved, a solution to the problem of accurate focus is provided.

The Modern Lens Is a Masterpiece of Precision

Important research carried on during the past few years has produced a means of minimizing flare and of actually increasing the light-transmitting properties of glass. It involves the treating of interior air-glass surfaces with a chemical. Naturally, it has started scientists off on new researches which will undoubtedly produce other refinements before long. The fine modern lens is a masterpiece of precision, but there is every indication that the lens of tomorrow, or the day after, will be a still finer thing.

By the way, if you've grown up with the old inferiority-complex notion that American-made lenses aren't as good as lenses made abroad, you'd better get rid of it. It simply isn't true. Our country's leadership in both lens and glass making has now become a well established fact. The Eastman Kodak Company, for example, has a radically new optical glass of a rare-element type. It is made from compounds of tantalum, tungsten, and lanthanum, and contains little or no silica, the basic component of other optical glasses. It is distinguished by its very high refractive index (light-bending power) and by low dispersion (spreading of the individual colors). Most of the advances in lens making have been made possible by the application of new kinds of glass, often differing only in a small degree from previous types. Even in the relatively short time it has been available to lens designers, this new glass has led to the production of lenses superior to any known before.

A LENS FOR YOUR CAMERA

The business of fitting a lens to a camera is not at all haphazard. It must be done with considerable care; otherwise the result could be grotesque— as grotesque as a light car fitted with a submarine Diesel engine.

The two major characteristics of a lens, the characteristics which give

30

the photographer the fundamental facts he must have before he starts to use a lens, are its focal length and its *f*-rating.

Focal Length (F) is almost a self-defining phrase. It means, simply, the distance from the lens to the plane (called the focal plane) where approaching parallel rays of light are brought to a point by the lens, so that a sharp image is formed.

←— INFINITY

(Lens simplified
for illustration)

F=FOCAL LENGTH

Since all rays of light approaching a lens from a point at infinity are parallel, the focal length is the distance of the image from the lens when the subject is at infinity. Even though focused on a close-up subject or completely removed from the camera, the lens' focal length never changes, for it is a result of the fundamental design to which the lens was ground.

A camera is generally fitted with a lens having a focal length roughly equal to the diagonal of the film to be used in that camera. The diagonal of a 2¼ x 3¼ film is slightly less than 4 inches; hence, most 2¼ x 3¼ cameras are equipped with 4-inch lenses. Some cameras are sold without lenses. In such cases, selection of the right lenses becomes a responsibility of the purchaser. So, remember the "rule of the diagonal."

Perspective

A word about perspective—the apparent relation between objects, as to position and distance, as seen from any given viewpoint. Lenses of differing focal lengths give you the same perspective but, because they vary in the area they cover, they create a different effect. The longer the focal length of a lens, the narrower its field of view. Yet if you enlarge a negative made with a short focus lens and limit its field of view to that of the

31

Exaggeration, by means of short and long focal length lenses.

longer focus lens, the pictures appear to have the same perspective. Thus, when using a camera with interchangeable lenses, you will find that the longer focal length lenses tend to shorten distances and dimensions in the direction in which the camera is pointed. Shorter focus lenses exaggerate distances and dimensions making near-by objects appear disproportionately large. For these reasons, the normal focal length is always best unless the desirable properties of the other lenses are needed. The short focal length lenses give you wide angles of view which are useful when photographing in cramped quarters, while long local length lenses enable you to make full-frame pictures of small objects at considerable distances.

The second major basis on which a lens is rated is that of its *f-number* —f/8 for example. It is a scientific way of stating a relationship which exists between the lens' opening and its focal length—and on this relationship depends the intensity of the light falling onto the film. Such a system

$$f/ = \frac{F}{d}$$

provides a common standard for exposure calculations, with all cameras and under all conditions.

There has been a lot of quite needless worry about $f/$, due, in part, to the fact that it looks vaguely like one of those abstract symbols so dear to the hearts of higher mathematicians. Here is the simple truth. The symbol f stands for focal length; the diagonal bar indicates a fraction, and the numeral beyond the bar gives you that fraction. An $f/8$ lens is one whose widest effective aperture has a diameter which measures ⅛ of its focal length. Obviously, an $f/4$ lens of the same focal length has an effective lens diameter twice as great as that of an $f/8$ lens. If the diameter is twice as great, the area is four times as great at $f/4$ as $f/8$; therefore, to achieve identical exposures only ¼ the time is required at $f/4$ as at $f/8$. In photographic language $f/4$ is "faster," and by four times.

It is important to look on this f business in an amiable way. With f as an unmysterious factor, you can make a lot of headway toward the understanding of photography, for f is important not only in the making of ordinary pictures but also in the use of special lenses, in enlarging, in the projection of slides, and in every operation involving a lens of any kind.

One of the things about f-*numbers* which tends to confuse is the fact that the smaller the number the "faster" is the lens. If you keep in mind the idea that an f-*number* is a fraction, the mystery subsides; ½ is greater than ¼, ¼ is greater than ⅛, ⅛ is greater than $\frac{1}{16}$, and so on.

Practically every good camera lens has an iris diaphragm built into it— an ingenious little mechanism of overlapping metal leaves by means of which the effective aperture of the lens can be varied. And, as the aperture is cut down, various stages in the process are marked so that you know exactly the f-ratio of each position. An $f/4$ lens, for example, is usually marked so that progressive *stopping down* can be fixed exactly at points where the f-ratio is 5.6, 8, 11, 16, 22, or 32. Those particular ratios are arbitrarily chosen because they give you a fairly precise mutual relationship. Closing the diaphragm from one f-number to the next larger in the following series: $f/1.0$, 1.4, 2.0, 2.8, 4.0, 5.6, 8, 11, 16, 22, 32, 45, 64, reduces the intensity of the light falling on the film by one half.

But now—what's the idea in stopping down a lens? If you have a good $f/4$ lens shouldn't you be happy about it and use it all the time? Well, you have 80 or more horsepower in the average modern car. How often do you call on all those horses to *give* for all they're worth?

With lenses it's much like that. Sometimes you need the full aperture

33

of your lens, but much more often you can do better by working at a considerably smaller lens opening.

The major difficulty with a wide-open, high-speed lens is the shallowness of its *depth of field*. "Shallow depth of field" sounds a little odd, of course, but *depth of field* is a specific, measurable quality and it can be either deep or shallow, depending on circumstances which you can con-

trol. The depth of field is the distance between the points nearest to and farthest from the camera that appears in sharp focus.

A glance at the sketches below will probably illumine this subject more effectively than words. But at worst, it's not a tough matter. Simply think back to those cones of converging light rays mentioned in the

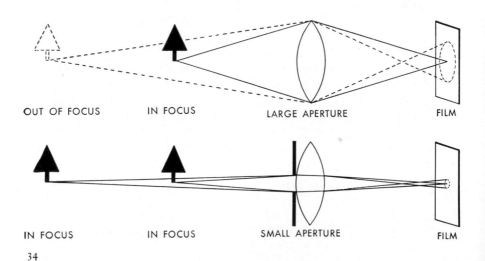

paragraphs on *focus*. When the lens aperture is relatively large, the angle between the converging rays from any point is large. Naturally, then, the circle of confusion becomes larger very quickly, fore and aft of the focal point. Because this is equally true for rays from all other distances, objects in front of or beyond that object quickly fall out of focus. In other words, the *depth of field* is shallow. But when you stop down your lens to, say, $f/22$ your converging cones are very slender, and the circles of confusion remain small for objects that are a considerable distance on either side of the one focused upon. Thus you obtain great *depth of field*.

It should be noted again that an extremely small circle of confusion does not produce a noticeable blur or out-of-focus effect. The eye may not even distinguish between a tiny circle and a point. It is within these limits of negligible circles of confusion that depth of field is calculated. How large the circles of confusion can be and still appear adequately sharp depends on the kind of work involved and the conditions under which the resulting pictures are viewed. The finer the detail to be repro- duced and the closer the pictures are to be viewed, the smaller the toler- able limits of the circles of confusion. Published data are usually for the average conditions for each particular lens. Because the size of an object in a negative is in proportion to the focal length of the lens the size of the tolerable circles of confusion is also in proportion to focal length. From experience with all the conditions involved it has been determined that an allowable maximum circle size of $1/1000$ of the focal length is quite satis- factory. Thus for a 2-inch lens the circle of confusion should not exceed $1/500$ inch, and for a 5-inch lens it can be as large as $1/200$.

Determining Depth

Some cameras have *depth of field* indicators—little dials by means of which you can determine the extent of the fore-and-aft sharpness in any picture you contemplate making. As you study such a dial you will dis- cover a very interesting phenomenon: *depth of field* tends to decrease rapidly as you close in on a subject. For example, in using a good modern lens in an average size camera you'll note that when you focus on a sub- ject 25 feet away, your depth of field at $f/4.5$ is from about 21 to 37 feet, and at $f/16$ from about 13 feet to infinity. But when you focus on a sub- ject only 6 feet away, the depth of field at $f/4.5$ is only from about 5¾ feet to 6½ feet, and at $f/16$ it is still only from 5 feet to about 7¾.

The reason for this interesting state of things will be found in another

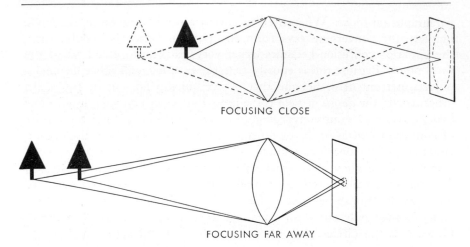

FOCUSING CLOSE

FOCUSING FAR AWAY

consideration of circles of confusion—and in careful viewing of the sketches. Since the images of more distant objects all fall into about the same plane, the depth of field for distant subjects is considerable. However, close-up subjects, even though very close together, are imaged in quite separate planes; hence, they cannot be simultaneously focused. The closer the subjects get to the lens, the greater the separation of their images—and the less the resulting depth of field.

Depth of field, then, depends upon four items. They are here listed, together with their effects when the other factors are held constant.

1. *Focal length.* The shorter the focal length the greater the depth of field. Miniature cameras have short focal length lenses and therefore greater depth of field. Relatively and geometrically, there is no difference between a long and a short focal length lens; the difference which accounts for the greater depth of field is simply one of the actual, measurable size of the lens opening. Thus a 4-inch lens has to be set at $f/8$ to give a geometric depth equal to that of a 2-inch lens set at $f/4$.

2. *The f-number.* The larger the f-number (smaller the opening) the greater the depth of field.

3. *The distance focused upon.* The farther the subject is from the lens the more will be in focus in front of and behind the subject.

4. *The circle of confusion.* The larger the circle of confusion to be tolerated before the picture is pronounced as unsharp—the greater the depth of field.

Putting three of the "depth" factors into mathematical combination the *hyperfocal distance* can be calculated and using this value as a mathematical stepping stone the depth of field can be determined.

$$\text{Hyperfocal distance (in feet)} = \frac{\text{The focal length (in inches) multiplied by itself}}{\text{f-number x circle of confusion (in inches) x 12}}$$

(The 12 converts the answer from inches to feet)

$$\text{or in formula} \quad HF = \frac{F^2}{f \text{ x c.c. x } 12}$$

Having determined the hyperfocal distance you can calculate the near and far points of sharp focus for any focus-distance setting, the fourth "depth" factor.

$$\text{Near Point (in feet)} = \frac{\text{Hyperfocal distance x distance (d) focused on (in feet)}}{HF + (d - \text{Focal length in feet})*}$$

$$\text{Far Point (in feet)} = \frac{HF \text{ x } d}{HF - (d - \text{Focal length in feet})*}$$

Note the necessity for expressing the focal length in feet to keep all units alike.

Depth of Field (in feet) = Far point – Near point

Example

What is the depth of field when using a camera with a 6-inch lens at $f/8$ focused at 10 feet and assuming a tolerable circle of confusion (c.c.) of 1/200 inch?

$$HF = \frac{F^2}{f \text{ x c.c. x } 12}$$

$$HF = \frac{36}{8 \text{ x } \frac{1}{200} \text{ x } 12} = \frac{36}{\frac{96}{200}} = 36 \text{ x } \frac{200}{96} = 75 \text{ feet}$$

$$\text{N.P.} = \frac{75 \text{ x } 10}{75 + (10 - .5)} = \frac{750}{75 + 9.5} = 9 \text{ feet}$$

$$\text{F.P.} = \frac{75 \text{ x } 10}{75 - (10 - .5)} = \frac{750}{65.5} = 11.5 \text{ feet}$$

Depth of Field = Far Point – Near Point

Depth of Field = 11.5 – 9 = 2.5 feet

37

There's an interesting side light on this business of depth of field. Many amateurs grow up in photography with the definite notion that a small lens aperture produces finer detail not merely over a deep field but even on the subject focused upon. If there was a billboard to be photographed at 50 feet, they religiously stopped down after focusing exactly for 50 feet. The truth of the matter is that stopping down gains little or nothing under those circumstances. If the focus is exact, you get the same definition in photographing a flat subject (perpendicular to the axis of the lens) no matter what aperture you use. This generality, like most, is

Small lens aperture, great depth . . . . Large aperture, less depth

Undesirable background eliminated by use of wide aperture.

subject to some limitations, for there is variation in lenses; some have what might be called *optimum* apertures, apertures at which they work best. The theoretically perfect lens provides best definition at full aperture; in practise, the better the lens, the greater the optimum aperture. Only experience will give you a full understanding of your lens.

Depth of Field Experiment

Object:

To determine the effect of lens aperture and subject distance on depth of field, and to compare results under practical picture-making conditions with mathematically computed depth.

Equipment:

A focusing camera (preferably 2¼x3¼ or larger) on which the lens aperture data is marked.

Procedure:

PART 1

Photograph a distant (infinity focus) subject, first with a small lens aperture, then with a large lens aperture, adjusting exposure time for correct exposure. Repeat procedure for a subject less than 10 feet distant. If possible, include both foreground and background objects. These will help show the effect of aperture size and subject distance on depth.

Mount the finished prints together on a notebook page for comparison.

PART 2

Calculate the depth of field for your camera when used with the lens wide open and focused on an object 6 feet away. Now make a picture under these conditions and from a contact print, viewed at about 12 inches, estimate the near and far points. The illustration below suggests a subject particularly suitable for this part of the experiment, as the distances can be easily and accurately measured.

Compare the computed figures with those of your observation.

Questions:

1. What factors affect depth of field and what is the nature of their effect?
2. If your observations do not agree with your calculations, might one of these factors account for the difference, (a) incorrect focus in making your picture (b) your liberal or critical observation of the sharpness (c) improper print viewing distance?

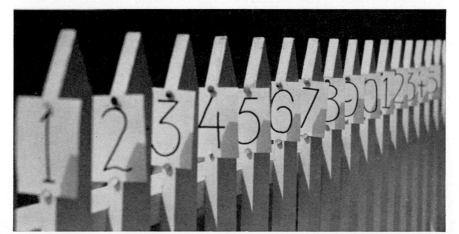

CHAPTER 4

Be Camera-Wise

THERE ARE good and bad camera habits, just as there are good and bad driving habits. And the good habits return large dividends, in terms of better pictures and greater personal satisfaction. Good habits, photographically speaking, are based on common sense and scientific facts. Photographs begin, for the most part, as intensely personal things—as ideas. Good photographs are accomplished through the application of established procedures. You can't buck these procedures very long or very successfully. It's a losing fight.

There's endless scope for ideas, inspiration, daring, and originality in photography as an art; it is when photography, the science, is called on as the medium for the art that "rules of the road" become essential.

It doesn't much matter what your basic attitude toward photography may be. For example, you may naturally tend to dream up a picture before you start out to make it. In that case you probably spend considerable time and effort to set the stage, to get models, and select locations before you unlimber your equipment. Your camera will be fairly large, and you'll use a tripod and a set of judiciously selected accessories. On the other hand, you may prefer to get your fun out of picturing spontaneous, unexpected, unrehearsed activity. Your little camera, hung about your neck, comes into play with a swish—and then when the flurry is over, it's forgotten. In either case, your success depends on your deep-seated photographic habits.

The good driver knows his car, knows the "feel" of it, knows when the going is easy or tough, knows what is possible, and what is not. Similarly, the good photographer knows his camera. He knows what it will and will not do; and he knows very accurately when he is pushing his luck. This business of knowing your camera is primarily a matter of experience, but it can be accelerated by a few hours of quiet study with the unloaded camera. Put it through its paces, get the feel of the various controls.

The better you know your camera, the better care you will give it. Here are a few suggestions for camera housekeeping. Consider them carefully.

The modern camera is a well-made, nicely adjusted mechanism. In average use, it is sturdy enough to go for a year or so without a major overhaul. But it cannot be expected to go on and on, indefinitely. A good camera, like a good watch, deserves respectful care. The wise photographer sees that proper care is administered; it's good picture insurance as well as common sense and economy.

For overhauls involving internal mechanism—the shutter, the iris diaphragm, and other mechanisms—only experts are qualified. Tinkering is definitely out.

But general camera housekeeping can be, and should be, done by the camera owner.

Camera Housekeeping

The most vulnerable part of your camera is its lens. It is precisely made, according to an exact formula; in most cases it is a combination of several glass elements, some of which are cemented together with a resin which is affected by prolonged exposure to light and by heat. So, the first rule of camera husbandry is to keep the lens clean and to protect it from needless harm.

Cleaning a lens is definitely not done by breathing humidly thereon as a prelude to brisk wiping with the nearest handkerchief. If the lens is so thickly coated with dust and grease that some sort of solvent is needed, use a drop or two of a lens cleaning fluid such as Kodak Lens Cleaner or similar solutions supplied by reputable manufacturers of optical goods. Then, wipe it carefully and lightly, with a piece of soft lens cleaning paper or a bit of lintless, clean linen. A soiled cloth may have dust in it which can easily scratch the carefully polished lens surface.

Most of the grease found on dirty lenses comes from fingers; it is an excellent idea, therefore, never to touch the glass surface. The chances of getting dust and grit on a lens are better during periods of camera inactivity than during actual picture making. If your lens doesn't fold back into the camera body where it is covered, keep your camera in its case or in a drawer where it will be well protected.

A flagrant—almost pictorial—case of lens flare.

Dust sometimes seeps into the interior of a camera, too, so make it a habit to keep the inner face of the lens and the inner surfaces of the camera itself as clean as possible. Free dust inside a camera is attracted to the smooth, faintly sticky surface of film—and dust on film means tiny black specks on your finished pictures.

Some photographers feel that a camera case is a bit of needless ostentation. They are sadly mistaken, for a case not only helps to keep a camera clean, but protects it from casual bumps and injuries. And cameras do need that protection. One of the easiest bad habits to acquire is that of stowing a camera in the glove compartment of an automobile. It is, true enough, a handy place for it, but it's a dangerous place too; for in summer it gets very hot in there, so hot that both film and lens can be seriously affected.

Among the good habits to cultivate, then, are camera cleanliness and protection from shocks and heat. To those add such other simple, common sense habits as these:

1. Load film only in subdued light, never in direct sunlight. The backing paper and packing provide excellent protection for films; with reasonable care all danger of light fog can be eliminated.

2. When the camera is idle, keep it in a dry, clean place.

3. All mechanical tensions should be relaxed during inactive periods. The shutter should not be left cocked. If you happen to own a focal plane camera of the Graflex type, be sure to cut the spring tension down

to zero when you put the camera away after use. Otherwise the spring tends to lose its strength and the shutter speeds will become unreliable.

4. If the youngsters in your home must have a camera to play with, get them an inexpensive box camera. Don't permit careless or mischievous hands to get at *your* camera, for bumps and dents do it definite harm. And marks from small, warm fingers can raise hob with any lens.

5. Have your camera inspected regularly—about once a year. Such an inspection should include a check for light leaks in the bellows and internal dirt in the lens. Too, the functioning of diaphragm and shutter should be tested, along with the means by which film is kept firmly flat in its proper place. Such an inspection need not be expensive nor time-consuming.

So much for camera care. Now about habits of camera use. Assume you are about to start off with your camera, with known or hoped-for picture opportunities ahead.

What kind of film is in your camera? If it has been a week or so since its last outing, you may have forgotten what type of film you loaded last time. And you've misplaced the empty carton. Of course, if you're using sheet film, you can identify the film, in a darkroom, by its notching code. But all that is a lot of trouble. So why not make it a habit to put a little tab of Scotch Tape on your camera or film septum when you load it? On that tab you can indicate the kind of film and the date. Thus your uncertainties are dissipated.

Another thing. If the camera is still loaded, was the film advanced after the last exposure? Once the question is raised, you're likely to get panicky and move to the next frame or film, just to play safe. More often than not, that means a wasted film. So spike that question and its attendant panic by establishing a rigid habit as to film winding. Two things favor winding the film after each exposure. For one, you are better prepared for a sudden picture opportunity. Then too, most people find it more natural to change the film *after* making the exposure. It's like spacing after a word when you're typing. There's an uncouth couplet that may amuse you and help in your habit formation. It runs,

> *You're out on a limb*
> *When you don't wind that "flim."*

Now to get on with preparations. How about extra film? There's seldom need to carry many extras, but ordinary reasonableness suggests one extra roll, or pack, or sheaf of film holders. At any rate, don't expose yourself to the tragedy of reaching the pictorial climax of your expedition—with all your film shot.

Make it a habit to carry along no more than the one or two filters which the weather and the type of pictures you hope to make call for. And, if you haven't learned how to make good pictures without filters, leave the filters at home.

Don't Shoot Until—

When it comes to actual picture-making habits, here's one that is so simple, so logical that it's easy to forget. *Use your view finder.* Your eyes and mind may be dazzled by some widespread view, but your camera simply isn't interested in anything beyond the confines of that rectangle of space shown in the finder. If yours is a direct view finder, with separate front and back sights, hold it close enough to your eye to enable you to see the inner frame of the forward sight. You may be able to do this with eyeglasses on, or you may have to take them off, depending on your vision and the type of glasses you wear.

Most view finders are designed so that their fields of view match those of the camera lenses at average snapshot ranges. However, with close-up subjects, the respective fields of view tend to separate because the lens and view finder are generally placed several inches apart. This discrepancy between the fields embraced by view finder and lens is what photographers refer to in speaking of *parallax*. To correct for it the camera must be pointed slightly toward the view finder side. The experiment following this chapter will aid you in determining the extent to which you will have to compensate for parallax.

If you've come to know your camera as well as you should, you'll

"Scalped" subjects are the commonest results of unconsidered parallax.

44

realize a small fact which many overlook. In all cameras whose lenses are equipped with iris diaphragms, it is entirely possible to set the lenses at points *between* the marked *f*-numbers. Thus, if you feel that *f*/5.6 is a shade too much and *f*/8 a bit on the tight side, there's nothing to prevent you from setting the lens between those two points, at about *f*/7, which is probably not a marked stop on your lens. This is not necessary in black-and-white photography because of the relatively wide exposure latitude of the film; in color work where exposure is more critical you may sometimes need to set the diaphragm between the marks.

The same type of practice is not suggested for shutter speeds.

Getting the Range

Now about safe and sane camera focusing. The basic rule is: For distances of less than 25 feet, your focus setting must be accurate; distances less than 6 feet require a tape measure, unless you are working at a very small aperture; for distances of 50 or 75 feet, your permissible error is fairly large; and for distances of 100 feet or more, set the lens at infinity.

Closely related to the focusing problem is the phenomenon of depth of field—or the extent to which your lens gives you sharp detail fore and aft of the point on which you focus. In most average work you probably want as much depth of field as possible—and you get it by using the smallest lens diaphragm opening consistent with adequate exposure. Sometimes, however, in making a close-up you may wish to obscure an undesirable background; you do it by using the maximum lens aperture. The optical laws governing depth of field were briefed in the chapter on lenses.

This business of depth of field explains why accurate focus is so important for close-ups and medium shots. Outdoors, where light is plentiful, you can gain a little leeway by closing down, but indoors, where the light is usually only fair, you are forced to be accurate really accurate.

If you have a range finder on your camera or as part of your equipment, use it as a means of checking your own distance judgment and not as a crutch on which you are helplessly dependent. If you have no range finder, you can check your estimates by walking them off. The average healthy adult walks along at the rate of five feet to two steps; thus you can check a distance by walking it, casually counting by fives at each second step.

Next to inaccurate focus for close-ups, the commonest source of trouble for most amateurs is camera shake—a movement of the camera, as the shutter is tripped, which results in loss of precise detail throughout the picture. Two preventives are respectfully offered. First, learn to handle your camera so that the shutter is worked by one finger, trigger fashion, while the other fingers and all of the other hand work together to hold the camera steady. Stand firmly, legs apart; give the camera support not only with your hands, but with your body; if you're using an eye-level finder, snuggle the camera up against your cheek bone. The second preventive is to use sufficient shutter speed. Even with average care with miniatures you'll need 1/100 and, for most folding Kodaks, 1/50.

Photography is a year 'round proposition and good habits are always in season. However, there is one additional point you should keep in mind during cold weather. Camera, lens, and film steam up when you take them from the cold into a warm room, but not when taken from warm to cold. Shutters may slow down, too, at low temperatures. So when you go on winter hikes, ski trips, and such, keep your camera under your coat or jacket, close to your body, removing it just in time to make your picture. When you take it into the house, allow time for the condensation to dry before you make any pictures.

The lens in any good camera is more versatile than you may suspect. You may be a long time in discovering its many aptitudes. And supplementary processes, especially enlarging, can make up for some of your lens' admitted inabilities. But, even so, the time will probably come when you need to make close-ups—portraits, copies of drawings or manuscripts, and similar close-range jobs—which your equipment, as it is, may not be able to handle. In that event, you can use a supplementary lens—a simple little affair that slips over the camera lens. There are several Kodak supplementary lenses—a portrait attachment for use with simpler cameras, and the Kodak Portra lenses, 1+, 2+, and 3+. To bring far objects closer, there's another series of supplementary lenses, the Kodak Telek 1—, 2—, and 3—, which need ground-glass focusing. Such supplementary lenses, properly used, can be among your most valuable accessories.

Speaking of accessories, there are so many of them, and they are all so interesting that the temptation is to load up with them. At the start, fight off that temptation. Later on, when you know exactly what you and your camera can do all by yourselves, you may discover that the appropriate gadgets really can help. But don't be impatient. Remember that a good camera, well used, will produce consistently better results than a mediocre camera cluttered up with extras.

Finally, don't count on luck. Luck is notoriously unreliable; the only certainty about it is that it will desert you when you need it most. If you know what you want to do, and how to do it, you can dismiss luck forever. And good riddance.

Parallax Experiment

Object:
To determine the degree to which a direct view finder departs from the camera view when used for composing close-up pictures.

Equipment:
A camera with a ground glass focusing back and a direct eye-level view finder having no parallax correction. A tripod.

Procedure:
Set the camera up on a tripod ready to make two exposures of a subject six feet from the camera. For the first of these, use the ground glass back for centering the subject on the film. For the second, use the direct view finder. Move

the camera up to four feet from the subject and take two more pictures, one centered by ground glass, one by the direct finder.

If you have a portrait attachment, slip that onto the lens. Make two exposures with the pictures centered as above.

Mount the prints for each distance side by side and decide just what allowances you must make for parallax when using the direct view finder for subjects close to the camera.

Question:
Why does the degree of parallax correction needed differ from one camera and finder to another?

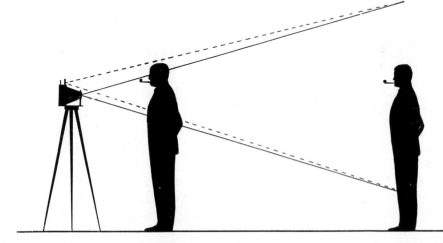

Camera Motion Experiment

Object:

To determine how fast the shutter speed must be to eliminate blurred images resulting from motion of the camera when hand-held.

Equipment:

A camera with adjustable shutter speeds.

Procedure:

Focus the camera on a subject composed of many right angle, sharp lines. The side of a house at a distance of 30 feet from the camera is excellent for the purpose. Hold the camera at waist or eye level. Make exposures at all marked shutter speeds, including a short "bulb" exposure and a time exposure of about 2 seconds. Adjust the diaphragm (*f*-number) in each instance to obtain correct exposure.

After development and printing, examine the prints with a magnifying glass. It will be readily noticeable that, as the shutter speed was increased, the lines became sharper and more clean cut. You may discover that 1/5 second gave you a sharper picture than 1/25. Put that down to sheer luck. Such accidents happen, but they are the exceptions which prove the rule that slow shutter speeds demand camera support.

From a study of the pictures you will readily determine the point, in the range of exposure speeds, at which it is safe to hand-hold a camera; for slower speeds, obviously, a tripod is indicated.

48

The effects of camera motion may not be apparent in small prints, but enlarged details thereof tell the story. Shutter speed, left, 1/25; right, 1/100. Moral: for hand held shots avoid slow shutter speeds.

CHAPTER 5

Films

To REPEAT, the most important part of any camera is the person who uses it; and a close runner-up is the camera's lens. But no camera, no matter how excellently lensed or how artfully handled, really amounts to much until there's a light-sensitive film in place within it, ready to record the image the lens permits it to "see" at the behest of the photographer

Oh sure—film. Film's the stuff you buy at your photographic dealer's. It comes in rolls or packs or sheets; you shove it into the camera and you're all set. Anybody knows what film is. There's no reason at all why people should regard film with any more respect than is accorded electric light bulbs or radios or newspapers or any of a hundred other commonplace modern miracles.

However, old timers cannot achieve that same casualness about today's film. They know how tough it used to be in the old days when they had to prepare their own plates for all their pictures. It was a tricky business, usually carried out under difficult conditions. For field work, a whole wagonload of equipment was necessary; a light-tight tent was one of the vital items. The plates were almost invariably glass, heavy, hard to handle, and very easy to break. To get the light-sensitive coating on smoothly was, even in the home studio, a combination of skill and luck.

Yet, the pioneer photographers not only succeeded in making plates, they made good plates and very good pictures. Possibly one reason why they made such good pictures is the fact that so much prayer, proficiency, and perspiration went into the preparation of each single plate. Every exposure *had* to be right. They simply couldn't afford hit-or-miss photography.

It is not suggested that today's neat, lightweight, convenient photographic film be revered merely because our uncles and grandfathers had to achieve its prototype in the hard way. But it is suggested that film be respected for itself alone and for its remarkable capabilities.

Every photographer, at an early point in his career, succumbs to the temptation to look at a piece of undeveloped film in full light. But there is no outward clue in the innocent looking thing to its almost magical potentialities. Ordinary film consists of a support of flexible, transparent material on which there is a smooth, cream-yellow coating. You can easily scratch this coating or wash it off with hot water. On the back of the film is a dye, perhaps blue, green, or red. But all such casual investigations mean nothing. For the miraculous virtues of film are totally invisible.

The Emulsion

Film achieves its photographic usefulness because it carries, suspended in that yellowish coating, millions of microscopic crystals of silver bromide. And silver bromide is light-sensitive; it registers its encounter with light by turning black later on, during the process of development. On that central fact depends the whole structure of photography—the science, the art, the "useful citizen," and the hobby that is photography.

The making of modern film is one of the most scrupulously controlled processes in industry. Maximum cleanliness is vital in every step, and many of those steps have to be taken in darkness. Temperatures have to be maintained at precise levels; relative humidity must be constant; the thickness of the supports and of the coatings must be uniform—and so on throughout the whole manufacturing process.

While a number of portrait and commercial photographers still prefer glass plates (made not by themselves, but by the same skilled technicians who make film), the preponderance of today's negatives are made on a flexible base of cellulose acetate.

The Support

This film support is, in itself, insensitive to light. Its purpose is to provide a transparent, firm, yet adequately flexible and chemically stable base for the film emulsion. In the manufacture of film support, cotton is first treated with acetic anhydride and subsequently dissolved in chemicals of which ether and wood alcohol are the major constituents. The result looks like a clear, thick syrup, affectionately known in the industry as "dope." It is, of course, highly volatile.

Huge, highly polished metal cylinders about 4 feet wide and 20 feet in diameter revolve slowly as dope is fed evenly onto them. In the course of less than one revolution enough of the solvents are driven off by heat and the dope has gained adequate body to permit its removal from the drums. It then wends its way through monstrous, continuously operating machines where it is fully dried and wound onto great rolls to await its life work as a support for the emulsion.

The supports for roll films and film packs are relatively thin; miniature films and motion picture films are thicker; sheet films generally are the thickest.

Film Manufacture

The making of emulsions (the light-sensitive coatings) is another story, which begins with silver. At Kodak Park where the Eastman Kodak Company makes its film, more than six tons of bar silver are used in an average week. Add the silver tonnage consumed in other photographic concerns and you have a very impressive lot of silver, all dedicated to the making of pictures.

To get back to our story . . . the bars of silver are dissolved in nitric acid, with silver nitrate as the result. Crystals of silver nitrate are formed as the water in the solution evaporates. Then the crystals are washed and purified.

Meantime, gelatin (chemically superior to the kind you buy at the corner store) has been prepared for its function as a vehicle for the light-sensitive emulsion. It is warmed to a syrupy consistency, and silver nitrate and potassium bromide added to it. At this stage, operations must be carried on in almost complete darkness, for the silver and the bromide combine to form light-sensitive silver bromide crystals. The potassium and nitrate unite as potassium nitrate, which is removed from the gelatin by washing. Thus, the crystals of silver bromide are left alone in the embrace of the gelatin. Photographically speaking, this is the emulsion.

Emulsion coating of the transparent film support requires that the emulsion be warmed to a liquid state, and kept at a precise temperature and a constant level in a large trough. From rolls, the film support loops down into the trough and picks up a "skin" of the emulsion. From there the film and its coating travel over a series of chilled drums designed to effect controlled cooling and uniform setting of the emulsion. Next, the coated support passes through long drying tunnels, after which it is wound onto huge rolls.

Applied much as are emulsions, the brightly dyed gelatin coating on the back of the film acts to absorb intense light which penetrates the emulsion and support during exposure. If not absorbed, these light rays may reflect from the back of the support or film holder, scatter and create a halo effect around bright points in the image. You've seen this halo in pictures of street lights at night. Because of its function, the light absorbing dye is called an *antihalation backing*. The color is completely removed during development, so as not to interfere with the printing or enlarging.

Here is a cross-section drawing of a typical modern film. It is precision-manufactured, according to an exact formula. Old timers never dared dream of such a thing.

After coating, the film is cut, prepared for use in rolls, packs, or sheets, packaged and made ready for shipment.

The manufacturing process here outlined applies to ordinary, black-and-white film. In the production of color films and special purpose films, many complications and variations are encountered. But, basically, the making of the film you use is much as we have described it.

WHY SO MANY KINDS OF FILM?

In any gathering of picture makers, there is much talk of film. Everyone seems to have his own favorite; obscure trade names are spoken glibly. And you hear knowing references to the "characteristic curve" of this or that film; its speed rating is discussed in terms of several systems; its most intimate qualities are flaunted for general admiration, amazement, or disapproval.

And that is all as it should be. Still, it is possible for the ardent hobbyist to become so preoccupied with these technical details that he never really settles down to picture making; he flits from film to film, seeking some miraculous combination that will automatically give him top speed, minimum grain, brilliance, full color sensitivity, and an exhibition print from every exposure. Obviously, there is no such golden mean. Modern film offers excellences and virtues undreamed of a generation ago, but the responsibility for good pictures still rests, as it always has and always will, with the individual photographer, his ability to see, his understanding of his camera, the intelligent use of whatever film he selects, and his command of fundamental photographic technique.

FILM'S FOUR BASIC CHARACTERISTICS

Films have these general qualities—color sensitivity, speed, graininess, and contrast. As these characteristics vary, the potentialities of the films vary.

Color Sensitivity

On color sensitivity depends the classification of the film as blue sensitive ("ordinary" or "regular"), orthochromatic, or panchromatic. (We are concerned here, of course, exclusively with the color responses of black-and-white or monochrome film. Color films and color photography are to be treated separately, later on.)

An important distinction between the sensitivity of black-and-white film and that of the human eye is that the film "sees" in terms of *brightness* only, while the eye discerns both *color and brightness*. Thus, while any film is capable of rendering a color and a shade of gray as identical tones; the eye knows better. It is in the selection of a film which will give the desired relation of brightnesses that the photographer must exercise both skill and judgment.

Silver bromide is ordinarily sensitive only to ultraviolet and blue light. However, the addition of certain sensitizing agents to the emulsion during manufacture renders the silver salts sensitive to other colors as well. The colors and the degrees to which the films are made sensitive to them depend upon the particular agents added.

Classed according to color sensitivity, there are three main groups or types of film; each has its own specific usefulness.

Blue-sensitive (ordinary or regular) film is sensitive to ultraviolet and blue only. Also, it is usually high in contrast, a fact which makes it well suited for copying black-and-white line drawings and manuscripts. Where color interpretation is unimportant, it makes an excellent film for com-mercial studio use.

Orthochromatic ("ortho") film responds to ultraviolet, to blue and

53

green. Such film finds wide usefulness in average snapshot making and in night photography by Photoflash. It is used widely by professional portrait photographers in making pictures of men, for it reproduces faces with full contrast and character. Ortho film is used commercially when its particular color rendition is desired. Its insensitivity to red means that it can be developed under a red light in the darkroom, a factor contributing to its popularity among those amateurs who do their own developing and printing.

Panchromatic ("pan") film, because it "sees" ultraviolet, blue, green, and red, gives the widest color response and the most natural-looking interpretation of colors in tones of the black-and-white scale.

Kodak panchromatic films are arbitrarily sub-typed A, B, and C in order of their increasing sensitivity to the longer (red) wave lengths of light.

Type A was the first panchromatic emulsion and was only slightly red sensitive. It is now obsolete.

Type B panchromatic film, slightly more red sensitive, has approximately the same brightness response as the human eye, except in the ultraviolet; it therefore interprets subject brightness about as we do. Where accurate color rendition is important, Type B panchromatic film is best suited, and its smooth rendition of skin tones makes it ideal for close-up portraits of women and children. In view of these several characteristics, Type B films are among the most popular modern emulsions.

Type C panchromatic film has maximum red sensitivity, hence highest speed in tungsten light, a fact which makes it tops for snapshots indoors at night. When used outdoors, this extreme red sensitivity means relatively less blue sensitivity and therefore pictures having good contrast between skies and clouds.

Ortho (left) and pan film differ in interpreting identical subjects.

Film Speed

Now about the second basic film quality, that of *speed*. This is, we are frequently reminded, the age of speed. Just as frequently, though less cheerfully, we are required to face the fact that speed involves sacrifices. Film speed is no shining exception to the rule.

Speed, in the film sense, is simply sensitivity. Greater speed means that good pictures can be made with less light. With less speed, more light is needed. It depends on manufacturing processes, including greater or less "cooking" or digesting of the emulsion prior to the coating. In general, the longer the cooking period, the larger the grains of silver bromide— and the larger those grains, the greater their sensitivity. In the last few years, films have been doubled and trebled in speed, with the result that, today, some of the most common snapshot films have a higher speed than specialized films could boast of, a dozen years ago. But the greater graininess of high speed films involves serious drawbacks.

Graininess

Graininess is usually not sensed in small prints, but when large-scale enlargements are made, it becomes all too visible, presenting a mottled appearance, especially in large, uniform, middle-toned areas.

Makers of film have made important advances in minimizing this graininess, both in manufacture and in evolving "fine grain" development processes; however, greater speed still means more graininess.

20X enlargements made from fine- and coarse-grain negatives.

Contrast

Contrast, the fourth important film characteristic, is the ability of the film to distinglish between closely related tones in the brightness scale. While the manufacturer controls it at the time the emulsion is prepared, this built-in contrast can be increased or decreased in film development and in printing. However, the wise photographer selects his film with its inherent contrast in mind.

High contrast films are used in copying line drawings, newspaper print, manuscripts or documents where maximum brightness differentiation is essential. In such cases maximum contrast is required, as only black-and-white tones are finally desired.

Lower contrasts in different degrees are desirable in most other forms of photography, such as snapshots and portraits.

There are other film characteristics or qualities which the well-rounded photographer understands, appreciates, and capitalizes. The characteristic curve, latitude, gamma, and resolving power—all these bits of camera-fan jargon—are meaningful and important, but specific discussion of them is postponed to the chapter, "Sensitometry."

THE LATENT IMAGE

Most mysterious and fascinating of all photographic phenomena is that of the latent image—the invisible image carried and retained in the film between the moment of exposure and the beginning of development. There have been innumerable instances of latent images lasting many years. Some exposures made at the time of the San Francisco fire in 1908 remained in a camera until 1937; on development they turned out creditably. An even more striking instance was discovered when the remains of the Andree polar expedition, which had set out in 1897, were found in 1930 in the far north. The men of the expedition had perished early in their explorations but the equipment was intact, including loaded cameras. When the films were developed, entirely usable images appeared. While perfect conditions for preservation of the film were, by accident, maintained in this instance, the persistence of the latent image under any ordinary conditions is a remarkable thing.

Exactly what the latent image is, no one knows with certainty. There are several theories. One of them maintains—on the basis of considerable evidence—that the latent image consists of a sub-microscopic silver speck on the silver bromide grain which renders the exposed grain developable.

Choosing Your Film

YOUR SUBJECT	KODAK ROLL AND PACK FILM	KODAK MINIATURE FILM	KODAK SHEET FILM
People, outdoors	VERICHROME (roll only)	PLUS-X	ORTHO-X
Close-ups of women	PLUS-X	PLUS-X	SUPER-XX OR PORTRAIT PAN
Interiors with existing light	SUPER-XX	SUPER-XX	TRI-X
Flash shots	VERICHROME OR PLUS-X	PLUS-X	ORTHO-X
General landscapes and cloud pictures	PLUS-X	PLUS-X	SUPER PAN PRESS TYPE B OR PANATOMIC-X
Copying line drawings High contrast work	PLUS-X WITH FULL DEVELOPMENT	MICRO-FILE	CONTRAST PROCESS (ORTHO OR PAN)

Fortunately for all of us, however, we know all we need to know in order to create a latent image and to develop it into a definite, visible, and usable one.

Making a Photographic Emulsion

Materials Required:
1. GELATIN. A good photographic grade gelatin can be purchased from leading photographic supply houses in 1 lb. lots. While not a photographic grade, gelatin suitable for the experiment can be purchased from the Eastman Organic Chemicals Dept., Distillation Products Industries, Rochester 3, N. Y., in lots of 250 grams for about $1.45 or 1 kilogram for about $4.20.
2. POTASSIUM BROMIDE — Available at any
3. POTASSIUM IODIDE — large photo-
4. SILVER NITRATE — graphic store.
5. GLASS. Any high grade thin glass will be satisfactory.

Proceed as Follows:
1. Dissolve 10 grams of gelatin in 360 cc. warm water. A stirring paddle of hardwood should be used; avoid resinous woods.
2. Add 32 grams potassium bromide and 0.8 grams potassium iodide and dissolve. Raise the temperature to 55° Centigrade (131°F.) and maintain it there.

    So far the work may be done in white light, but all subsequent steps must be carried out under the ruby light of the darkroom.
3. Dissolve 40 grams of silver nitrate in 400 cc. water. Add this to the potassium bromide solution at the rate of 20 cc. every half minute for ten minutes. Stir constantly.

4. Hold the temperature at 55° Centigrade for 10 minutes to allow ripening, then let the temperature drop slowly.
5. Add 40 grams gelatin to set the emulsion. Keep the mixture cool until it has set thoroughly. This requires from 3 to 4 hours.
6. Shred the emulsion by forcing it through cheesecloth. Onto the shreds pour 3 liters (approximately 3 quarts) of water, leave 2½ minutes, pour off 2 liters, and add 2 liters more. Repeat five times. This washes out the excess potassium bromide, potassium iodide and potassium nitrate.
7. Heat for 15 minutes at 55° Centigrade for further ripening. Slowly cool to 40° Centigrade (104°F.).
8. Pour 4 cc. of the emulsion onto a clean 3¼ x 4¼-inch glass plate, spread to form a uniform coat, place on a level chilled metal plate until the emulsion sets, and is dry. The plate is now ready for use.

The Exposure:
Outdoors in bright sunlight an exposure at $f/8$ and 1/25 second will be approximately correct. For development, use any of the active, fast-working film developers.

Questions:
1. Have you made a regular, orthochromatic, or a panchromatic emulsion?
2. List the relative advantages and disadvantages of glass plates and the flexible types of film support.

CHAPTER 6

Developing Film

YOU'VE "TAKEN" your picture. The latent image, wrapped in mysterious invisibility, lies in the film. To make that latent image come to life, you take the next step. You develop it. You do this by placing the film in a chemical solution called, oddly enough, the developer. After a few moments you remove the film from the developer, rinse it in water, and put it into another solution called the fixing bath. After another few minutes you switch on the light, and peer anxiously at the result.

There's your image, but it's strangely different from the subject. It's a negative; that which was white in the scene you "took" is now black, the blacks are clear transparency. Everything in the black-and-white scale is reversed. It's a little disconcerting. To get the positive print, a picture you can look at and enjoy, you make a contact exposure on photographic paper. And the image you get on paper is a *negative of the negative*. Obviously, two negatives make a positive. That's your picture.

This is a good negative   **and this a good print**

Shadow and highlight detail, recorded in the negative, are preserved in the print

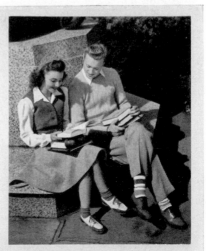

59

If your first encounter with the development of film prompts you to mutter something about "black magic," even the most literal minded, most technical enthusiasts will pardon you. For there is certainly something of magic in the process; and it is more than likely to be carried out in darkness. But "black magic" carries an unpleasant connotation; in that respect the phrase is wholly inappropriate.

Like most other forms of magic, development turns out to be remarkably simple. All it takes is a little understanding.

Specifically, what happens in the process of development? Physically, of course, the latent image is made visible. Chemically, the developer attacks the exposed grains of silver bromide, reducing them to metallic silver and a form of bromine. The metallic silver is deposited on the film support. The bromine is liberated, eventually to go down the sink.

Undoubtedly, the way to clarify all this is to get some practical experience. So consider, now, ways and means thereto.

THE DARKROOM AND EQUIPMENT

The darkroom and equipment for developing need not be elaborate. Any room from which *all* outside light can be excluded will serve. Many a photographic career started in a "blacked-out" kitchen, bathroom, fruit cellar, or a space under the basement stairs. How dark is dark enough? Try this little test. Turn out all lights; wait three or four minutes until your eyes become accustomed to the darkness. Then, if you can't see a sheet of plain white paper on the workbench in front of you—it's dark enough. To have a darkroom in the basement is the fond ambition of most enthusiasts. There all materials can be stored, and facilities for developing and printing kept readily accessible.

Only the following items of equipment are essential in film development and print making:

1. Four clean enamel or glass trays, approximately five by seven inches in size.
2. An accurate thermometer.
3. A graduate or liquid measure.
4. Bottles for storing solutions.
5. A safelight.
6. A printing frame or box (to be described in the next chapter).

Small kits of such equipment are available at low cost. These kits may also include the chemicals necessary in the process.

Inasmuch as the film is light-sensitive until the processing is nearly complete, it is necessary to develop the images under subdued light of a controlled color and brightness. As mentioned earlier, films of the "chrome" type, Kodak Verichrome for example, are insensitive to red light and therefore can be developed under a ruby colored *safelight*. Some ordinary red electric bulbs are satisfactory, but should not be relied upon as entirely safe unless supplied specifically for the job. Otherwise, test them. Note the experiment at the end of this chapter. If light other than red strikes the "chrome" type film during development, a general veiling or *fog* over the entire surface of the film results. The Wratten Series 2, (deep red) safelight slide, used with a 10-watt bulb at a distance of four feet from the film will be entirely safe. A good safelight is good insurance. Panchromatic films, fully sensitive to all colors, are developed in total darkness.

THE DEVELOPER

If you are a beginner you will find it best to go to your local photographic dealer to obtain developer. There you will find packets, cans, and bottles of ready-mixed chemicals on sale, and in almost any quantity desired. For use, these chemicals need only be dissolved in water according to printed instructions on the labels. Once you start using packaged developers, you probably will stick by them for good. You'll find that, in addition to being easy to mix, they are economical, clean, and space- and time-saving. Most important, there's no chance for variation from one batch of solution to the next.

If you prefer to mix your own solutions, you may wish to use the following formula which is exceptionally good for film development.

KODAK DEVELOPER DK-60a

	Avoirdupois		Metric	
Water, about 125°F. (50°C.)	96	ounces	750	cc.
Kodak Elon Developing Agent	145	grains	2.5	grams
Kodak Sodium Sulfite, desiccated	6¾	ounces	50	grams
Kodak Hydroquinone	145	grains	2.5	grams
Kodalk Balanced Alkali	2 oz. 290	grains	20	grams
Kodak Potassium Bromide	30	grains	0.5	gram
Water to make	1	gallon	1.0	liter

Dissolve chemicals in order given.
Average development time for deep tank about 7 minutes at 68°F. (20°C.)
See instruction sheets packed with materials for specific development times.

As you become more experienced you will want to try several different developers and determine for yourself which one best fits your needs. You'll find many different ones listed in the various Kodak Data Books and the Kodak Reference Handbook.

What the Developer Does

The process of developing invisible images into visible ones requires three quite distinct steps.

1. Softening and swelling of the gelatin so that the solution can get at the exposed crystals of silver bromide.
2. The dissociation of the silver and bromine.
3. The exposed silver bromide crystals are transformed into tangles of extruded silver, commonly called the developed "grains."

Naturally, no one chemical can accomplish this whole task. So a developer contains many chemicals and, because the chemical quantities can be varied with varying results, there are hundreds of formulas. Essentially, though, they contain the same ingredients.

1. A SOLVENT, water. Chemical reactions of the nature of film development require solutions. Obviously dry chemicals could never accomplish even the first stage, the softening.

2. A REDUCER whose task it is to do the actual breaking up of the exposed silver salts. Elon is one. When used alone in a formula Elon produces images rapidly but they are low in contrast. The action of Elon is little affected by slight changes in the temperature of the developer.

Hydroquinone is another reducing agent. Its images generally are slow to appear, but have good contrast. Elon and hydroquinone are frequently combined and the best properties of each utilized in compounding a developer which works fairly rapidly, gives good brilliance, and is only moderately affected by temperature changes.

Pyro or pyrogallic acid, distilled from gall nuts imported from China, was not so many years ago in wide use, but has largely been replaced by these newer and more efficient reducers. Pyro oxidizes rapidly and turns brown, staining hands, negatives, or anything it contacts. This same stain is deposited upon the film almost in proportion to the amount of silver deposited. Much silver means lots of stain; a little silver a little stain. Thus negatives developed in pyro gain added printing contrast.

3. AN ACTIVATOR. To function properly, most reducers require that the solution be alkaline rather than acid or neutral. Sodium carbonate,

borax, or Kodalk supply this extra energy to the reducer. In addition, the alkali softens the gelatin more rapidly than plain water and thereby assists in the physical diffusion of the developer through the film.

Sodium carbonate has long been most commonly used, but it has some drawbacks. Notable of these is the formation of carbon dioxide gas as the film, with warm developer in and on it, is carried into the fixing bath containing acetic acid. The emulsion is soft from the warm carbonate and unable to resist the pressure of the tiny bubbles of carbon dioxide which form within the emulsion. As the bubbles break they pit the emulsion surface.

Kodalk, originally introduced as an activator for developers that might have to be used at excessively high temperatures, causes no volatile gas formation even at 80°F. It is now being used in many everyday developers for both amateur and professional photofinishers.

Borax, less active, is used with semi-fine grain formulas.

4. A PRESERVATIVE. Reducing agents are greedy for oxygen. If they get it they "rust" themselves away until they become photographically inactive and deposit rust-colored stains on the film. They take oxygen from both air and water. The inclusion of sodium sulfite in the solution preserves the reducer by retarding the oxidation or "rusting;" the formation of the colored compounds that stain film is thereby prevented. When large amounts of sulfite are used, it tends to dissolve part of the silver, making for finer-grain images.

5. A RESTRAINER. While suitable developing agents will work only on exposed silver grains, even the best developing agent may reduce some of those not exposed. Thus a general veil of gray—"fog"—is deposited on the film surface. Potassium bromide, the restrainer, makes the developer more selective, makes it harder for any unexposed grains to get themselves developed. It *prevents fog*.

Why Follow Recommendations?

With each formula goes a recommendation for the proper development time and temperature. These are more than suggestions. They are the results of scientific experiments and are backed up by many practical tests. If you follow them, you're almost certain of good results. Occasionally, of course, there's reason to change from the recommended technique, but this should be done cautiously and deliberately.

Start out by following instructions, not just one time, but consistently.

You probably will need to make no adjustments. But if you find that your picture-making system (which includes camera, printer, enlarger, etc.) gives negatives that require a contrasty printing paper, such as No. 4, increase the development time slightly. With any developer, an increase in time over normal increases the contrast. Conversely, you can lower your contrast by shortening the time. Keep the temperature constant, at 68°F.

High developer temperatures cause undue softening and swelling of the emulsion, making it readily susceptible to finger marks and scratches.

Then, too, remember that if sodium carbonate is used in the developing solution, there is a tendency for carbon dioxide gas to form within the emulsion as, soaked with developer, it is dipped into subsequent acid baths. An emulsion unduly softened during development at a high temperature cannot resist the force of these tiny carbon dioxide bubbles. On the other hand, the soft, warm, newly developed emulsion may try to shrink back to its original state too rapidly in subsequent cold baths. This results in a crackled appearance called *reticulation*. Get in the habit right now of keeping all your solutions at the same temperature.

An increase in either time or temperature is accompanied by additional graininess and a rise in the fog level. In fact, anything which increases the general activity of a solution adds to the contrast, softness of the emulsion, graininess, and fog.

Agitation

Films *must* be given good agitation throughout processing. In development, by-products of the reduction are formed, for example, sodium bromide. These are heavy and settle down on the films in trays or cling to films hanging vertically. A development restraining coating thus covers the emulsion and a fresh supply of developer is unable to get through to the emulsion. These by-products often collect in spots; grouped at random over the surface of the film, they retard development unevenly. The result is a mottled appearance. Good agitation gives good contrast, as it increases greatly the effectiveness of the solutions. Agitation, therefore, is a specific and important part of the development process. Usually it need involve nothing more than a gentle rocking of the tank for a few seconds every minute or two during the development period. Tray development usually involves ample agitation in the course of routine handling of the film.

But "developing" alone, even though properly done, does not complete the development process. After the film has been bathed in the developer, it carries metallic silver where light originally struck it, plus the still light-sensitive emulsion where no light struck it.

So, before it is safe to turn on the white room lights it is necessary to rinse the developer from the film with fresh water and then to bathe it in what is called a *fixing bath*. The fixing bath dissolves the unexposed and undeveloped crystals from the film, leaving an image of metallic silver on the clear support.

FIXING BATHS

There are three types of fixing baths. The principal ingredients are water and sodium thiosulphate, traditionally called "hypo." The hypo does the fixing, although in some baths other chemicals are added.

1. NON-HARDENING FIXER. It is used infrequently and then for special processes such as color printing, and for prints to be hand-colored. A 25% to 35% solution of hypo fixes most rapidly. Adding more hypo does not speed up the rate of fixation. Sodium bisulfite is generally added to non-hardening fixing baths to neutralize the alkali of the developer, and sodium sulfite is included to prevent sulphurization.

2. ACID HARDENING FIXER. In addition to hypo and sulfite, acetic acid and a hardening agent such as potassium alum or potassium chrome alum are included. The acid neutralizes the alkalinity of the developer and stops its action. Alum hardens the gelatin originally softened by the water and carbonate of the developing solution. Sodium sulfite serves as a preservative and also prevents the sulphurization of the hypo due to the presence of acetic acid and alum. It is by far the most widely used type of fixing bath today.

3. ULTRA-RAPID FIXER. Since ordinary hypo baths are of the most efficient concentration, faster working baths require other forms of hypo. Because of the instability of these forms as dry chemicals, they are supplied in concentrated solution. They completely fix film in three minutes, and paper in 1½ minutes. Slightly more expensive than other forms, rapid fixers are used principally by news photographers and others to whom speed is essential.

Like developer, fixing baths can be purchased in package form and dissolved in water for use. If you prefer to mix your own hypo, here's a standard formula which lists the chemicals and amounts for one quart of fixing bath, to be used without further dilution. Dissolve the chemicals in the order of their listing.

KODAK F-5 FIXING BATH
For Films and Papers

	Avoirdupois	Metric
Water, about 125°F. (50°C.)	20 ounces	600 cc.
Kodak Sodium Thiosulfate (Hypo)	8 ounces	240.0 grams
Kodak Sodium Sulfite, desiccated.	½ ounce	15.0 grams
*Kodak Acetic Acid (28% pure)	1½ fluid oz.	48.0 cc.
**Kodak Boric Acid, crystals.	¼ ounce	7.5 grams
Kodak Potassium Alum.	½ ounce	15.0 grams
Cold water to make.	32 ounces	1.0 liter

*To make 28% acetic acid from glacial acetic acid, dilute three parts of glacial acetic acid with eight parts of water.
**Crystalline boric acid should be used as specified. Powdered boric acid dissolves only with great difficulty, and its use should be avoided.

Films or plates should be fixed properly in 10 minutes (cleared in 5 minutes) in a freshly prepared bath. The bath need not be discarded until the fixing time (twice the time to clear) becomes excessive, that is, over 20 minutes. One quart of the above formula will satisfactorily fix the equivalent of 40 to 50—5 x 7-inch films, provided the films are rinsed in water between development and fixation.

DEVELOPING YOUR FILM

Fortunately for all of us, the mechanics of film development are infinitely simpler than the many reactions that take place while the films are immersed in the various solutions. There are two general methods for developing films, known respectively as the *tray method* and the *tank method*.

The Tray Method

1. Is principally for the beginner, but
2. Should be a part of everyone's photographic technique; you never know when or where you're going to be called on to develop a roll of film without benefit of your usual "accessories."
3. Is suited more to "ortho" film development. You need the safelight to see what you're doing. But, again, be prepared to do a roll of "pan" in total darkness if need be.
4. Is not advisable when the development time is longer than 10 minutes.
5. Is one for you to know and outgrow.

The Tank Method

1. Is economical. You will spill and splatter less; therefore it
2. Is cleaner to use, too.
3. It means cleaner negatives. There's no need for touching films until they're ready for drying.
4. Makes it easier to control your solution temperature.
5. Prevents any toxic chemicals from getting onto your hands.
6. Requires no darkroom when a day-loading type tank is used.

First, here's how to develop your roll films via the tray method.

Arrange three trays side by side in a sink or on a covered table or bench. The tray on the left is most convenient for the developer, the center for a rinse water, and one on the right for the fixing bath.

After you have poured the chemicals into the trays ready for use and turned off all but the safelights, remove the film from the paper roll or container which has served as its protection from unwanted light. Depending upon the type of camera used in making the exposure, you will encounter one of four types of film packing. Each type requires a slightly different handling during development.

1. ROLL FILM. Roll film is a strip of sensitive film backed by an attached paper strip which excludes light while the film is being loaded into, and removed from the camera. The film is attached to the protective paper only at the end first pulled through the camera. In the darkroom, before developing, remove the paper and unroll the film.

It is advisable to rinse the film in clear water before development. This lessens its tendency to curl and buckle, and makes uniform development much easier. Hold the long film strip at both ends, emulsion side down, and loop or dip it into the water. (Films curl slightly toward the emulsion side, the dull surface on the inner side of the roll.) The film will then be in a "U" shape, with only the bottom of the "U" immersed in the water. In order that all parts of the film can be equally wetted, the film is drawn through the water by a smooth seesaw action of right and left hands.

After rinsing the film in this manner for one minute, lift it out, turn it over emulsion side up and run it through the developer for the required time. The looping action must be sufficient for complete immersion of both ends in their turn.

After the development time, which may be from 5 to 10 minutes, depending upon the film and formula used, lift the film loop to the rinse bath tray where clear water will remove the developing chemicals from the surface of the film.

Fix the film by immersing it in the fixing bath in the third tray. At this point the opalescent coating which was not blackened during development will be dissolved from the film surface. During fixation, the film image will not only be made photographically permanent, but the alum in the "hypo" will harden the emulsion enough to prevent scratches or abrasion marks during ordinary handling of the finished negatives.

As the film is first placed in the hypo, the rinsing action should be continued. This will insure that all parts of the film are fixed evenly. If the available tray is large enough and the quantity of hypo used is sufficient to cover the film, the strip may be carefully folded back and forth across the long dimension of the tray and allowed to soak in that position for the greater part of the fixation time. About every two minutes move the film about in the tray to give it the benefits of uniform fixation.

It is difficult to tell you just how long the film must be in the hypo before it is 100% safe to turn on the room lights. There is really no point in turning on the white room lights before the film has been "cleared" of the yellowish emulsion, for not until it is clear will you be able to tell whether or not the negative fulfills your hopes. Fresh hypo completely fixes film in ten minutes, about half of which time is required for clearing. With adequate safelight protection, you can determine when your film is clear by inspection; double the clearing time for full fixation.

After fixation, wash the film for at least thirty minutes in running water to remove all chemicals used in processing. If these are allowed to remain

Primitive, but it works   **The modern, convenient way**

on the film, stains or image fading will result. One of the three trays can be used for washing. A larger washing tray is an advantage, however, as the film can circulate with the motion of the running water, and will not need to be rinsed by hand at such frequent intervals.

Now, about tank development. The tank for developing roll film includes either a plastic apron or a plastic or metal reel into which the dry, undeveloped film is wound. The apron with the film wound into it is inserted in the tank and after the lid is fastened in place the room lights can be turned on. All further treatment takes place within the tank, as small lighttight pouring holes in the lid permit the easy addition and removal of developer, rinse water, and fixing bath. The agitation required to provide uniform development is accomplished by moving the tank in a quick circular motion, first in one direction and then the other. This provides a less active rate of development than the continual rinse of the tray method and therefore requires about 20 per cent more time. The film may be washed by running water through the apron or reel either in the tank or a tray.

2. MINIATURE FILMS. The very nature of miniature photography makes tank development the only answer. You're almost always dealing with pan film, hence development in total darkness is required; too, handling of the film has its dangers, for dust spots or abrasion marks will be magnified later on in the course of enlarging.

Finally, of course, it just isn't convenient to loop five feet of narrow film back and forth through a small tray. It leads to comedy, consternation, constriction, and catastrophe.

3. THE FILM PACK. To remove the exposed sheets from the pack for development, the metal cap is removed, the back of the pack opened, and the paper-backed film lifted out—all in darkness, or safelight, of course. For tray development, the paper backing and the film should be separated from one another. Films can be developed individually in the tray, if kept well under the surface of the developer and properly agitated by rocking the tray. This method, however, requires too much time for a pack of 12 sheets; you will find it better to develop the 12 sheet films simultaneously, or to do two batches of 6 each.

In developing a full pack in the same tray, extreme care is required. Films must be handled only by the very edges. Moist fingers touching the surface of the film cause finger prints which cannot be corrected by any convenient means later in the process.

69

The tank's a "must" for miniature film and for sheet film in quantity

With twelve sheets of film in the same tray, two methods of agitation or rinsing are advisable. Either the tray should be rocked continuously, or the films should be constantly and smoothly changed in the tray from bottom to top to avoid any possibility of them sticking together.

Films from the pack may be rinsed and fixed in the same manner as they are developed.

Washing of film pack films is somewhat easier than the washing of roll film, as their size permits more motion within the tray, thus lessening the need for manual rinsing.

Developing tanks, similar to those used in the processing of roll film, are helpful in processing packs, because twelve sheets may be developed simultaneously and the danger of finger marks largely avoided. An inner cage provides a separate compartment for each sheet of film. After the cage is loaded with the exposed film, placed in the tank, and the lid screwed on, the room lights can safely be turned on for the development period.

4. SHEET FILM. Sheet films are used primarily by advanced amateur and professional photographers. Somewhat thicker than either the pack or roll film, this type is easy to handle and convenient when only one or two pictures are to be made on a particular assignment. The tray method of development is best suited to amateur processing of sheet film. The steps in the procedure are much like the steps in the developing of film packs by the tray method.

Professional photographers slip the film sheets into grooved hanger racks. The racks are lowered into large tanks or individual compartments for developer, rinse water and fixing bath, in order. Such a system permits the processing of several times as many films daily as would ever be possible with tray development.

DRYING THE FILM

For drying, the film should be hung in a place where the air circulates freely, for without this circulation the drying time is unduly long. Before removing the film from the wash water, swab it with cotton. This will remove any sandy or gritty particles that may have filtered through your water pipes. After the film is lifted from the washing tray, and the excess water allowed to drip from it, the strip or sheet is hung from a line much the same as Monday's laundry. Several clips or pins are available for this purpose, one of the most satisfactory being the common spring clothes pin.

At this point you will notice that many small droplets of water are on the film surfaces. If not removed, these will spot the film, due to uneven shrinkage of the swollen, water-soaked emulsion as it dries. To remove this excess water, the films are slowly wiped down with a dampened cloth chamois, or sponge, immediately after removal from the washing tray.

Soft viscose sponges are used by many photographers for wiping films. These have only one disadvantage—and that a serious one. Grit particles are apt to become embedded in the sponges, and may later come to the surface to scratch another film. Laundering easily cleans the cloths and chamois, removes the dirt, grit and chemicals that might be absorbed by them, and makes them completely safe for repeated use. But sponges can't be laundered quite so successfully.

A slow, gentle wiping of both film surfaces from top to bottom is most effective. If the action is too rapid, the water drops are not absorbed. The time for complete drying will vary with different conditions of humidity and air circulation.

When dry, the films are removed from the clips, the roll-film strip cut into single picture sections, and the negatives filed in an appropriately identified envelope or folder. The wise beginner starts a film file with his first roll. Divisions may be made according to the date of exposure or subject matter. Complete data regarding both exposure and processing should be written on the filing envelopes. Thus you build up a usable backlog of technical data.

Safelight Test

Object:

To determine the length of time that film or paper can be exposed to a darkroom safelight without a harmful fog resulting, on development.

Equipment:

Developing and printing facilities. The safelight or safelights you use in your darkroom.

Procedure:

Arrange the safelight you intend using for film development at the usual distance above your working space. Turn off all lights, including the safelight. Place a small piece of film on the table, with the emulsion side facing the safelight and with one end covered with black paper. Turn on the safelight. After one minute, cover an additional narrow strip across one end of the test film with the black paper. After each successive minute, for fifteen minutes, cover an additional strip of the sensitive film by sliding the black paper over its surface.

After this exposure, develop in total darkness, fix, wash, and dry this test in customary fashion.

If the test strip of film shows fogging, the safety time for your safelight-film combination equals the time of exposure just shorter than the one producing a detectable fog.

Repeat this procedure, using any safelight and film or paper combination. The safety factor is determined in the same manner.

Question:

Would a dark blue safelight be suitable for use while developing?

| 0 | 3 | 6 | 9 | 12 | 15 |

Exposure time, in minutes

Safelight test strip, on Kodabromide F-2, at 3 feet from a Wratten 0A Safelight, used with a 10-watt bulb.

Since films and papers that have previously been exposed in the camera, printer, or enlarger are somewhat more susceptible to safelight fog than those not previously exposed, it is advisable to make a final check on the results of the experiment by repeating it, using exposed film or paper for the test. Because this imposes extreme conditions, it constitutes a thoroughly reliable guide to the safe handling of sensitive materials. In actual darkroom practice, film or paper is seldom exposed directly to the safelight for any considerable period. During tray development when exposure to a safelight is apt to be most direct, the material is somewhat less sensitive, hence less likely to fog.

Agitation Test

Object:

To compare the effects of agitating and not agitating films during the course of development.

Equipment:

A camera for exposing two sheets of film. Developing trays.

Procedure:

Properly expose two identical sheets of film. Develop one alone in a tray, rocking the tray continuously, as development proceeds, for the recommended time. In developing the second sheet, simply slip it into the developer and leave it there unagitated and for the same length of time as the first negative.

When fixed, washed, and dried, print the two negatives simultaneously onto the same sheet of paper. Use a paper, exposure time, etc., which give the best obtainable print for the properly developed negative. As an alternative, the two negatives may be cut down the center and opposite halves of each joined together to make a single print. While it is sometimes possible to correct during printing for low contrast caused by lack of agitation, there are no means for correcting unevenness, mottle and spottiness that also invariably arise from lack of agitation.

Mount these prints in a conspicuous place as constant reminders of the importance of agitation.

Questions:

1. What effect does agitation have on negative density? Contrast?
2. What function does agitation play in development?

Developed without agitation . . . . and with continuous agitation

Time of Development Experiment

Object:

To determine the effect of development time on the contrast of a negative, and to demonstrate how Elon and hydroquinone differ as developing agents, both in the rate of image growth and resulting contrast.

Equipment:

A camera for making film pack or sheet film exposures. A tripod will be helpful. Facilities for developing films and making prints.

Procedure:

Select a subject with a wide range of brightnesses. Expose 24 correctly timed negatives. Develop 8 of these in Kodak formula DK60a, one for each of the following times: ½, 1, 3, 7, 11, 15, 25, and 60 minutes all at 68°F. Fix, wash, and dry them.

Prepare a small quantity of DK60a, omitting hydroquinone. Bring to 68°F., and develop 8 films in that; one for each of the times indicated above. The quantity of solution required will depend upon the size of the tray or tank used. Fix, wash, and dry.

Prepare another quantity of developer, using the DK60a formula but omitting the Elon. Bring to 68°F., and develop 8 films for the same times as above. Fix, wash, and dry.

Keep the negatives separated by groups, and as soon as they are dry, mark them with identifying numbers.

Make the best possible print from the negative developed 7 minutes in the regular Kodak DK60a. Using that same grade of paper, make prints from all negatives developed for this experiment. In so doing, expose each sheet of paper just long enough so that the dark shadows of the subject match in all prints. Fix, wash, and dry the prints.

For study, arrange the prints in sequence, in three rows with the corresponding times of development in the same vertical column. Mount on a card or notebook sheet for keeping.

Questions:

1. Which works faster, Elon or hydroquinone?
2. What would logically be the principal reducing agent in a developer used for reproducing line drawings of high contrast?
3. How does the time of development affect the contrast of a correctly exposed negative? What happens to the detail in the bright portions of the subject with overdevelopment?
4. What is the function of the alkali in the developer?
5. What effect does the age of the developer have on development?
6. What is fog? How long does the development time have to be before the fog is especially noticeable?
7. What effect does fog have on the picture?

Top row: DK-60a. 3-7-25 minutes. Developed with moderate speed and contrast.

Middle row: DK-60a *without Elon.* 7-25 minutes. Hydroquinone alone produced no image in less than 7 minutes. Contrast built up quickly.

Bottom row: DK-60a *without Hydroquinone.* 3-7-25 minutes. Elon alone worked rapidly, but with little contrast.

Temperature of Development Experiment _____

Object:

To determine the effect of the temperature of a developer on its action and the degrees to which temperature changes affect Elon and hydroquinone.

Equipment:

A camera for making film pack or sheet film exposures. A tripod will be helpful. Facilities for developing films and making prints.

Procedure:

Expose 9 identical negatives of a subject such as a doorway, landscape, or street scene with a wide range of brightnesses. Develop one negative under each of these 9 conditions.

1. Kodak DK-60a ....7 minutes   68°F.
2. DK-60a ....7 minutes   58°F.
3. DK-60a ....7 minutes   78°F.
4. DK-60a formula with hydroquinone
    omitted ....15 minutes   68°F.
5. DK-60a formula with hydroquinone
    omitted ....15 minutes   58°F.
6. DK-60a formula with hydroquinone
    omitted ....15 minutes   78°F.
7. DK-60a formula with Elon
    omitted ....25 minutes   68°F.
8. DK-60a formula with Elon
    omitted ....25 minutes   58°F.
9. DK-60a formula with Elon
    omitted ....25 minutes   78°F.

Fix, wash, and dry.

Make the best print possible from negative number 1. Using the same grade of paper, print all other negatives, matching the blacks of the shadows in each case with the number 1 negative.

Arrange the dried prints in order and mount on a card or notebook sheet for study.

Questions:

1. How does a temperature change affect the reducing action of hydroquinone? Elon?

2. What are the properties of Kodalk?

3. What is the recommended temperature for fixing baths?

4. How does temperature affect the rate of fixing?

5. How does temperature affect the rate of washing?

6. What is reticulation?

Illustrations (right)

Top row: DK-60a, 7 minutes, 58°F., 68°F., 78°F.

Middle row: DK-60a, no Elon; 15 minutes, 58°F., 68°F., 78°F.

Bottom row: DK-60a, no Hydroquinone, 25 minutes, 58°F., 68°F., 78°F.

CHAPTER 7

Photographic Paper and Printing

WITH FILM development complete, you have on your hands one or more negatives—supple, dark, useless-looking things. Hold one up to the light. The image you see there is the reverse of the subject you took; blacks are white, whites are black. All very interesting but, as a picture, it simply doesn't make sense.

To achieve a positive, real-looking image on paper, another process is necessary—the process of photographic printing.

Photographic printing is simply a process of passing light through a negative so that it forms a corresponding image in the sensitive emulsion of a photographic paper. When the emulsion side of the negative is in uniform contact with the emulsion side of the paper, the image passed to the paper is exactly the same size as that of the negative. A print so made is called a *contact print*. It has the advantage of perfect "synchronization;" being in contact with the negative, it picks up its every detail automatically. Prints made by projection—enlargements and reductions—must depend on the precision of the optical system of the projector and on the sometimes fallible focusing ability of the operator. Hence, contact prints automatically achieve a sharpness which only real precision attains in projection prints. But there are advantages in projection printing, too, as may appear a little later on.

PRINTING BY CONTACT

The process of printing consists of four basic steps:
1. Exposure
2. Development
3. Fixing
4. Washing

The first two are fascinating, so fascinating that many amateurs tend to overlook the last two, not realizing—or forgetting—that inadequate fixing and washing mean impermanent prints.

First, how dark must the room be? Surprise! If you use Kodak's Velite paper it doesn't have to be dark. Velite carries a special kind of emulsion —it's not particularly sensitive to the normal level of artificial room illumination. But being highly sensitive to very bright light Velite is easily exposed in the printing boxes to be described later. Thus Velite is ideal for the beginner at printing—by working in room light you can concentrate attention on good print quality without having your judgment affected by the darkness of the room.

More conventional paper emulsions are slow relative to film, and sensitive only to blue light, hence a fairly high level of illumination is permissible, so long as the light present does not contain blue. Window shades should be drawn at night to exclude direct rays from street lights, neighboring houses, or passing cars. If you have a regular darkroom lamp, use the Wratten Series OO or OA safelight with a 10-watt bulb. Some orange and ruby colored bulbs are safe but should be carefully tested before you expose any quantity of your paper to them. (See "Safelight Test," page 72.)

Trays and Chemicals

Three trays are placed side by side in the sink or on a covered table. The left-hand tray, for convenience, is used for the developer, the center one for a rinse, called a stop bath, and the one on the right for the fixer.

Paper processing chemicals differ slightly from those used with film, although some developers such as Universal Developer and that contained in the Tri Chem Pack can be used for both. Paper developers work more rapidly. If you make an occasional small batch of prints you'll find the small packets of prepared developer convenient. Kodak Dektol, a paper 79

Packaged chemicals for convenience and accuracy

Arrange your trays like this

developer, is supplied in larger quantities if you work more frequently and make a greater number of prints. Following is the formula for Kodak D-72, if you care to mix your own solutions from bulk chemicals:

KODAK DEVELOPER D-72

	Avoirdupois		Metric
Water, about 125°F. (50°C.)	16	ounces	500 cc.
Kodak Elon Developing Agent.	45	grains	3.0 grams
Kodak Sodium Sulfite, desiccated. . . .	1½	ounces	45.0 grams
Kodak Hydroquinone	175	grains	12.0 grams
Kodak Sodium Carbonate,			
monohydrated	2 oz. 290	grains	80.0 grams
Kodak Potassium Bromide	30	grains	2.0 grams
Water to make.	32	ounces	1.0 liter

Dissolve chemicals in the order given.

For papers, dilute 1 to 2 and develop about 60 seconds at 68°F.

This formula can also be used for films and plates. See recommendations listed on instruction sheets packed with materials.

The acid stop bath for the center tray is prepared by diluting 1½ ounces of 28% acetic acid with water to make 32 ounces. Its purpose is two-fold. First, it neutralizes the alkali in the developer carried over on prints, thereby putting an abrupt stop to development and preventing uneven markings or development streaks. It also prolongs the life of the fixing bath by preventing the developer alkali from being carried into the hypo by the prints.

In the third tray is the fixing bath. You can use the same fixing bath for prints as for films if you use the formula suggested in the chapter on "Developing Film."

Make some provision for washing your prints in running water after they're fixed.

The Printing Frame and Printing Box

There are two standard means by which contact print exposures are made —the *printing frame* and the *printing box*. You'll need one or the other.

The printing frame is very much like a small picture frame, except that it is far sturdier and the back is easily removable. Too, the back is equipped with spring steel clips which assure a firm, squeezing pressure, so that paper and film are held in sure contact between the glass front of the frame and the stiff, felted back.

In practice—and in safely subdued light—the printing frame is placed,

The printing frame is simple and adequate   But a printing box is more efficient

glass side down, on the work table, and the spring clamps turned so that the back can be lifted out. Then the film is laid on the glass, *emulsion side up*. (That's the dull-surfaced side.) Over it goes the paper, *emulsion side down*. (Photographic paper tends to curl toward the emulsion side.) Then the back is put on, the clamps tightened, and all is ready for the exposure to white light.

Make certain that all other unused printing paper is safely covered. For the printing exposure, the frame is held, glass side foremost, about a foot from an ordinary 40-watt electric light, and the light turned on for a few seconds. After the bright light is turned off and the exposed paper removed from the frame, it is ready for development.

The printing-frame is a make-shift. It works, but it's not the most convenient arrangement in the world. Since it requires an open light, it means covering all sensitive materials between exposures. And, unless you're careful to have the frame in exactly the same position relative to the light for every exposure, you have no sound basis for comparing results on successive exposures. It is quite easily possible to build a simple apparatus so that light and printing frame are always at one set distance, but if you go to that trouble, you might just as well go a little farther and enjoy the greater benefits of a printing box.

A printing box, whether you buy, build, or borrow it, is simply a box with the necessary light inside of it. The top is covered by a piece of strong, clear glass, over which a pressure pad, made of two pieces of felt-covered wood or metal, hinged together, clamps down. The negative to be printed is placed on the glass, emulsion up, with the paper over it. When the pad comes down, negative and paper are in perfect contact.

In the ready-made boxes, the clamping down of the pressure pad

81

switches on the lamps. In addition to the lights used for making the exposure, good printers also contain a small ruby lamp which remains lighted throughout the working time of the box. Its purpose is simply to facilitate positioning of the film, the adjustment of the marginal masks for white borders, and the placement of the paper over film and masks.

The printing box is so convenient, so quick, that you'll lose interest in printing frames after your first printing box experience. For one thing, the box is lighttight during the exposure; hence, you are spared that panicking worry about "did I or didn't I cover up that paper before I switched this light on?"

Printing Exposures

It is physically and scientifically possible to work out an automatic or an arbitrary exposure guide for contact printing. But, for most of us, there's no necessity for any such setup. For, with a little experience, it is a relatively easy matter to determine the right exposure. If you are profligate with paper, the trial-and-error system will serve. If you are both economical and efficient, you'll cut a single sheet of paper into four or five narrow strips and expose each strip for a precise time, varying your exposures in some such order as 4 seconds, 8 seconds, 16 seconds. Mark the respective exposure times on the back of the strips, in pencil, so that after normal development, you can compare the results.

82

Four test strips will usually give you the key to the right exposure. With more experience, you'll need fewer tests

| 1 Second | 2 Seconds | 4 Seconds | 10 Seconds |

Here and now get into the habit of exposing for proper appearance when the print is developed according to the recommended time and temperature. It is impossible to get the best that's in your negative if you try to compensate for all printing errors by either shortening or forcing development.

If one of your test strips looks right, make your full-sized print accordingly; if not, make another test for a longer, shorter, or "in between" time as indicated by your first results. With experience, you'll learn to estimate the proper exposure for different types of negatives with fair accuracy and a minimum of waste paper.

Development

Slip the exposed paper neatly and quickly into the developer. Be sure that all of the paper gets under quickly, so that development will be even and uniform. In a few seconds—as you rock the tray gently—you'll see the image begin to come up, the strongest blacks first, then the middle tones and, finally, the highlights. If the exposure is normal, the print should appear to be complete in about 45 seconds. Give it an extra 10 or 15 seconds for the sake of full-bodied, rich tones and full contrasts. Too, the dim light tends to make the print seem dark, so be wary about yanking the print from the developer too soon.

With development complete, the print is slipped into the center tray for a chemical rinse in the stop bath and, after five seconds or so, shifted over into the hypo.

Prints on single-weight paper, such as Azo, Velox, and Velite, are fixed sufficiently in twenty minutes, provided they receive good agitation in the fixing bath during that period. Not only should the tray be rocked back and forth every minute or two, but the prints themselves should be rotated in the tray, so none of them becomes firmly matted to another. If a heavy, double weight paper is used, even more agitation is in order during fixation.

But—you don't have to wait until the prints are fully fixed to turn on the white room lights for a real inspection of your work. Two or three minutes in the hypo should be sufficient to preclude fogging.

Is the Print a Good One?

Take a good long look at the finished print. Does it have the richness, the full range of tones it should have? If it does; all is well. If it doesn't, there are two immediately possible remedies. One, a different exposure. For example, a longer exposure will correct for over-all lightness and lack of depth or darkness. Longer than normal development will do little more than invite over-all fog and staining. If the print is too black, try a shorter exposure. If the print is gray, lacks brilliance, sparkle and snap, consider the second possible remedy—a paper of a *different contrast*.

In the description of the printing process reference to the "contrast grade" of paper used has so far deliberately been omitted.

In an ideal world, in which all subjects and exposures would be perfect and all photographers ditto, there would be need for only one grade of paper, for all negatives would print on normal paper. Fortunately, the world is not that dull. Light values vary, shutter speeds vary, judgment sometimes misses, and even darkroom control has been known to slip up. Hence, there are many negatives that are not normal. Yet they may be made to produce beautiful and useful prints. This amiable situation is brought about through the use of papers which help to compensate for the negatives' shortcomings. Thus, a too contrasty negative is printed on a "soft" contrast grade of paper, while a low-contrast negative may be forced to stand and deliver a usable print by printing it on high-contrast paper. Simple, isn't it?

Contrast grades usually run from 0 to 5; normal contrast paper is a No. 2 or No. 3. Numbers 4 and 5 are contrasty papers, whereas numbers 1 and 0 are, respectively, soft and softer. For the average amateur's purposes, a supply of 1, 2, and 4 should serve to meet most requirements. Naturally, a larger supply of 2 should be carried, for the relatively normal negative, it is to be hoped, will predominate. The extreme grades of paper are, like life preservers or parachutes, handy to have around in a crisis, but are not to be used as a steady diet.

Azo and Velox are two outstanding contact printing papers used both by professionals and amateurs. Both are supplied in varying surfaces and a full range of contrasts. Velox is noted for its uniformity of tone throughout all contrast grades, a fact which makes it popular among photo-finishers.

Washing and Drying Prints

Assuming that you've made amends for any printing difficulties, and that you are reasonably satisfied with the prints in your hypo tray, let's finish the process. Prints, like films, must be carefully washed after fixation. In fact, prints need even more thorough washing, for paper absorbs more of the chemical solutions than does film. Those chemicals have to be washed out.

Laboratory tests show that even small quantities of hypo, if allowed to remain in the paper, will tend to produce faded images. To overcome this, several chemical "hypo eliminators" have been devised. However, fresh water can be relied on to do the job properly, if you're patient about it. About an hour's wash in running water, or twelve changes of water—five minutes each—should suffice. If long time permanence is wanted, use the hypo eliminator, Kodak HE-1 *after* washing.

After the fixing bath has been removed from the prints, and the excess wash water allowed to drip from them, they may be laid down on flat photo blotters or a clean water-absorbing cloth, or may be rolled in a blotter roll for drying. The tendency of prints to curl on drying will in no way harm them, as they may be easily stretched flat by pulling them gently over the smooth edge of a table or bench.

In order to produce prints with a high gloss surface like those frequently supplied by photofinishers, it is necessary to glaze or "ferrotype" them after washing. This is a process of rolling the wet prints, emulsion side down, onto a highly polished "ferrotype tin," where they remain until dry. Not all papers ferrotype properly. Those designated for the purpose, Azo F and Velox F, carry an overcoating of clear gelatin which, when rolled onto the highly polished tin, assumes a similar surface on drying. As the prints dry, they peel away from the tin easily.

PRINTING IS AN ART

Possibly "craft" is a better word than "art," but the point is that an experienced printer utilizes many tricks and devices to achieve his ends.

Thus, to *hold back* a portion of a negative so that the rest of it has an extra opportunity to register, he sometimes interposes tissue paper between the printing light and the part of the negative to be *held back*. Many printing boxes are equipped with panes of clear glass, below the diffusing glass, the purpose of which is to serve as shelves for tissue. This process is known by the pleasantly vivid name of *dodging*. Thus, the "artful dodger," of whom you may have heard, may have been simply a skilled and ingenious photographic printer.

You may have noticed some workers trying to accelerate development by rubbing their finger tips vigorously over the part of the print that seems slow in coming up. Heat, of course, speeds up all chemical reactions and, in this case, the heat of the fingers might hurry development in one particular area. This procedure, however, is not advisable; for, while heat accelerates development, it also accelerates staining due to over-oxidizing of the developer.

Sometimes printers even resort to extreme measures of this type: they'll yank the partially developed print from the developer, douse it in fresh, cold water to arrest development, and then go over the balky areas with a finger or a bit of cotton dipped in developer. If they get the desired result, the print then goes back into the bath for complete development.

And so it goes.

Such devices, interesting as they may be, again belong in the life-saver or parachute class. It's simply good sense to aim at the production of the best possible prints by orthodox methods. And that implies good negatives to begin with.

PAPER EMULSIONS

If you think the modern photographic industry provides a large variety of film emulsions, take a look at the paper situation.

In the first place, there are three basic types of paper—slow emulsions for contact prints, fast emulsions for easy enlarging, and an in-between type which can be used for both contact and projection printing. These types are known, respectively, as chloride, bromide, and chloro-bromide papers.

Speed in papers is not comparable to film speed. There's no real need for it; in fact, the advantage is all the other way 'round; for the slower emulsions used with paper permit a far greater degree of control during exposure.

Within each of the three general paper types there are dozens of sub-types distinguished by the character of the surface—matte, semi-matte, lustre, glossy—or by the paper tint—natural, white, cream, ivory,—or by the "warmth" of the emulsion (blue-blacks are cold, brownish blacks are warm). These characteristics in Kodak papers are denoted by a letter, F, G, R, E, etc. Then, for these sub-types there are the different contrast grades, 0, 1, 2, 3, 4, 5. And, in many instances, different grades are available in both single and double weight.

When you stop to consider the multiplicity of these paper types and the scores of sizes in which most of them are available, it's plain to see that there are headaches in stocking and selling photographic papers.

There are styles or fashions in papers, just as in dogs or books. One year the photographers may develop a mass fondness for hard-as-nails glossy prints; and the next may find a special demand for novelty surfaces. The intelligent photographer will try to avoid fads and to select his papers on the basis of the individual picture to be printed and on the purpose for which it is intended. For commercial work, with reproduction by photoengraving involved, it's best to use full contrast and a glossy finish. For pictures to be seen at first hand, a less commercial finish is desirable.

It is only by actual experience and experiment that you will discover which papers best meet your requirements.

PHOTOGRAPHIC PAPER

In the course of making a print, you may find yourself suddenly impressed with the fact that you're dunking a piece of paper into chemical solutions and much plain water—and that the paper remains paper.

You can't do that with ordinary paper. Drop a piece of newspaper into water. In a matter of seconds it has lost its strength, its color, and its usefulness. The same thing happens to almost all the other forms of paper when subjected to water. But photographic paper, the paper on which a photograph is ultimately realized for all the world to see and to admire, is made of much sterner stuff. It has to be. For it undergoes an ordeal by water that would leave ordinary papers limp and unlovely.

Photographic paper is not only tough; it is very much purer than the driven snow. Again, it has to be. If it contained traces of iron, copper, or other chemical impurities, they might easily be the ruination of the photographic emulsion-coating. Too, they could easily stir up trouble during the chemical reactions involved in development.

Before the light-sensitive emulsion is coated on the paper (by a process very similar to that used in film coating), the paper has first to be seasoned for a time and then to be coated with a milky white substance called baryta (barium sulphate and gelatin). Baryta, which is chemically inert, fills the surface pores of the paper and provides a smoothly uniform surface as a foundation for the photographic emulsion. It keeps the emulsion from soaking into the fibres of the paper, with inevitably uneven results. The consistency of the baryta is the major factor in the establishment of the matte (dull) or gloss finish of the paper.

Paper Contrast Experiment

Object:

To illustrate the characteristics of the different contrast grades of contact printing paper.

Equipment:

Facilities for printing. An average negative, one making a good print on a normal contrast grade of paper.

Procedure:

Using the selected negative, make the best obtainable print on all contrast grades of a standard contact printing paper, such as Azo or Velox. The printing time will vary with the contrast grade, so keep a record of those times.

You will profit by repeating this procedure, using a negative low in contrast, or flat, and then a contrasty negative, or one printing best on a low contrast paper.

Mount in order on a card or notebook sheet for comparisons.

Questions:

1. What is wrong in highlights, shadows, etc., in each print that appears in your estimation to be off in contrast?
2. How do the speeds of the different paper grades compare?

Average contrast negative

Low contrast paper is too soft

Normal contrast paper, good print

High contrast paper, harsh highlights, empty shadows

Low contrast negative

High contrast negative

Low contrast paper is extremely flat

Low contrast paper makes a good print

Normal contrast paper, still too flat

Normal contrast paper, too contrasty

High contrast paper makes a good print

High contrast paper, extreme contrast

Washing Test

Object:

To determine whether or not films or prints are reasonably free from hypo and sufficiently washed to prevent fading of images.

Procedure:

Mix 250 cc. of hypo test solution as follows:

Distilled water .... 180 cc.
Potassium permanganate.. 3 grams
Sodium Hydroxide
  (caustic soda) .... 6 grams
Add enough distilled water
  to make .... 250 cc. of solution

To Test Films for Completeness of Washing:

1. Dilute 2 drops of the above solution with 250 cc. of pure water.
2. Lift an eight-exposure roll of No. 116 film or the equivalent (about 80 square inches) from the wash and allow the excess water to drip into the diluted test solution. If hypo is present, the solution will change from violet to orange or yellow. If no hypo is present no change in color will result.

To Test Papers for Completeness of Washing:

1. Dilute 2 drops of the stock solution with 125 cc. of pure water. Use 15 cc. of this in a glass for your test.
2. Take about 120 square inches of prints (for example, 10 prints from No. 116 negatives) from the wash and let the excess water drip into the test solution. If hypo is present, the solution will turn yellow then lose its color, if no hypo is present, no color change will take place.

Both films and papers should be washed until the wash water from them does not change the color of the test solution.

To Insure Accuracy of the Test:

Add a sample of tap water equal to the volume of water from the films or paper, to a sample of the fresh test solution. If there is no color change, the tap water you are using for washing is free from certain chemicals which might otherwise render your washing test inaccurate. If there is a slight change in the color of the violet test solution upon addition of the tap water, the tap water test should be run alongside the wash water tests. Comparisons of the two test solution colors will then indicate freedom from hypo when both tap and wash water give equal color changes.

CHAPTER 8

Enlarging

THERE'S A THRILL to enlarging. The very fact that you're able to produce a big, framable picture from a negative that may be as small as a postage stamp is, in itself, exciting. Bigness always is.

But there's more to enlarging than the mere "blowing up" of an image. The control you exercise in making an enlargement is so extensive that you can almost create new pictures from your old negatives. It is eternally true that the expert photographer sees his finished picture in the view finder of his camera; after the exposure each succeeding step in the photographic process serves merely to carry him straight to the realization of that picture. But we are not all so expert. If we find a means by which some of our shortcomings can be remedied, we embrace it. Enlarging is such a means.

Far more important, however, is the fact that enlarging is a method of glorifying pictures—of translating them into terms which carry far more force than those of album-sized snapshots. By skillfully enlarging an image you bring it somehow closer to reality, or the illusion of reality. And that illusion is one of the important intangibles in any art form.

One factor contributing to this illusion is that you generally view enlargements from a distance which enables you to see the correct perspective in the picture. To see the same perspective in a contact print you must hold it only a few inches from your eyes—and that, naturally, you seldom do.

Enlarging, as intimated in Chapter 7, is simply a form of photographic printing. It differs from contact printing in that the negative image is projected, much as a lantern slide is projected. The image is focused onto a sheet of light-sensitive enlarging paper which is subsequently developed.

The enlarging apparatus is, essentially, a camera in reverse. Instead of receiving an image, it projects one. There's a strong light source, the rays

The control it affords . . . . **is one of enlarging's features**

from which pass through the negative (which stops or passes them according to the varying densities of the image) to a lens which transmits them in an expanding cone to the enlarging paper. Obviously the farther the paper is from the lens, the greater the expansion of the cone of projection—and the larger the projected image.

With this arrangement, it is apparent that you are dealing with a simpler problem than that of a camera, as far as proper focusing is concerned. For both the negative and the enlarging paper are flat; hence you need have no concern for depth of field. You simply watch the projected negative image for maximum sharpness as you move the lens in or out, in relation to the negative. The best working aperture for the projection lens is usually somewhat less than wide open; and one which permits a convenient and controllable exposure time—say, 10 seconds.

Under these circumstances, it is plainly important that the enlarger be designed to project a uniform intensity of light. There are three principal systems of illumination, capable of achieving such uniformity, without a "hot spot." And enlargers are "typed" accordingly.

Diffusion Enlargers

Diffusion enlargers seek to get a uniform supply of light to the negative in either of two ways. One of these is by the use of a lamp house shaped to scramble the rays of light completely—or integrate them—as the technical men describe it. In the other system uniformity at the negative surface is accomplished by means of a diffusing medium, usually a piece of ground or opal glass, placed between the lamp and the negative.

The newest enlarger designs utilize the first of the two above methods in combination with fluorescent lamps which themselves provide quite well scattered or diffuse light. In these enlargers the lamps are generally circular and of greater diameter than the negative. If so they are recessed in the outer edges of the lamp houses so all the light reaching the negative area is "indirect"—and of maximum uniformity. Enlargers with fluorescent lamps have the added advantage of cool operation, which avoids buckling of negatives in glassless carriers, and saves tempers that flare when you accidentally touch your forehead to the lamp house of the older variety.

The degree of uniformity obtained by the use of a diffusing glass is also influenced by such factors as lamp house shape, size and type of the tungsten lamp used and its location in the housing.

The diffusion referred to, thus far, is that which takes place *before* the light reaches the negative. An enlarger with a perfect diffusion system affords enlarged print quality equaling that of contact prints. A good enlarger must be so constructed that, *after* the light passes through the negative, it is not reflected from the inside of the bellows, lens board or other parts. If it is, the stray light tends to wander into areas where there's supposed to be no light: reflection of this sort means gray, dimmed highlights in your enlargements.

Some of the finest enlargers, both professional and amateur, are of the diffusion type. Portrait studios use them because they can deliver matching contact prints and enlargements to their customers. The Kodak Flurolite Enlarger, an example of the "integrator" type, is outstanding among diffusion types for amateurs.

Condenser Enlargers

The old-time condenser enlarger had no diffusion whatsoever. The result was high optical efficiency accompanied by exaggeration of graininess and defects and by extreme contrast. To understand this increase in contrast, it is only necessary to consider the fact that the effective density of a negative depends upon (a) its light-stopping properties and (b) its light-scattering characteristics.

Thus, in a diffusion enlarger, the difference between two densities is wholly a matter of how much light each one stops. In the condenser enlarger the lower density stops some light and scatters some, while the higher density not only stops more but also scatters more, thereby creating

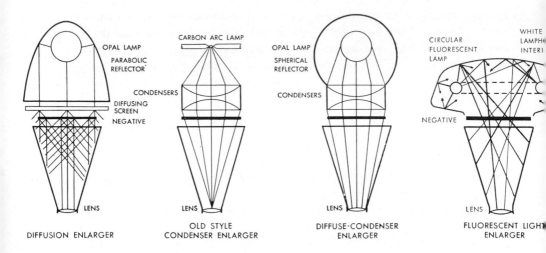

OPAL LAMP
PARABOLIC REFLECTOR
CONDENSERS
DIFFUSING SCREEN
NEGATIVE
LENS
DIFFUSION ENLARGER

CARBON ARC LAMP
CONDENSERS
LENS
OLD STYLE CONDENSER ENLARGER

OPAL LAMP
SPHERICAL REFLECTOR
CONDENSERS
LENS
DIFFUSE-CONDENSER ENLARGER

CIRCULAR FLUORESCENT LAMP
WHITE LAMPH INTERI
NEGATIVE
LENS
FLUORESCENT LIGHT ENLARGER

a greater effective difference between the two silver deposits. In the condenser enlarger, with no diffusion, the resulting gain in contrast was too great for most practical uses.

This meant also that the "grain" in the film and all the tiny blemishes, scratches, and dust spots were projected as exaggerated parts of the image. And even the cleanest negative showed these defects when the enlargement was great. Thus, while the condenser enlarger was optically efficient it did tend to keep its owner and user humble with its uncompromising presentation of minute defects.

Another point about this enlarger: because it depends on a precise optical system, the relative positions of the lamp filament and the condenser elements must be changed as lenses of varying focal lengths are used, or separate sets of condensers must be used with the different projection lenses.

Today the use of the pure condenser enlarger is limited almost exclusively to a few technical applications that are fairly remote from popular photography. But the condenser idea has been adapted and improved in the third basic enlarger type, the diffuse-condenser enlarger, diagrammed above and described below.

Diffuse-Condenser Enlargers

In this type of enlarger an opal bulb is substituted for the clear bulb of the original condenser type. Thus the optical system has diffuse light to work with. The results are better, for it affords slightly more contrast than a straight diffuser outfit, yet not quite as much as the clear bulb-condenser type, and tends to be less revealing as far as negative defects and graininess are concerned.

Negatives enlarged with the opal bulb-condenser enlarger may require a paper which is one contrast grade softer than that needed for best results in contact printing or diffusion type enlarging.

Lenses for Enlargers

In general, any well-corrected lens, the focal length of which is at least equal to the diagonal of the largest negative to be enlarged, will serve in enlarging. Lenses made particularly for enlarging are corrected for those distances generally used in enlarging—and thus may differ slightly from ordinary camera lenses. However, many a successful amateur finds it both economical and efficient to use his camera lens in his enlarger.

This practice in general is more apt to prove satisfactory if you use a miniature lens and enlarge miniature negatives than if you enlarge larger negatives with longer focal length lenses. In the former case the magnification is greater and the lens is therefore used closer to the point of maximum correction.

Some lenses are unsatisfactory for enlarger use because, due to improper color correction, they fail to produce a visible image in exactly the same plane as the photographically effective image. Hence, focusing on the enlarger's paper board or easel with such a lens becomes a matter of approximation and guess work. With any good lens, however, trouble of this sort is automatically eliminated. Kodak Ektar and Ektanon lenses, fully corrected for enlarging, are supplied in a number of focal lengths and can easily be fitted to any size enlarger lens board.

Automatic shutters are not usually needed in enlarging, as exposures are in terms of seconds, rather than hundredths of a second. The exposure is made by turning the light on and off rather than by any mechanism at or in the lens. A light switch which can be operated by foot pressure is advantageous, in that it leaves the operator's hands free for various manipulations during the exposure.

Practically every enlarger is equipped with a red safety screen which can be swung into position over the lens to permit safe readjustment of focus, or any other adjustment *after* the sensitive paper is in place.

ENLARGING PAPERS

The chief difference between enlarging and contact papers is one of speed. In contact work, the printing lights are concentrated (and relatively close to the negative and paper) so that high speed is not important. In enlarging, the light passing through your negative is spread over a large sheet of paper and must pass through a small opening in a lens to get there, hence greater sensitivity becomes important.

Enlarging paper emulsions are generally mixtures of silver chloride and silver bromide—thus commonly referred to as chloro-bromides. By carefully controlling the proportions and characteristics of these two sensitive salts the manufacturer can obtain a wide range of the photographic qualities including speed and contrast. The size of the developed silver grains imparts tone or color to the image. Finely divided silver grains give the print a brownish or warm tone while larger grains appear to be more bluish-black or colder in tone.

Enlarging papers, like contact papers, are to be had in great variety, ranging all the way from the glossy, super-smooth papers intended for ferrotyping, to papers with extremely coarse surface texture or pattern—papers whose use is limited (or should be) to those subjects which can justify them. In addition to variations in surface, there are variations in color, in weight and, of course, in contrast.

For a number of years Kodabromide and Opal have been "standard" among enlarging papers. Kodabromide is a fast, all-purpose paper with wide exposure and development latitude. Opal is slower, warmer in tone and ideally suited to the requirements of the pictorialist.

Recently two new papers have been added to the Kodak line, Medalist and Ektalure. Medalist paper is unique; you can vary the exposure and development ratio to obtain contrasts between the four available contrast grades. It tones well in standard toners. Ektalure has a brown-black tone and is noteworthy for its ability to retain good detail in deep shadow areas.

The table on the opposite page lists the paper surfaces and tints appropriate for various picture subjects. Make an extra 8x10 print from each new surface you use, put it into a notebook and you'll soon have a very helpful paper-subject reference book to which you can turn when choosing papers for particular types of negatives.

Selecting Your Enlarging Paper

YOUR SUBJECT OR THE USE FOR YOUR PRINT	PAPER SURFACE, TINT, AND BRILLIANCE	PAPERS AND GRADES
Scientific subjects *Photographs for publication* *For maximum brilliance and detail*	SMOOTH, GLOSSY WHITE	KODABROMIDE F MEDALIST F
Commercial subjects *Display photographs* *Album enlargements*	SMOOTH, LUSTRE WHITE	KODABROMIDE N MEDALIST J (High Lustre)
Snow scenes *Portraits in high key* *Smooth skin texture*	FINE GRAIN, LUSTRE WHITE	KODABROMIDE E
General pictorial *and portrait work*	FINE GRAIN, LUSTRE WHITE	KODABROMIDE E
	FINE GRAIN, LUSTRE CREAM WHITE	KODABROMIDE G MEDALIST G
Character portraits *Large size pictorial prints* *Extreme enlargements from* * miniature films* *Table tops with massive areas*	ROUGH, LUSTRE CREAM WHITE	OPAL L
	FINE GRAIN, LUSTRE CREAM WHITE	EKTALURE G OPAL G
	TWEED, LUSTRE OLD IVORY	OPAL S
Specialized portrait or * pictorial effects*	TAPESTRY, LUSTRE OLD IVORY	OPAL Z
	SUEDE, MATTE CREAM WHITE or OLD IVORY	OPAL V OPAL W
	SILK, LUSTRE CREAM	OPAL Y

ENLARGING

The enlarging process, itself, is a fascinating one. For one thing, you have more at stake; a sheet of enlarging paper costs good money. Hence there's more than artistic aspiration involved as you prepare for action.

Preparations

Developer, stop-bath, hypo, and rinse are prepared and brought to the proper temperature just as for contact printing. The trays should all be a little larger than the largest print you contemplate making at any one session.

Be sure the enlarger lens is clean. *And* the negative. *And* the negative holder, especially if it is of the "glass sandwich" type. Remember you're going to enlarge; dust and dirt enlarge just as much as details of the image itself.

A safe light for enlarging is less bright than is permissible in contact work. The yellow-green, Wratten OA Safelight should be used. Better run a test to be sure that you're not using too bright a bulb or using the light too close to your working area.

Have your paper handy, so that a sheet can be selected quickly and the package closed to prevent fogging when you turn on the white light for print inspection. Some amateurs have built light-tight paper drawers into their work benches just below their enlargers; good idea.

Procedure

Put a pencil back of your ear, don your apron, and get going.

1. Place the negative to be enlarged in the negative holder of the enlarger, emulsion side toward the lens.

2. Put a sheet of plain white, non-photographic paper in position on the paper board.

3. Open the lens to its fullest opening and—white light off, now—turn on the enlarger lamp. You'll see the projected negative image on the paper. By changing the lens-to-paper distance you get the size you want; a little further manipulation of the lens-to-negative relationship will give you exact focus. And *exact* it must be.

4. That done, switch off the enlarger lamp and place a test strip of enlarging paper on the paper board. A test strip for an 8 x 10 enlargement can be a very narrow slice (one 8 x 10 sheet can be cut into a dozen test strips, easily) but it should be placed so that it gets a representative assortment of the intensities in the projected image. Otherwise, it can afford no conclusive test.

5. Close down your lens to its best working aperture and make a test exposure series of, for example, 4, 8, and 16 seconds. This can be done by covering the strip, step by step, with a sheet of black paper during exposure. Mark the times on the back of the strip and,

6. Develop it for the recommended time. If one of the times seems right, make a full test strip at that time for a check. If development shows too obvious over- or underexposure on all steps of the first test, discard it and make another series, halving or doubling the times, as the case may demand. With the seemingly correct strip safely in the hypo, give it a moment or so and then—

7. Turn on the white light for a real inspection. Check it for focus, of course, but primarily for density and contrast. If everything looks right, that's fine. If it lacks brilliance, a test on contrastier paper should be made.

Thus, by trial-and-error, correct exposure on the right paper is determined. Another, and very neat, method of establishing correct enlarging exposure is offered in the Kodak Projection Print Scale. By means of a single test exposure, it gives you visual evidence of the best exposure time plus a plainly legible figure showing the necessary exposure time.

At first you may have to make tests on several contrast grades for comparison before discovering which one is the right one. Most beginners seem to have a tendency to make prints that are just a bit too flat. Perhaps it's because prints lose some contrast and brilliance as they dry. There may be another reason which you can avoid easily by timing your enlarging exposures for proper development in the recommended time. Pulling prints out of the developer before they've been in the full time, just because they're "dark enough," means a loss in contrast, too. Still another reason is that, in the dim light, prints look darker than they actually are.

8. So you go ahead with a full-size enlargement. Develop, rinse, fix, and wash carefully. An hour's good washing should be about right.

9. Dry the print, face down, on a big clean white blotter (you can buy photo-blotters quite reasonably) or on a piece of cheesecloth stretched on a rack.

And there you have a straight enlargement. It is just like a contact print, only bigger. It may be very good, too—exactly what you wanted. But the chances are that it can be improved. Here are some of the means by which true glorification of a picture can be realized:

Manipulation

CROPPING, which consists of enlarging only a portion of the negative, eliminates the undesirable parts. This can be done either by masking or framing the desired part of the negative itself, or by utilizing only a portion of the projected image. Cropping can be used to add emphasis, to improve composition, or to straighten either horizontal or vertical lines. Practically every negative, no matter how carefully composed can be improved by slight cropping.

SHADING of parts of the image during the exposure reduces the exposure of those parts and lightens them relative to the unshaded areas. A small black paper disc on the end of a wire is used to shade central areas while a black card can be used near the margins. This is also referred to as *dodging*. The dodgers should be held a few inches away from the paper and kept in slight motion during exposure to insure blending.

PRINTING IN is the local addition of exposure to selected parts of the enlargement on top of the overall exposure. Perhaps the entire sky needs more exposure, or the corners of the print need darkening to afford a natural frame. Frequently one or two small bright portions need extra time. A large black card with a hole cut in it is held between the lens and the paper; the hole allows light to get to the desired portion, while the card holds it back from the rest of the picture. As in shading, the *printing in* must blend naturally into the remainder of the picture, so the card needs to be kept in gentle motion.

Fine of the baby, not so good of mother. A straight enlargement doesn't help but, with vignetting, mother and background disappear

100

VIGNETTING is a sort of glorified shading. It is an effect gained by shading all of the picture except for one central feature, leaving that emphasized. Used mostly, of course, in portrait photography, it is a convenient trick when you want an enlarged picture of one particular person in a group photograph.

DIFFUSING. Sometimes pictorial and portrait photographers achieve a soft "atmospheric" effect in their prints. In enlarging this may be done by holding a *diffusion disk* directly next to the enlarger lens during the exposure. This disk is a flat glass with slightly raised concentric rings pressed onto it. Light passing through the disk has its path altered just enough to break the sharpness of a straight line. Usually it is best to give half the exposure without the diffusion, and half with diffusion.

Crumpled cellophane and black net are sometimes used in place of the glass disk, but are not as suitable because they greatly reduce contrast and cause too much scattering or diffusing.

The negative had plenty of sky detail, but an enlargement, exposed for the foreground, failed to reveal it. By dodging, the sky was given the necessary additional printing exposure 101

Photographically, an uncorrected enlargement was satisfactory, but geometrically it was not. Tilting the enlarger easel corrected the distortion.

CORRECTING DISTORTION. Enlarging allows for the possible correction of what may logically be termed distorted perspective. In the average snapshot of a building, made at close range, the sides of the building seem to lean in toward the center of the picture and the building appears to be falling back. The top of the building is farther away from the camera and is therefore reproduced on the film as smaller. Hence, some snapshots, otherwise beyond criticism, look quite unnatural.

To correct for this effect in enlarging, tilt the easel or paper board so the projected image of the bottom of the building is closer to the lens than the top part. Then the bottom of the building will be magnified less; if the tilt is of the proper degree, the combination of camera distortion and the reverse enlarger distortion will be one of cancellation and the print will appear normal.

Some enlarger easels or paper boards have adjustable legs for tilting; with others you can simply lean one end of the board on a couple of books with the same result. Focus the image in the center and stop the lens down as far as possible for all-over sharpness.

The final enlarged print may represent a combination of all the above "doctors." Don't lose sight, however, of the fact that the more care you exercise in the original exposure and negative development, the less manipulating you'll be required to do.

CHECKING UP

Here are a few questions you might ask yourself as a sort of measuring stick for the quality of your enlarging.

1. "Have I selected the right contrast grade of paper?"

   You have, if your print shows the full tone range of which the paper is capable, and if you can see detail in both the picture highlights and shadows. There should be modeling and brilliance in any faces that show.

2. "Is the paper surface right for the subject?"

   It is, if it jibes with the chart in this chapter, or if it seems pleasing to you and to others.

3. "Have I exposed and developed it properly?"

   You have, if your print was so timed as to be fully developed in the recommended time. It will be free from streaks and stains if you kept it *well agitated* in the developer, stop bath, and hypo, and used fresh solutions.

4. "Is my print sharp?"

   It will be if your negative was sharp to begin with and you were careful in focusing your enlarger. Enlarger vibration during exposure will, of course, ruin the over-all sharpness and definition of the print.

5. "Will I—or anyone else—be able to enjoy this enlargement a few years from now?"

   Certainly—if fixation and washing are carried out according to both the letter and the spirit of the laws governing those processes. If you're doubtful, remember there's a test you can make. Check the experiment on page 90.

Printing Latitude Experiment

Object:

To determine the extent to which over- and underexposure of printing and enlarging papers may be compensated for by over- and underdevelopment.

Equipment:

Facilities for printing and enlarging.

Procedure:

Using a negative of good quality, make the best possible contact print or enlargement on the paper to be tested. Follow the recommended development technique, but adjust the intensity of the printing light to provide a paper exposure of approximately twenty seconds for this good print.

Perhaps the best print from the negative you select will come from a short exposure. In that case smaller bulbs may be substituted for those in the printer, or a few sheets of white typewriter paper can be inserted between the lamps and the negative. In enlarging, simply adjust the diaphragm of the enlarger to give the suggested twenty second exposure.

Record your exact exposure and development times. Then make a series of prints, reducing the exposure time by three seconds for each successive one. Develop each print long enough to compensate for the lack of exposure. Make another series of prints with longer exposures, with a three-second increase in exposure time for each successive print in the series. Develop these

Extreme overexposure and underdevelopment result in a flat, muddy print

for shorter times in an attempt to compensate for the over-exposure.

Carry both the over- and under-exposure series to the point where the resulting quality is definitely inferior.

Mount in order, for study and comparison. It will be obvious that while passable prints may be obtained through a considerable range, best prints result from correct timing and processing.

Questions:

1. What is the passable range?
2. How many prints are equally as fine as the correctly handled one?
3. How does contrast vary with the time of development?
4. What is wrong with the prints that are not wholly acceptable to you? Are they flat and muddy looking? Are they stained and yellowish?

Properly exposed and developed, this print covers the full tonal scale

Extreme underexposure and overdevelopment produce flatness, fog, and stain

CHAPTER 9

Sensitometry

WHEN YOU TAKE A PICTURE you have one specific result or effect in mind. "Trial and error" is one way of getting what you want, but it's uncertain, inconvenient, uneconomical, and often just plain impossible. Obviously, the better way is to be able to define your aim in terms of print quality, and to set about getting it systematically. That's where science comes in.

A good print, generally speaking, is one in which the full scale of the paper from white to black is utilized, and in which there is detail in both the highlight and shadow regions. But a really good print cannot be achieved without a good negative; negative quality is fundamental.

On the basis of very extensive study, photographic scientists have been able to make definite recommendations for the use of film, paper, and chemicals, all aimed at a good picture as the final objective. *Sensitometry* is the name attached to this phase of photography. It is concerned, as its name implies, with the measurement of sensitivity and the study of all technical factors effecting the use of sensitized materials.

In sensitometry the measurements and the language are specific and quantitative. They are the backbone of the exposure and development recommendations which accompany sensitive materials. Take them lightly for granted if you wish, but the fact remains that they are based on the fundamentals of the science of photographic materials. If you know these fundamentals, you are in a far better position to take full advantage of film and paper than one who does not; just as one who knows automotive mechanics is reasonably sure to get better mileage and smoother driving.

THE TERMINOLOGY

While most of the words of sensitometry are familiar enough, many have special meaning when applied in photography. For example, there's *exposure, opacity, transmission, density, speed, latitude,* etc. It is of course possible to go through a fairly successful photographic life serenely unaware of them. It is also possible to live today without considering what's involved in such terms as 50 miles per hour speed, 60 watt lamps, 90 horse power engines, 70 degrees Fahrenheit, 1430 on the radio dial, or 20 miles-to-a-gallon motoring efficiency; it's possible—but hardly practical.

Exposure

Speaking specifically of *exposure*, photo-scientists properly regard it as the root of all photographic good and evil. For exposures result in silver deposits in the film emulsion, and at precisely that point the success or failure of the eventual picture hangs in the balance.

Exposure implies the total action of light on the sensitive film at any particular point. It is a composite, the product of the illumination *(I)*, as it reaches the film, and of the *time (t)* that light is allowed to act on the film. It's a nicely symbolic coincidence that the basic equation of photography reads thus:—

$$E = It$$

For *exposure* is unquestionably "It" in photography.

During the instant the shutter of your camera is open, as you "take" a picture, many different light intensities from the scene fall onto the film, all for the same length of time. This means many varied exposures, all of which go to make up the image or negative after development. The scene is visible in real life and on the film only because of these intensity differences.

In addition, *I* is controlled by adjusting the lens aperture, which uniformly raises or lowers the intensities of light reaching the film. If the lens aperture is opened too far, under average conditions, the highest intensities (the highlights) of the subject are overexposed; cut down the aperture too far, and the low intensities (the shadows) become too weak to register adequately.

The other variable, *time* or *t*, is a matter of shutter speeds. Change from the conventional 1/50 second to 1/25 second and you obviously get double the exposure. Many modern cameras give you a range of shutter speeds from 1/400 second to one second, hence your factor, *t*, is really quite variable.

Density

The result of exposure is, on development, a silver deposit on the film—and that deposit is quite important, too. For on its adequacy and on the inter-relationship of all the deposits on the film depends the quality of the eventual picture.

Roughly, here is the mathematical approach to density, or the all-important light-stopping qualities of the silver deposit.

1. Here's a developed film. In one section of it, in an area concerned with some such monotone subject as, for example, the side of a barn, there's a silver deposit labeled "A."

2. Suppose the deposit is just enough to permit half of the incident light to pass through.
3. Since the *transmission*, or light-passing characteristic, of any medium equals the light passed divided by the light incident, the transmission of A = ½.
4. Divide the incident light by the light passed and you have the reciprocal of transmission, or a quality which is called *opacity*.*
5. The *opacity* of A = 1 ÷ ½ or 2.

So far, so good. But opacity, as a basis for photographic computations, is clumsy, and not directly related to our visual impressions. The opacity of silver deposits in current films might easily vary from 0 to 500 or more. A chart, drawn to represent the growth of opacity in the film, might have to extend over vast expanses of graph paper. But, more important, the eye does not recognize tone differences in arithmetic proportions; it sees them in terms of logarithmic differences. Density is the term applied to the logarithm of opacity. If the opacity of the deposit A, mentioned two or three paragraphs ago, is 2, the density of that deposit is the logarithm of 2, which happens to be .3.

This term *density*, in its specialized photographic sense, is freely used in technical discussions. For example, you may be casually informed that some specific area has a density of 2.3. To figure out what that means,

*The science of photography needs some expert word craftsmen, for *opacity* is a poor word. It comes from "opaque" which is an absolute conception, not a relative one. Think it over.

arithmetically in terms of *transmission*, you grab your nearest "Handbook of Chemistry and Physics" and look up the antilog of 2.3 (the number which has 2.3 for its logarithm). It turns out to be 200. Therefore, backing into the equations, you establish that:

$$\text{Opacity} = 200$$

and that the corresponding transmission is 1/200.

In other words, only 1/200 of the incident light is transmitted.

In film testing laboratories, light sources of definitely known intensities and precisely measured exposure times are used. The instrument for exposing film in this exacting fashion is called a *sensitometer*. Your camera is a sensitometer minus the precise controls. You expose for known times, but not at known intensities.

There are also *densitometers*. These are used for measuring the densities of small areas of silver deposits. They are simply scientific extensions of the judgment you use when, scanning a negative, you announce that it is thin, or dense. Such optical or electrical devices are relatively expensive, but indispensible in such professional fields as the motion picture industry. If you wish to do a limited amount of density reading, such as for occasional color printing at home, you'll find the Kodak Densiguide useful. It contains a strip of measured densities which you can use for comparison with your film gray scale densities, and arrive at a reasonably accurate measurement.

The density of a silver image on paper is figured in quite the same way as those of film, except in place of transmission the amount of light reflected is measured. Paper densitometers illuminate the area to be measured with light from 45° angles and use a viewing direction which is at right angles to the paper.

All of this may seem to belong in the "interesting if true" category, but in the manufacture of film it is put to work in a number of constructive ways, ways which can be of real value to you as a user of the products. By comparing and controlling the relationship between exposure and density in films, remarkable uniformity can be maintained in the manufacture of the many types of films, and specific, pratical exposure recommendations can be made.

The Characteristic Curve

On the basis of such precision, it is possible—and useful—to establish exact relationships between exposure and density and to plot those relationships on a graph. Because *density* is a logarithmic expression, *exposure* is transposed into logarithmic terms and becomes known as "log E," or the logarithm of the two factors which determine exposure, $I \times t$.

The curve which results when density and log E are plotted as a function of one another looks like this for film.

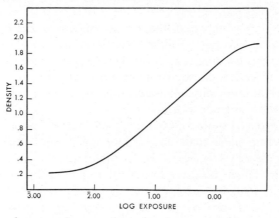

Each film and processing combination bears a unique curve which describes the response of the material under a specific set of development conditions including the solution, time, temperature, and agitation. Such curves are known as characteristic curves.

One might rightfully expect that if the log exposure is doubled or tripled, the resulting density should double or triple, but film doesn't see things that way. If it did we'd have a graph like this—

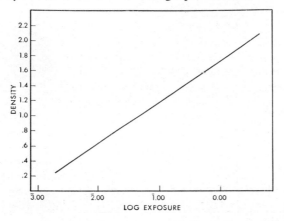

But film actually responds in a much less direct way. With no exposure there is no response, except for possible safelight or developer fog. There may not even be a response to a little exposure. You've sensed this in trying to make pictures at night. There was light—for you could see your subject—yet there was not enough of it to affect the film, for it was blank after being developed.

As the exposure is increased, there is an increase in the response of the film, though it is less than proportional to the exposure increase. However, the increases become greater as the exposure becomes greater, until finally they do reach a constant rate—for a while. Beyond another point the rate drops off until subsequent additions of exposure result in no more density; the film is as black as it can get.

Compare it to a locomotive as it starts out of the station with its train. The first horrific snort may do nothing much more than spill a little coffee into somebody's saucer, back in the diner. Another three or four very impressive efforts contrive to get the train actually in motion. Fairly soon, speed picks up almost in proportion to the extent the engineer opens the throttle. Then, out of the yards, it's straight going, with speed responding to power. But eventually, at high speed, more power produces less and less added speed until finally the train is going as fast as it can; "full-out" power adds nothing.

Whenever you make a picture you register a *series of exposures* on your film. These eventually are developed to densities. Technically, you locate your picture at some section along the characteristic curve.

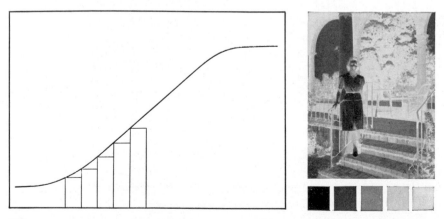

If there is too much light, or the shutter is left open too long, the exposure is uniformly multiplied and the scene moved farther out to the right on the curve, like this.

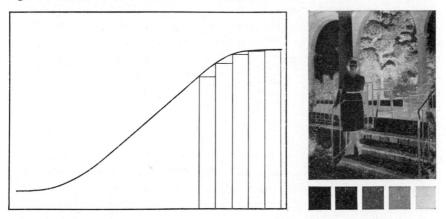

Here there is very little difference between the various subject brightnesses. They all look almost alike on the film, because they tend toward all-over blackness. The portion of the curve here used is called the *shoulder*.

Conversely, as less and less exposure is given the film, the section used shifts to the left on the curve. As it shifts, the darker parts of the picture

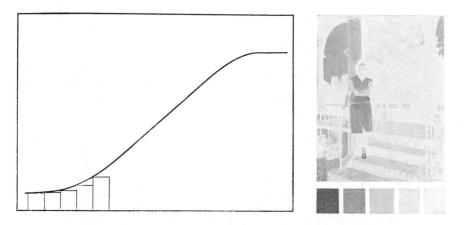

lose their separation from one another. Finally, with too little exposure, all but the brightest parts of the subject are the same—blank.

Such a picture is said to be made partly on and partly off the "toe" of the curve, and is underexposed.

One glance, then, at a characteristic curve tells us there are three more or less distinct parts to it. There is first a toe, then a straight line portion where density increases uniformly as the log exposure increases, and then a shoulder. All of these show degrees of density differences resulting from differences in exposure. Incidentally, be sure you keep in mind that density itself means little—it's almost entirely a matter of the relationship of all densities to one another that determines what kind of photograph you get.

Films which differ in the position of their curves along the log E axis respond to exposure quite differently. It is this fact that makes it necessary to have specific exposure recommendations for each type of film. It is the sole purpose of exposure guides to tell you what aperture and shutter speed you should use, at different levels of illumination. In following this guidance, you place your negative at such a position on the curve that, when it is developed and printed, you'll have a good picture.

Several additional terms serve to describe the characteristic curve, its shape and its parts, the first of these being *gradient*. Gradient is the slope of a line drawn tangent to the curve at any point. It represents the rate of density growth at that point. Thus on the extreme or flat end of the toe of the curve gradient is zero, but as you move to the right gradient increases until it reaches its maximum on the straight line portion where it is called *gamma*. In your negative this means that shadows falling on the flat part of the curve have zero contrast; if they fall on the toe they have moderate contrast. (See curve on opposite page.)

$$\text{Gradient (G)} = \frac{AB}{BC} = 0.24$$

Then there is *average gradient*, the mathematical average of the gradient values for all the points on the curve between the points of minimum and maximum exposure. It is a quantitative measure of what has heretofore been referred to as negative contrast and depends upon such items as the film used, subject conditions, lens flare and development.

Extensive tests have shown that to be a wholly acceptable negative, that is, one capable of yielding an excellent print, the gradient at the point of minimum exposure must equal .3 of the average gradient. This means that at least a part of the subject is located on the toe of the curve, the shadows

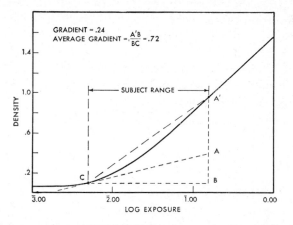

having moderate contrast, the high lights more contrast. More exposure—giving negatives located farther to the right on the curve—is permissible, but not less exposure, for with less exposure the shadows lose their detail. Exposure guides and calculators recommend times and apertures aimed to keep your negatives safely above the minimum, and provide leeway for any slight human errors in judging light and mechanical errors in equipment.

When you develop your negative you control the slope of the curve, hence the average gradient for your negative. Little development means a flat, low-contrast negative; longer development means normal or higher contrast. The degree of development is measured in terms of *gamma*. Gamma compares the density increases with exposure increases on the straight line portion of the curve. It is entirely independent of camera exposure or subject, but is important in comparing results with different materials.

Characteristic curves are generally accompanied by a "time-gamma curve," for the customary developer. This is the result of plotting gamma as a function of the development time.

TYPICAL TIME-GAMMA CURVE

If you want to develop your film to a particular gamma, locate that value on the upright axis of the chart, draw a line through it parallel to the time axis. From where this line intersects the curve, drop a perpendicular to the time axis. The intersection of this perpendicular and the time axis gives you the development time for the desired gamma.

In view of the several factors over which you can exercise control it becomes apparent that on your shoulders rests a large part of the success of the negative. In case of doubt, follow recommended procedures; they are firmly rooted in facts.

PAPER CHARACTERISTICS

A photographic paper emulsion responds to light in essentially the same way that film does, and a characteristic curve shows the relationship between density and log exposure. While you can change the slope of a film curve by changes in development, a paper curve is fairly fixed. It is for this reason that there are usually several different contrast grades of each paper type. Here's the curve for Velox No. 3. Note that its toe

rises slowly but that at higher densities the contrast is much greater. Remember now that the negative becomes the "subject" for printing. The shadows of a good negative are a bit low in contrast; they transmit considerable printing light to produce the higher print densities in the regions where paper contrast is high. Conversely, the highlights in the negative are higher in contrast and are reproduced by the flatter, sweeping toe portion of paper. In other words, the shapes of film and paper curves have been engineered to fit each other.

Papers of lower and higher than normal contrast permit compensation for some errors in exposure, processing, variations in subjects, and variations in equipment, but can by no means be thought of as cure-alls.

SPEED

The less camera exposure required in making a good negative, the faster the film is said to be, or the greater its *speed*. In terms of the curve, the farther the characteristic curve of the film comes to the left or low log E values, the "faster" the film is. From a more practical viewpoint the former definition is much more important. Considerable discussion has arisen as to just how comparative film speeds should be determined.

The American Standards Association system of speed determination is based on the minimum exposure required for an excellent negative. For application of this value, a safety factor is added; the factor depends on the exposure latitude of the film, and on the characteristics of the exposure-determining device with which the figure will be used.

The result is put into words on Kodaguides and into numbers called exposure indexes or speed numbers, for use with photo electric meters.

Speed considerations are important when it comes to determining actual camera exposures, that is, you must know how fast your film is. Beyond that point the importance of speed diminishes rapidly. Almost all films are fast enough for anything you are apt to be required to photograph. Extreme speed is attained only at the expense of other qualities—fine grain, for example. Ratings in terms of speed are not clues to quality which is so much more important in making good pictures. Uniformity in manufacture, color sensitivity, graininess—those are the points to look for rather than buying for speed alone.

LATITUDE

The classic definition of the word "Latitude" has always stated that it was the horizontal extent of the straight line portion of the characteristic curve. However, as the definitions of sensitometry have been shifted toward a more practical side, this concept has given way to what might better be called *camera exposure latitude*. This is the difference in camera exposure between the shortest and longest exposure resulting in negatives capable of printing into excellent pictures. (Since camera exposure latitude is influenced by the optical system used in the camera, no specific values can be assigned.) Most of the camera exposure latitude falls on the overexposure side, since recommendations are made to permit the use of nearly the least practical exposure.

RESOLVING POWER

Resolving power is the ability of a film to distinguish between very finely divided lines, hence to produce fine detail on extreme enlargement. This is naturally an important consideration in choosing films, especially in miniature photography where considerable enlargement is the rule.

If you try handwriting in small letters with pen and ink on blotting paper, all the detail runs together and is lost. On a hard-surfaced paper, microscopically fine ink lines can be kept separate and can be distinguished easily with an eyeglass.

With films it's much the same—only you write with light on film. The ability to produce critically sharp images—that is, resolving power—is measured in lines per millimeter, and

1. Increases with contrast of the test object.
2. Increases with contrast due to development.
3. Decreases with overexposure.
4. Varies from film to film.
5. Decreases with coarser grain size.

The illustrations show a resolving power test.

Kodak Panatomic-X Film Developed in D-76

Prints reproduced here represent resolving power at 75 times enlargement.

Upper Left: Underexposure and normal (12 minutes) development. Result: Loss of both resolution and detail.

Lower Left: Normal exposure and normal development. Result: Maximum resolution.

Upper Right: Overexposure and normal development. Result: Spread of light obscures fine detail.

Lower Right: Normal exposure and overdevelopment (36 minutes). Result: No apparent loss of resolving power, as compared to normal.

Moral: Correct exposure.

117

SO WHAT!

About now you are thinking—"How can I apply any of these things to my work to get more consistent results?" Here are some suggestions.

1. Follow directions; it's easiest and safest. If for one reason or another the directions don't fit your working conditions, vary your procedure as necessary.

2. If you have become accustomed to a particular type of film and have had excellent results by developing for a time which results in a gamma of .8, you can switch to another film whose characteristic curve is similar in shape to your first film, develop it to a gamma of .8 and expect the same picture contrast.

3. If you switch developers, say to get finer grain images, select the time which gives you the degree of development (gamma) you've found best, and you'll get the same contrast as originally. Developers vary considerably in the rate at which they work, but results at any gamma value are the same as far as contrast is concerned. This assumes the image in all cases is black, not brown, and is unstained.

4. A time-gamma curve will tell you the number of minutes required for any desired gamma in a given developer and temperature. By consulting the same curve you can tell how much you must increase or decrease your development time to make an appreciable change in the contrast of your negative. Similarly, you can tell just how accurate you must be in timing your development. If the gamma value to which you work falls on the flat portion of the time-gamma curve, extreme accuracy is not essential. If the value falls on the rapidly rising portion, accurate timing is necessary.

5. If you encounter a scene involving an unusually long brightness scale, make certain your exposure is sufficient to register the shadows far enough up on the toe of the curve to allow a differentiation of detail.

6. When you tackle the job of making color prints by separation negatives, it will be necessary to make three negatives through color filters. To be satisfactory the density and contrast must be nearly identical. This involves adjusting development times and balancing exposures. Density readings will be necessary and if you do not have a densitometer available, use a Kodak Densiguide.

7. If your system of picture making, including camera, usual subject

matter, film, development and printing, or enlarging requires on the average a No. 3 contrast grade paper, and you wish to use No. 2 paper, increase the *gamma* to which you develop by 20%. Conversely, if you're getting too much contrast and are forced to print most of your negatives on No. 1 paper, decrease your development time to reduce your gamma by 20%. For the changes in time required, consult the time gamma curve.

So runs the language of sensitometry, a living science. And because that science is dynamic and useful, it's a good thing to understand a little of it. There is no need to make a fetish of gamma or to consult the characteristic curve of your film before every shot. But it is a comfort to know that a lot of scientific spade work has been done by the photographic industry, not to impress or mystify but to permit more intelligent achievement of the ends of modern photography. Those ends are, simply, better pictures.

Latitude and Speed Test

Object:
To show the wide range of negative exposures which are capable of being printed into good pictures.

Equipment:
A camera with variable aperture and shutter speeds. (The shutter speeds should ideally extend from one second to 1/400th of a second. With those cameras not capable of that range, the experiment may be contracted.) Super-XX, or another panchromatic film. Facilities for printing.

Procedure:
On a bright, cloudless day select a subject in full sunlight and make the following exposures with the lens set at f/22:

1/400, 1/200, 1/100, 1/25, 1/5,
1, 8, 16 seconds.

After the films are developed according to recommended procedure, make the best print possible from each negative, using any of the six contrast grades of paper available.

Mount the prints in sequence on a notebook page or card. Encircle the ones with the least and longest exposures which printed satisfactorily. The longest printable exposure divided by the shortest will give the latitude, expressed as the exposure relationship between the extreme prints. For example: if the test shows that all negatives including the 1/200th of a second exposure and the 8 second exposure limits gave passable prints, the range would be 1,600 times.

If this test is repeated for several films, it can be used as a test of film speed. Film is fast only if you can make prints from negatives made with little exposure. If film A gives a print from the 1/200th negative and film B only from the 1/100th negative, film A is approximately 2 times as fast as B.

To compare camera exposure latitude of black-and-white and Kodachrome film, make five exposures on the latter; one at the normal or recommended setting, one at one stop less than normal, one two stops less, one at one stop more than normal, and one two stops more.

Questions:

1. Compare the negative from which the first excellent print was obtained with the one having one step less exposure. What's missing in the one with less exposure which is present in the one with more exposure?

2. While good prints may have been obtained through a considerable range, how do those on the under- and overexposure side differ from the one correctly exposed?

A negative is satisfactory if a good print can be made from it. For this series, six negatives were exposed at, respectively, 1/100, 1/25, 1/5, 1, 2, and 8 seconds, all at f/22. Without recourse to high-contrast paper the over- and underexposed negatives would have been unprintable. Therefore latitude appears to be a function of both film and paper.

120

CHAPTER 10

Filters

UNLESS you are an unusually astute—or lucky—person, something of this sort will have happened to you by this time:

Down along the shore, one fine day, you observe a beautiful scene—a scene which demands and deserves picturing. The sky is blue, the clouds are big and billowy; against this "back drop" a white lighthouse rears its slender form. In the foreground there are trees and rocks. The whole thing composes easily and well. In short, it is a ready-made picture, and you turn your camera loose on it with fine enthusiasm. It is a natural.

But when the negative is developed and a print made, you discover that something has gone haywire. There is no sign of that beautiful sky, the clouds have faded into insignificance, and the lighthouse itself has been lost, save for its windows and the glassed-in light chamber. Blues and whites have merged into blankness. The foreground is perfect. But the picture—the beautiful scene that tempted, beguiled, and inspired you —is gone.

It's discouraging, of course, but it is more mystifying. How is it possible that so much should drop out of a picture, leaving you nothing but negligible remnants? You experiment. You make similar shots on other days, under other light conditions, and with other exposures. Sometimes you get passable results, too. You discover that a really deep blue sky does tend to give you more cloud-sky contrast; and you may observe that a bit of underexposure helps to achieve the same ends. And various films, of course, vary in their color response. But your experimentation reveals to you no sound-and-certain technique until—usually at some veteran's suggestion—you decide to see what happens when you slip a color filter over your camera's lens. And when you do find out what happens, you immediately become filter-conscious, for filters are very important to you and to your pictures.

121

The sky was the same when both exposures were made; a yellow filter
over the lens made the difference

What Is a Filter?

A light filter consists of a piece of dyed gelatin or glass, held in place
immediately in front of the camera lens during the exposure. Rays of
light from the subject, striking the filter, are either absorbed or transmitted, depending on their color relationship to the filter. It is sort of an
optical strainer for light waves. You use a filter which will absorb the
colors you want to appear darkened in the print and which will transmit
the colors you want relatively brightened.

Because the usefulness of filters depends on the nature of light, and
because it is a short step from filters to color photography, this is a good
point at which to delve a little deeper into some of light's characteristics.

Light travels in waves. The length of these waves from crest to crest
determines the color of the light. Red waves are long, green waves
shorter, blue waves shortest. Within these general wave length groups,
the shades of red, green, and blue vary with smaller wave changes.

Of course, if there are no waves, there is no light. If all the waves
travel together, the result is white—the presence of all colors. A mixture
of less but relatively equal parts of red, green, and blue results in gray—
in any "neutral" tone from black to white.

Red and green waves combine to form yellow. A yellow book is one that reflects both red and green, absorbs blue. Likewise, all other colors are combinations of the three *primary light colors*—red, green, and blue.

Orange = red + some green

Yellow = red + green in equal parts

Pink = red + blue in equal parts

Darker pink = less red and less blue

Due to the very nature of filters, their ability to absorb certain wave lengths of light, they appear colored when held in front of a white light. A filter looks green if it *transmits* green, absorbs blue and red. Thus through a green filter, green objects look light—other colors not containing green are absorbed and appear black.

A yellow filter absorbs only blue and allows light from both green and red objects to pass through to the eye or film.

There are over a hundred light filters, all of different absorptive characteristics, hence of different colors. Those of real practical value to most photographers are limited to about half a dozen; the others afford a means of exact control over light for special purposes in commercial and scientific photography.

Which Filter to Use

Filters cannot be used without regard for the film in the camera. The film must be sensitive to the light passed by the filter; otherwise no image can be recorded. Orthochromatic films cannot be used to make negatives through a red filter, as they are sensitive only to blue and green, and these colors are absorbed by a red filter. Because of their sensitivity to the full range of colors, panchromatic films can be used with all filters.

In photographic usage there are three arbitrary words employed to describe filtered and unfiltered effects. A picture in which the tones have the same relative brightnesses that we see in the subject (assuming that we have normal color vision) is said to be *correct*.

When negatives are made under ordinary conditions and without a filter, the relatively high blue sensitivity of photographic emulsions records the blues in the subject as too bright. That's why the lighthouse, the sky, and the clouds all emerged as white. Panchromatic (Type C) films also record subject *reds* as too bright, in terms of what the eye sees. Such pictures suffer from *undercorrection*. When used in conjunction with the right films, certain filters absorb the too-active rays and allow a balanced or correct effect. These are referred to as *correction* filters.

123

Other filters cut out too much of the blue light and produce exaggerated effects, such as black skies. These are known as *overcorrection* filters. A somewhat incongruous term, it simply means "correction," carried to an extreme.

Listed here are the most widely used filters, together with their properties and major fields of usefulness.

Choosing Your Filter

YOUR SUBJECT		YOUR FILTER	YOUR FILM
	For smooth skin texture and "corrected" skies	YELLOW FILTER WRATTEN K2	PAN B FILM SUCH AS PLUS-X, SUPER-XX
	For haze penetration, contrast in marine scenes, sky-cloud contrast	ORANGE FILTER WRATTEN G	ANY PAN FILM
	For exaggerated sky— cloud contrast, storm pictures, etc.	RED FILTER WRATTEN A	PAN B OR C FILM SUCH AS PLUS-X, SUPER-XX, TRI-X
	For natural reproductions of blossoms, foliage, outdoor portraits against sky	BRIGHT GREEN FILTER WRATTEN X1	PAN B OR C FILM

124

Sometimes we hear reference to "contrast filters." This term refers more to the effect obtained than to any unusual characteristic of the filter by itself. The effect is a distortion of the brightness values so that two colors of about equal visual brightness photograph quite differently. The filter absorbs one, transmits the other. Almost any filter can produce this sort of subject contrast when used in the right place with a film capable of properly recording the differences the filter sets up. For example—a red filter is a "contrast" filter when used to photograph blueprints. Maximum contrast between the white lines and the blue background is obtained as the red filter transmits the red component of the white lines and absorbs all the blue from the background. If the subject were a red and yellow beach umbrella, the red filter could not be considered as adding contrast. Through a red filter both red and yellow look the same—and photograph the same.

The Kodak Master Photoguide contains a sample set of four filters through which you can view your subject to determine the effect of those filters on contrast. Frequent reference to this handy guide will provide good training in filter sense and when unusual color combinations pop up it will give you the answer.

Wratten Filters

Originally of English manufacture, and now produced by the Eastman Kodak Company, Wratten Light Filters have become more or less standard the world over in the past 30 years. They are available for photographic use in any or all of these three forms.

(1) *Dyed gelatin.* Made in gelatin sheets much like film support, the color absorption and transmission characteristics come from organic dyes of great purity. Both the supporting gelatin and the colors are held to extremely close physical and optical tolerances in manufacture.

Filters supplied in gelatin sheets are less expensive than in any other form. At the same time, they are less conveniently attached to the camera for use, and the finger prints and scratches that naturally accrue from handling cannot satisfactorily be removed.

(2) *Dyed gelatin cemented between glass.* Two distinct grades of glass are used. One, "B" glass, with a dyed gelatin filter cemented between it, provides perhaps the best combination available for average use. The same high standards of color purity are maintained as in the gelatin filter alone. The glass protects the filter from scratches and abra-

125

sions; finger marks can be more easily removed, and it is easily attached to the camera by means of a slip-on holder ring which fits neatly onto the lens mounting. "B" glass is sufficiently accurate optically to permit its use in most phases of amateur photography. And the price is such that every photographer can afford at least one such filter.

The other glass, a hand-ground and polished optical flat, is referred to as "*A*" glass. Filters of gelatin cemented between pieces of "*A*" glass are expensive but almost indispensable in aerial photography, photoengraving and other work in which perfect measurements and sharpness must be maintained. "A" glass has no magnifying power; hence it permits photographing to the extreme accuracies required in aerial surveys and mapping.

Filter Identification

Wratten Filters are assigned arbitrary letters or numbers for identification —K2, X1, A, B, C, etc. These are in no way concerned with the separate letters used to denote the kind of glass between which they are mounted. One merely has to remember the letter designation assigned to the filter of the color he uses.

You may have heard of using ordinary sunglasses as filters; it can be done, but it should be reserved for use only in dire emergencies. The tinting of such glasses has little photographic significance, the colors are seldom uniform, and the glass itself may not be optically respectable.

Filter Factors

Thus far, only one aspect of filters has been considered; their ability to change the relative print brightnesses of the subject colors. But equally important is the fact that a filter may cut out from ⅓ to ⅔ of the light available for making the picture. Naturally, therefore, a longer camera exposure is needed when a filter is used over the lens. The number of times which the proper unfiltered exposure must be increased when a filter is used is called the *filter factor*.

The filter factor depends upon the filter itself, the film, and the light source. And there is a nice interdependence between these three. For example, a red-transmitting filter used with a red-sensitive film does not involve as large a filter factor as one which transmits less red light.

The filter factor is also dependent on the light source. Outdoor light is bluish; most artificial light is reddish. A bluish filter used outdoors therefore absorbs little of the existing light, and the exposure need not be increased materially to equal the exposure without a filter. Indoors with tungsten light, mostly red, a blue filter cuts out all but a small portion of the light and the blue-filtered exposure necessitates a relatively high factor.

In applying a filter factor to the calculation of exposure, you can work in three different ways. Assume the factor to be 4, and the normal "no-filter" exposure to be 1/50 at $f/11$. If you increase the time by 4, you have 1/12.5 second; 1/10 is close, so you can shoot at 1/10 at $f/11$ with the filter. If, on the other hand, you need to use 1/50 shutter speed, apply the factor to the lens aperture. Opening the diaphragm two stops quadruples your light volume; hence you can work at 1/50 at $f/5.6$. Or you can compromise by doubling both time and aperture; that gives you 1/25 at $f/8$.

Determining Filter Factors

Object:
To determine the filter factor for any film, filter and light source combination, using only ordinary camera equipment.

Equipment:
Any camera, plus the film and filter in question.

Procedure:
1. Obtain sheets of white, medium gray, dark gray, and black paper, each one foot square. Attach these to one another in order to form a strip four feet long.
2. Photograph this chart with no filter under lighting conditions similar to those to be used for pictures to be made subsequently with the film and filter, i. e. sun light or flood light. Obtain correct exposure, by trial if necessary, and correctly expose one film for later development.
3. Now photograph the chart under the same lighting conditions, but with the filter over the camera lens.

Make three exposures. For the first one, use twice the exposure given when no filter was used. Double that for the second—and double the second one for the third test. This will provide *filtered* pictures with 2-4-8 times normal exposure.

4. Develop the above 4 exposures simultaneously.
5. Compare the negatives visually by transmitted light. From the negatives made through the filter, select the one whose chart parallels in density the unfiltered chart. The increase in exposure represented by the matching filter negative, over the normal *no filter* exposure, is the filter factor and can safely be used as such under similar conditions at any time in the future.

If none of the three filter pictures matches the first exposure, make additional tests, increasing or decreasing the time as necessary until a close match is obtained.

Panchromatic Film

Without a filter

With a red filter

Orthochromatic Film

Without a filter

With a yellow filter

Pan film with a yellow filter produces the most normal-looking black-and-white interpretation of the colors in the original scene

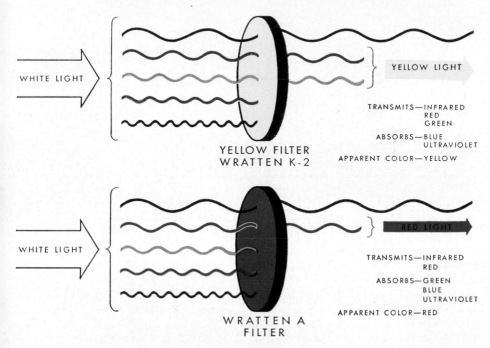

WHITE LIGHT

YELLOW LIGHT

TRANSMITS—INFRARED
RED
GREEN

ABSORBS—BLUE
ULTRAVIOLET

APPARENT COLOR—YELLOW

**YELLOW FILTER
WRATTEN K-2**

WHITE LIGHT

RED LIGHT

TRANSMITS—INFRARED
RED

ABSORBS—GREEN
BLUE
ULTRAVIOLET

APPARENT COLOR—RED

**WRATTEN A
FILTER**

The "mechanics" of filter action

Color Subtraction

Cyan, magenta, and yellow are over-lapped to produce red, green, blue, and black subtractively.

Color Addition

Red, green, and blue, mixed addi-tively, produce cyan, magenta, yel-low, and white.

Color Wheel

The color wheel, re-duced to twelve arbi-trary hues. Opposite hues are complemen-tary; hues touched by the triangle, as it is rotated, tend to be harmonious.

CHAPTER 11

Color Photography

As far as most people are concerned, taking color pictures is exactly as simple as is black-and-white. The film is different, but it loads like black-and-white and requires only a little change in the basic exposure. You get transparencies for projection, paper prints, movies. And the quality is excellent. No particular knowledge of color itself is essential but—for that matter—it takes no special knowledge of what's behind the scenes to take black-and-white snapshots, either.

"This is Photography" assumes an interest—beyond the snapshot stage —in those things fundamental to photography, both color and black-and-white. An understanding of the fundamentals of color is particularly important if consistently superior results are to be gained, and if the full enjoyment of color photography is to be realized. This chapter and the next one are devoted to these important fundamentals.

While taking pictures in color, as has been said, is not particularly difficult, a clear understanding of the basic principles of color is not always easy to achieve. And for very good reasons! From the cradle up, we have all been exposed to color, its identification, and specification. We have not always been aware of this exposure, but it has been a continuous one. Some of our notions are quite correct and some are partially so. But many of them are just plain wrong. So let's start from scratch, shedding all we have "known" about color all these years. This is really the hardest part of all.

COLOR IS A SENSATION

Hot and cold are sensations, too. Touch an iron from which energy—in the form of heat waves—is being radiated and at once nerves in your fingertips shoot a message to your brain where headquarters decodes it, flashes the "HOT!" sign, and activates muscles which pull your fingers away, fast. Color is possibly a little less violent sensation but the means by which it is perceived are even more fantastic. Light waves are waves of energy, too, and differ only in size from heat waves. While the nerves in our fingertips are not sensitive to light waves, this form of radiation does stimulate the incredibly complicated system of receptors in our eyes. The receptors pass the word along to the brain where the interpretations are made, and we report that the color is red, yellow, blue, brown, etc. Whether or not we like what we see is, at the moment, unimportant. But it is worthwhile at this point to warn you of the disturbing fact that the same energy does not always produce exactly the same perception. More about this in the next chapter. We mention it here only to indicate that color is full of puzzlements.

The fundamental fact, which is basic to all color and thus to color photography, was discovered and proved just about 150 years ago. Scientists then showed that the visual appearanceof any color could be matched by appropriate mixtures of red, green, and blue light. (Light! Not paint.) To demonstrate, they projected colored light from three lanterns (ancestors of our slide projectors), mixing red, green, and blue light on a screen. By changing the proportions of the projected colors, they obtained the required combinations.

Red, green, and blue emerged, therefore, as the *primary* colors; primaries because they were and are all that we need to match any known color. This fact seems to support the contention of most scientists that the receptor system in our eyes is a three-color system with one receptor group sensitive to red, one sensitive to green, and a third sensitive to blue. Thus every color we perceive depends on the extent to which these three receptor groups are stimulated. If all three primary colors are present in about equal amounts, the sensation produced is white or gray. If none is present, there is no light. We see no color, so we call it black.

What has been said in the two previous paragraphs doesn't quite conform to what we learned about those so-called primaries in our first grade paint boxes. But it is true, and should be nailed down once and for all, as basic. But remember, we're talking about light, not paint. We'll get to the paint problem shortly.

COLOR ADDITION

A demonstration of the fundamentals of color is pictured on page 130, upper right hand corner. Except for the modern projectors, it's much the same arrangement as that used about 1802 when the principles involved were first illustrated. Red, green, and blue light are converging on the screen from three projectors, but not "in register." With the displacement or overlapping of the three beams of light, as photographed, we therefore see not only the three primary colors but four simple combinations. For example, where red and green light mix, the result is *yellow*. Right here we face up with another fundamental involved in these mixtures. The primary colors in the mixture lose their identity and the new color often seems to give no clue to its components.

Red and blue light, when seen together in mixture, result in pink or *magenta*, as color photographers know the color. Blue and green combined produce a little more obvious color, blue-green, or more technically correct, *cyan*. Where the three primaries combine in the center of the screen, the result is white. But there's more to color mixture than these simple combinations. Let's go on. Suppose we vary the amounts of red, green, and blue on the screen. We can do this by changing the aperture of each of the three projector lenses. (Holes cut in cardboard will do the trick.) The ultimate result of such experimentation will verify the fundamental fact that any color can be created on the screen by combining various amounts of the three primaries. If you're the "pure science" type, you'll go on to calculate the relative amounts of each primary color required to match any given sample.

In this demonstration the colors were added, as required, to the screen. The starting points were the three primary colors and their presence on the screen was controlled by apertures of various sizes. The same measure of control could be accomplished photographically by inserting black-and-white slides in each projector. In this case the density of the slides determines how much of each color reaches each part of the screen.

Whenever color is produced by mixing the three primary colors of light from three separate sources regardless of the particular method used to control the amounts, the color mixing is referred to as *additive color*.

COLOR SUBTRACTION

For a somewhat different method of color mixing, refer to the pattern of circles in the upper left hand corner of page 130. In this case, the starting point is the white paper page of the book. It's white because it reflects red, green, and blue light about equally. This of course assumes that you're reading your book under fairly normal conditions of illumination. Now let's see what happens when we start overlaying white with various dyes (or pigments or printing inks). If we overlay the paper with an ink having the ability to filter out or absorb blue light, only the red and green will remain of the white reflected by the paper. This red and green light combine to give us the color we call yellow. Remember? Now that's precisely why yellow ink or yellow paint appears yellow. It absorbs or subtracts blue light and reflects or transmits the red and green; these remaining colors appear together as yellow. If lesser concentrations of yellow ink are used, less blue will be absorbed and the resulting yellow will be weaker, that is, closer to white.

An ink or dye of different chemical composition will absorb other colors. For another example, let's think about one that absorbs green light. When this happens we see what is left of the primary colors reflected by the white paper, namely, red and blue, or magenta. Magenta ink thus has that particular color simply because it absorbs green light. The extent to which it absorbs green controls the depth of the magenta. The third printing ink shown in the illustration absorbs red, allowing only green and blue, or cyan, to be transmitted from the paper. If less blue-green, or cyan ink, had been used, less red would have been absorbed with the resulting cyan being lighter or closer to white.

Now, where the pigments overlap in the illustration, we see four combinations. Where all three of the inks are present, no light emerges from the white sheet. The yellow ink absorbs blue light, magenta ink absorbs green, and cyan ink absorbs red—so there's nothing left. Where yellow and cyan overlap, they absorb blue and red respectively, and only green remains. Magenta and cyan together absorb or subtract green and red, so that only blue remains. By varying the concentrations of yellow, magenta, and cyan inks, all degrees of blue, green, and red absorption can be accomplished. Thus by mixtures of various proportions of these three inks, or dyes, or pigments, any desired color can be produced by absorption or by *subtraction*. The color wheel on page 130 is an example of 12 subtractive mixtures with each color resulting from particular amounts of blue, green, and red having been absorbed by the inks. This is a direct example of the principle of subtractive color mixing.

We have called red, green, and blue *primary* colors. What shall we call yellow, magenta, and cyan? Certainly the terminology has not been clear or consistent and since it's an author's prerogative to crusade a bit, maybe this is the time. First, since every color we see comes to us in the form of light, and since our eyes analyze that light in terms of red, green, and blue, let's restrict the word primary to these three colors. It really applies —it's a descriptive and valid name. Yellow, magenta, and cyan dyes can be, and in color photography are, used to obtain all colors by controlling the amounts of the three primary light colors we are permitted to see. So how about calling them *basic control colors*. In the past they have been given various other names including the words "secondary" and "complementary," but neither of these really describes their function.

Remember your first grade paint box? You were probably given to understand that the colors in the box were yellow, red, and blue, and that these were the primary colors. This is just plain wrong! In the first place, the colors were not yellow, red, and blue—the blue was really blue-green, or cyan. That's why you could mix it with yellow to get green. Thus, the colors were not properly identified, they were not primary colors, nor were they basic control colors. They were *convenient* colors, arbitrarily selected to do an adequate job on the kinds of painting most of us were interested in doing in the first grade. No wonder we have been confused!

Let's review the fundamentals just once more.

1. All colors can be matched by appropriate mixtures of red, green, and blue light.
2. Red, green, and blue light can be added from separate sources to match any desired color.
3. Red, green, and blue light can be subtracted from white by cyan, magenta, and yellow pigments or dyes to produce any desired color.

NOW, COLOR PHOTOGRAPHY

Fundamentally, color photography involves simply recording the extent to which red, green, and blue are present in a scene and the utilization of those photographic images to control the amounts of red, green, and blue seen by the person looking at the picture. Different color processes accomplish the recording of the colors and the production of color for the observer in different ways. Some utilize the principle of color addition. Others, color subtraction. But you will realize even now that the difference lies in the method, not in the principle.

Commercially available color processes are nearly all subtractive in character, but since the additive process was the forerunner of all of them, it is described first here.

THE ADDITIVE PROCESS

For an example of additive color photography, consider the following sequence of steps.

1. A color chart is photographed onto three separate sheets of black-and-white panchromatic film, one of which is exposed through a red filter, one through a green filter, and one through a blue filter. In each case, light from the subject which is the same in color as the filter passes, unchallenged, onto the film where it is recorded by varying degrees of silver densities. Red goes through the red filter, and so on. Where the color is complex, as with yellow, pink, or white, the light passes through all filters whose colors are represented in the subject color. Light from a yellow object goes through the green and red filters, and from a white object, naturally, through all three—because, red, green, and blue are all represented in white. The three resulting negatives are silver records on film of the amounts of the primary colors in the subjects. They are appropriately referred to as *separation* negatives, for they separate the primary colors onto separate films.

2. Each of these negatives is next printed onto another black-and-white film, giving a positive image. The *clear film spaces* in each positive represent the corresponding primary color in the subject. The black, or silver, areas indicate an absence of the primary color in those particular areas.

3. If the positive on which the clear spaces represent *red* is projected onto a screen by means of red light, the red of the subject will be reproduced in its entirety. Red will appear on the screen where there was red, and in lighter tints where there was pink, yellow, or white in the original. The same reasoning follows for the green and for the blue records.

4. If the three color records are projected simultaneously and the images superimposed, the full color reproduction will appear. Red and green, as projected, combine to form yellow; blue and red combine to form magenta, and blue and green to form cyan. Varying intensities or saturations of the basic hues give an infinite variety of colors, bold or subtle. Only primary colors are used to gain the desired effect, an effect possible because these colors can be mixed to give *any* color. They are *added;* hence the technical term *additive process.*

This example is additive color photography in its most rudimentary form. Obviously you would be limited to motionless subject, but it requires only black-and-white materials and produces excellent color results.

The inherently good quality has led scientists by the hundreds to try to find a way of making it into a convenient system.

You have undoubtedly heard of the Lumiere Autochrome color process, of Dufaycolor, and of Finlay Color, all based on the application of so-called additive principles. These have been developed so that pictures can be taken on single films and viewed or projected directly as color transparencies. These are referred to commonly as screen plate processes, for a pattern or screen of microscopically small red, green, and blue color patches covers the film emulsion. During exposure these color patches act as filters, and respectively pass or withhold the subject colors. The resulting negative is a patchwork of separation negatives, all on one film surface. The developed image is photographically reversed to a positive either by bleaching, re-exposing, and redeveloping, or by making a print on another film or plate. In contact with the color screen, this positive acts as a mask; when held before a viewing light, only the color of the unmasked patches appears—these patches acting as independent sources of the three primary colors.

THE SUBTRACTIVE PROCESS

Subtractive color processes depend upon the subtraction of unwanted colors from white light to reproduce the colors of the original.

They work this way, speaking schematically:

1. Three separation negatives are made on black-and-white films through filters of the three primary colors—red, green, and blue. As with the additive process, the silver on each film negative represents the presence of the primary color in the subject; clear spaces indicate an absence of that primary.

2. Film positives are made from the separation negatives. Silver in each positive indicates the extent to which the corresponding primary color must be subtracted from white light to produce the color picture.

The trick, then, becomes one of substituting dyes for the silver deposits —dyes which will subtract only the unwanted colors. Cyan dye (blue-green) is substituted for the silver deposits on the positive made from the red-filter negative, and it filters the red from the white viewing light. Similarly, magenta coloring is substituted for the silver on the positive made from the green-filter negative, and yellow for the silver on the positive from the blue-filter negative.

3. Suppose, now, that these three colored images are superimposed and

matched, or registered, and viewed against a white surface. The white surface—being a source of white light—is giving off red, green, and blue. The three dyes, the basic control colors, which are present in a wide variety of concentrations, will combine to subtract red, green, and blue to various degrees to produce a color picture.

COLOR PROCESSES

Currently available subtractive color processes can be classified in either or both of two ways. On one basis, they could be classified as transparency or print processes, depending on whether they are intended for viewing by transmitted light as in the case of motion pictures, or by reflected light as we see album prints. Then, too, they can be divided into reversal or negative-positive processes, depending on the photographic means involved in arriving at the end result.

Reversal Processes

In a reversal process the negative image is developed in the conventional manner. Then, rather than removing the unused emulsion with a fixing bath, the silver image is removed with a chemical bleach. The remaining emulsion is exposed to light and developed. This produces a positive image on the same film used for the camera exposure. Examples of reversal color processes are Kodachrome and Ektachrome.

Kodachrome Process

By far the best known of all subtractive color processes is Kodachrome. Kodachrome film consists of three film layers on a single support; in other words, it is a film sandwich. When exposed in the camera, each emulsion makes a negative record of one of the three primary colors. When processed in especially equipped processing stations, the negative images are developed, reversed to positives, and cyan, magenta, and yellow dyes are substituted for silver in the appropriate layers. The same piece of film you rolled through your camera comes back with the same three layers—with the cyan, magenta, and yellow, the basic control colors, subtracting from white light to give the brilliant full-color transparency.

Kodachrome film for still pictures is available for cameras using 35-mm. or 828 film. For movies in full color it is supplied for both 16mm. and 8-mm. cameras. There are two different Kodachrome emulsions; one, Daylight Type for outdoor pictures, the other, Type A for use indoors with photoflood lamps.

Ektachrome Process

Ektachrome film also consists of three sensitive emulsions, but differs from Kodachrome in one important respect. In the case of Kodachrome, the dyes are formed during processing, by reactions with color-forming ingredients in several processing solutions. In Ektachrome the color formers are incorporated in the emulsion layers and all three colors can be formed simultaneously. This reduces both the complexity and number of solutions required, and simplifies processing to the point where any careful darkroom worker can satisfactorily develop his own color pictures. Or he may prefer to use the services of a color processing laboratory; there is probably such a laboratory in the large city nearest you.

Ektachrome is supplied in sheet film sizes and as roll film in 620 and 120 sizes. The resulting pictures are transparencies and except for size can scarcely be distinguished from Kodachrome pictures. Ektachrome is available in both Daylight and tungsten types, the latter, Type B, being balanced for use with 3200°K Mazda lamps.

Negative-Positive Processes

Negative-positive color processes are closely akin to the usual black-and-white procedure. The film exposed in the camera is developed, fixed, washed, and dried. This negative is then printed by contact or enlargement onto another color material which is processed in solutions similar to those used in developing the negative. In a color negative, not only are lights dark and darks light—the colors are negative, too. Blue skies show up as yellow, green grass is magenta, and red barns are cyan. When printed, the colors, as well as lights and darks, get back to the proper relationship. Kodacolor and Ektacolor are examples of negative-positive processes.

Kodacolor Process

Like Kodachrome and Ektachrome, Kodacolor is a multiple-layer emulsion in which the primary colors are recorded on the separate layers.

Development of Kodacolor film produces negative silver images in all layers. As this takes place, by-products of development react with special chemical couplers, included in the film during manufacture, to form the three colored dyes.

The most startling aspect of developed Kodacolor film is the appearance of the unexposed portions—they are a fiery orange-red. This is unused color former or coupler, the color of which was carefully chosen so that when the negatives containing it are printed, prints of improved color quality are obtained.

From such Kodacolor negatives you can order color prints to be made by the same Kodak Laboratories that processed your Kodacolor film. The paper on which the negatives are printed carries an emulsion very similar to the film itself, except that the color formers are colorless and do not interfere with the final picture. Small color enlargements can also be obtained from Kodacolor negatives.

Kodacolor film, in both daylight and photoflood types, is available in the principal roll film sizes, including the small 828 size. This means full color for the amateur on a snapshot basis. It seems like a fairly simple, logical process but its success depends on a great deal of scientific control at every step in the manufacture and processing of the materials.

Ektacolor Process

Ektacolor film is the sheet film counterpart of Kodacolor film—with some notable differences. While the negative material is essentially alike in both, Ektacolor can be processed by the photographer himself, using packaged chemicals supplied for the purpose.

Prints from Ektacolor can be made by the photographer with the Dye Transfer Process. This means making three separation positives from the negative by exposing through red, green, and blue filters onto Pan Matrix film. The processed films produce gelatin-relief images and they are dyed cyan, magenta, and yellow. The dyes are then transferred successively and in precise register to a specially prepared white paper, to produce the finished print.

Positive transparencies can be made by contact printing or enlarging the negative directly onto Ektacolor Print film. It's a three-layer material and can be processed by the photographer using essentially the same steps as in developing the Ektacolor negative.

While research in color goes on (as, for that matter, it does in black-and-white) color photography is well beyond the experimental stage. It is here. It is good. It is usable. You can have it in snapshots, projectable transparencies, home movies, in professional portraits, and in commercial illustration. You will want to experence it in as many forms as your cameras will encompass. And master the one that meets your need.

CHAPTER 12

Shooting in Color

Having delved, briefly, into the theories of color and their application to color photography, it is in order, now, to consider some of the practical aspects of making pictures in color.

Yet, no matter how practical we may try to be, we run smack into the fact that color photography cannot ever be fully divorced from color theory or from psychology. Most emphatically, psychology.

From the very start of the era of color, back in the 30's, photographers —amateur and professional—made the uncomfortable discovery that there were discrepancies betwixt colors as seen, colors as photographed, and colors as remembered. There were even strange differences observed in subsequent viewings of the same pictures. In short, the human eye and mind conspire together to complicate color photography's job—especially for those more serious about their pictures than the casual snapshooter.

But, let's be specific. What are some of the factors involved when colors in a photograph differ from those the photographer saw in the scene?

First, of course, no manufacturer of color films makes the claim that his film is perfect for all colors, even under ideal conditions of use. It is true, for instance, that blues often reproduce slightly darker than they are in the scene but, by-and-large, these inherent discrepancies are slight, the quality excellent. Our concern here is with the differences that are introduced during exposure.

The Nature of Light

During the mid part of the day, when the sun is shining brightly, the light, we say, is white—with about equal parts of red, green, and blue. Your white house, or the one across the street, is its whitest white, and in a properly exposed color photograph the house and all its surroundings are revealed in their true color and tone relationship.

But on a cloudy day the same house, looking to you just as white though perhaps not quite as bright, photographs as bluish; sometimes early in the morning as reddish or yellow. Why should this be? It *looked* white all the time. Herein lies the problem, one of the most perplexing to the uninitiated.

The real character of daylight varies widely, even during a single day, and much more so around the calendar. Sometimes it's blue, sometimes red, often pink, purple, or yellow. Yet we can scarcely see these differences unless they are extreme—for our eyes and minds are always compensating, always discounting changes, to save us from the unpleasant experiences which might otherwise be ours. So our houses look white and faces appear normal in color even though they may be illuminated by rather highly colored light. Psychologists call this color adaptation.

Color films cannot adapt; they are "adapted" by the manufacturer for use with a specific kind of light, the kind most likely to prevail when most people want to take color pictures outdoors or indoors. Variations in the color of light thus show up on film even though we are unaware of their presence.

Two examples. It's a clear day, the sun's out, sky's blue. The side of your white house not illuminated by direct sunlight is *blue*. Does it look blue? No! But it must be, for it is illuminated only by blue sky light. It will photograph as blue. Same way with snow shadows.

Late in the day when your white house is lighted by the low afternoon sunlight, does it appear reddish? Not noticeably so—but it will photograph reddish. Naturally other colors besides white houses are affected by light changes too. A white house just seemed like a good obvious example.

Then, let's sum up the problem this way:
1. The color of "daylight" varies radically.
2. Our eyes adapt to the light—so it seems constant in color.
3. Color films cannot adapt—they detect and record these color variations.
   Now then, what to do about it?

If you want your color pictures to be as nearly like the scene as you see it, take your pictures during the mid part of a clear day. If you take them under other light conditions don't be surprised if you come up with some color differences.

Don't get the idea it's never good to take color pictures at odd hours. Sometimes the highly colored results give you results far more beautiful than your recollection of the scene. But learn the directions in which you can expect the results to go — use the unusual conditions for pictorial effects; but when you want your film to "see" things as you see them — be cautious.

Thus, while the words *Daylight Type* on color film boxes seem to imply that the film can be used with abandon whenever there is daylight, there are limitations.

With tungsten type films, Type A and Type B, it's a little different; the instructions specify, "for use with photoflood lamps," or, "for use with 3200°K lamps." Most photographers observe these more specific instructions, hence fewer color problems are encountered than with daylight. Occasionally, though, one of us is tempted to use ordinary house lamps instead of photofloods because "they look the same." They aren't the same, they contain relatively less blue; hence pictures made with them on films intended for photofloods are bound to be yellow.

Regarding "light" variations, the question is often asked, "Isn't there a meter that will tell me the exact color of the light?" The answer: Not one that's practical for the photographer to use outdoors where the problem is most serious. Even if there were a usable meter, it would take a thousand and one filters to compensate adequately for all the variations.

The difficulty lies in the fact that daylight does not have a true color temperature, therefore its determination is complex. In the case of yellow light from a low sun, shaded parts of the scene are lighted by blue light. Correcting for the sunlight color makes the shaded parts worse.

THE LANGUAGE OF COLOR

Even the least color-conscious of us is aware that all reds are not the same and that there are shades of color that are hard to classify. In fact, the variations in color are almost limitless; for practical purposes, however, color can be fairly accurately described in terms of three different qualities—*hue, value,* and *chroma.*

Hue is what most of us mean when we say "color." Red, orange, yellow, green, blue, and violet are the major hues, with such in-between hues as yellow-green, green-blue, and red-violet.

Then, within each hue there is *value* or brightness. A value scale in color corresponds to a gray scale in black and white; it is lightness or darkness.

Finally, there is *chroma* which is a reference to the purity of a color, or to the extent that it is free from gray. Obviously the less gray there

143

is in a color, the purer it is and the higher its "chroma."

On the basis of these three qualities any color can be accurately described. Progress is being made, especially among users of printing inks and paints, toward a system by which a series of index numbers can be used to describe any color—and with considerable precision, too. Thus, according to the Munsell system—the one which scientists seem to favor — a specific red can be designated as "R 4/14." R is for the *hue*, red; the 4 shows the *value* thereof, and the 14 refers to its *chroma*.

Such indices are of no immediate use to the casual photographer, save as they indicate that the world of color is expanding both in comprehension and importance to the point where precise evaluations are necessary.

In color, as in light and many another branch of science, relativity plays a part. A specific blue-green, for example, appears to change not only in value but in hue when surrounded by different colors. Surround the blue-green with yellow, and it looks darker; center it in a field of dark green, and it appears lighter. A blue background brings out the green color by contrast, the same blue-green appears blue in front of a green backing. In black-and-white photography a similar phenomenon makes a medium gray seem darker on a white background than on a black one. This phenomenon is known as "simultaneous contrast."

Right there is a usable tool for workers in color photography. Nail it down.

Developing this theme a little farther, consider the uses of color to provide contrast. As you experiment with color, you will notice that any composition in which all the colors are of the same value tends to become a "color hash," without emphasis and therefore without meaning. Change-of-pace is just as important to the successful color worker as it is to an All-American halfback. This, however, is not a likely source of trouble, for color films tend to exaggerate color differences, thereby giving you, automatically, plenty of color contrast. Your problem may easily become one of subduing rather than intensifying those contrasts.

Many of us have grown up with a kind of fear of color—a fear which, like so many other fears, is born of ignorance. We have been told that some colors simply don't go together, yet those very colors have been utilized by "daring" designers to achieve notable results. We failed to note that the apparent flouting of the "rule" was, in reality, a clever use of subtly chosen values and chromas of the forbidden hue combinations. There is no escaping the fact that two colors of similar value and strong

144

chroma do not make good neighbors. Take a strong red and its complementary color, blue-green; placed side by side they "vibrate" very unpleasantly. But vary the value or chroma of either, and you can achieve something usable.

Having mentioned complementary color, let's back up a moment. The various major and intermediate hues arrange themselves naturally in a kind of color wheel, as indicated in the diagram opposite page 131. It can be made to serve a useful purpose. The two colors directly opposite one another on the wheel are complementary; any three of the colors touched by an isosceles triangle, rotated within the circle, are likely to be harmonious; and a combination of colors embracing an arc of several neighboring hues can be used to set the color key or mood. Thus, an autumn scene is very reasonably made up of the warm, ripe colors in the neighborhood of red. Along the roadside there's a delightful mixture of brilliant red, rusty red, reddish brown, brown, golden red, and yellow. For backgrounds there is the deep blue of a fall sky and the rich green of the pines, a perfect natural harmony. A "cold" picture, on the other hand, logically includes an arc of the green, blue-greens, blues, and so on.

It may be that the generally accepted ideas of the proper use of color stem directly from the color combinations of nature. At any rate, the great out-of-doors does provide the best textbook available on color harmony. Study it faithfully and you'll gradually absorb a real sense of color.

Speaking of "mixers," if you are contemplating indoor portraiture or table-top photography in color, you'll find medium blue and gold backgrounds friendly with almost all subjects. If one isn't, the other is. Outdoor sky blue is good background too, blending especially well with flesh tones.

Color and mood, or emotion, is another consideration that has baffled some of us. Red, we have been told, is angry, passionate, hot, and warlike. Yet what is more cheerful than the red of Christmas decorations? Blue and green, they say, are cool, restful, and full of peace; yet we speak dourly of "the blues."

The answer to these seeming difficulties lies, of course, in the functioning of the human judgment—based on an understanding of all the factors involved. The skillful artist sometimes appears to break the rules; actually he is only using them to gain an effect.

Kodachrome and its derivative color processes have given us the means for vast new photographic pleasures and achievements. Those processes are not foolproof—but they are exciting and inciting. To succeed with color means more than making a snap of a pretty girl in a red coat; it means creating a setting and a composition which will reveal the girl most charmingly. The problem is not always simple, but it can be solved.

Lighting for Color

Use flat, even light, and let the colors take care of contrast and emphasis. So runs the basic rule of lighting for color photography. Like many another rule, it can be and has been successfully violated, but only by experts who knew what they were about.

Like all honest rules, it is no mere arbitrary matter. It makes sense. By simple, all-over lighting you give all of your colors a chance to rise up and be seen. The minute you add an emphasis with special lighting, or throw in a shadow for dramatic effect, you complicate things; for the colors do not behave as tones of black-and-white do. The colors take on totally new personalities, in terms of value and chroma, and may fall completely out of harmony with your color scheme.

Illuminate your shadows, don't let them go empty and black. In using anyone of the several color films, you will discover that your best pictures —especially portraits—are made in sunlight when the sky is slightly hazy rather than perfectly clear. The same lens aperture as for clear sun will usually do.

While front lighting is preferable, it need not be *full* front lighting. Even in color, such lighting tends to be a little unhappy looking, especially in shots of people. Let the sun come in a little over your right or left shoulder; in so doing you gain facial modeling without sacrificing color and color values. Close-ups made in bright sunlight under a clear blue sky may require a reflector to throw light into the shadow side.

In picturing groups, it is even more important in color than in black-and-white work to be sure that all the members of the group have about the same light. If a few are in heavy shade, while the others are in direct sunlight, your picture will not be satisfactory.

Back-lighted color work is tricky; sometimes it can be very effective and dramatically beautiful. But don't bother with it until you are fairly sure of yourself with ordinary lighting. If and when the time comes for some back-lighted shots, you'll do well to provide some degree of frontal lighting, either by a flat reflector or a synchronized flash. Here again, be

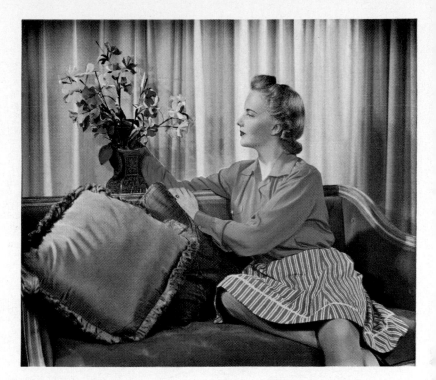

Much or vociferous color may almost drown your picture.

Color, for Color's Sake, is Not Enough

Subtle color carefully used, can be far more vivid and effective.

If You Are Color-Conscious . . .

You will remember that sunset light is much redder than midday light.

You will prefer open shade to contrasty lighting for outdoor portraits.

You will avoid unattractive color reflections, as from light green foliage.

careful of the color of that frontal lighting. If you use a reflector, use a white one; if you use a flash, it should be a blue-tinted bulb such as the No. 22B or 5B Photoflash lamps, if used for supplementing outdoor light. Such fill-in lighting for back-lighted subjects is possible, of course, only at relatively close range.

Exposure Latitude with Color Film

With black-and-white film you may sometimes over- or underexpose to a considerable extent, and still compensate for the error in printing. But no such compensation is possible in color work, for when you're "off the beam" in exposing color film, the colors themselves suffer. You get an image, but the colors are not correct.

Reversal color films require more exact exposures. When using them, your variation from correct exposure cannot, with success, be more than half a stop, over- or under. Negative-positive processes, with greater latitude, afford leeway of as much as a full stop under, and somewhat more on the overexposure side.

Fortunately it is not difficult to achieve the necessary degree of accuracy in using color films. The instructions enclosed with the films are specific for a wide variety of picture making conditions.

Take Care of Color Films

All films need and deserve careful storage. Color films and transparencies rate even greater care.

Before exposure, color film has very good "keeping" qualities. Of course, the film must be kept reasonably cool and dry.

After exposure, the film should be sent off for processing as soon as possible. If it is impossible to get it away promptly, give it every possible consideration. In the tropics or sub-tropics, seal the film against humidity after drying it first, and keep it in an icebox, if there's one handy.

When the processed film is returned to you, you'll be wise to see that it is given clean, dry, average temperature storage. Use and enjoy it, of course, but don't be careless with it, for you're dealing not with stable silver deposits on film, but with dyes. And dyes are delicate. Bright light, especially sunlight, has a deleterious effect on them. The particular dyes used in Kodachrome and Kodacolor Films, and in color prints, are as stable as possible, consistent with their other requirements. With care, you will be able to enjoy them over a long period.

COLOR SHOWMANSHIP

Photographic color can be shown to your admiring friends in a manner which will hold their friendship and increase their admiration.

If you're showing miniature Kodachrome transparencies, *don't* pass the little slides out casually, for squinting scrutiny by the nearest light, whatever its intensity or color. If you cannot project them, at the moment, contrive somehow to give them a reasonably fair showing. You can, of course, buy little battery-operated devices which give you an illuminated and sometimes magnified view of a transparency. A simple viewer can be made easily with two sheets of cardboard, each about 5 x 7 inches in size. In one cut a centered opening 1¾ inches square; in the other one, the opening should be 2 x 2. Cement the two together, registering the two openings. You'll find that a color slide fits neatly into the 2 x 2 space, and is held from falling out by the smaller opening. Hold this viewer about a foot above a sheet of white matte card on which a good strong light is directed. And there you are.

Table viewers are commercially produced which give excellent presentation of your slides for groups of three or four. Slides, inserted in such a viewer, are projected *inside* the viewer body, from mirror to mirror, and finally on to the back of a translucent viewing screen, where they are seen magnified by a factor of 4 or more. Such a viewer can be used in an undarkened room.

But projection, of course, is the classic way to present your color slides. The glowing image on the screen in a darkened room automatically invites and retains the attention; it is big and easy to see and understand. The optical system of a good projector reveals the full beauty of the transparency; and the distractions of other colored objects are eliminated.

It is a good idea, in all such showings, to give your audience and your transparencies the benefit of a smooth performance. Try to have your screen up, the projector in place, and the focus adjusted before your audience gathers. Have your slides in logical order, ready to show. Arrange your pictures in a crescendo of interest, the best for the last. All such preparations, if performed before your audience, are distracting.

Many users of color slides have gone far in their showmanship. Musical accompaniment, in a series of especially selected records, is one of the favored devices. The reading of great nature poems to accompany scenics is another. Methods and plans, of course, will vary with your pictures and your audience. Sometimes you can ask nothing better than the spontaneous running-fire comment of your guests.

ABOUT COLOR PRINT QUALITY

For one thing, the color print seldom gets the benefit of the "showmanship" which frequently attends the presentation of a color transparency. There is no darkened room, no brilliant image on a screen to attract and hold our undivided attention. While it may rival the transparency in technical excellence, the print has to struggle against the handicap of being looked at just as an ordinary picture is viewed—in the hand or as an enlargement, mounted and framed, on a wall. The light may be good or bad, and the distractions — including the other colors in the room — many. Thus, some color prints may seem disappointing.

We tend to scrutinize a color print with great care, quibbling over its hues and tones. Details which pass unobserved in a transparency are noted, and defects which cause us small concern in ordinary prints are accorded undue emphasis.

Contributing to this situation is the fact that in viewing projected transparencies in a darkened room our color perception is not distorted by surrounding walls, furniture, etc.; our eyes are free to adjust themselves to the color of the projected image. In viewing color prints, the colors are very likely to be affected in both value and hue by the color of our environment.

There's another angle — and a typically human one, too. True photographic color has been so long in arriving that we tend to be over-critical of it. Undoubtedly, this is a more healthful situation than would be the complacent acceptance of any color print as "wonderful" just because it is in color. But it's tough on the print.

Black-and-White Prints from Kodachrome Transparencies

Because Kodachrome Film images are dye images and not silver grain images, there is almost complete freedom from graininess. This offers a real advantage, in that black-and-white prints, or even enlargements of considerable size, can be made from sheet film or 35-mm. or 828 Kodachrome transparency originals. This can be done by making projected black-and-white negatives and then paper prints as follows:

1. Place the Kodachrome transparency in an enlarger with the emulsion side facing away from the enlarger lens. Focus the positive image

onto a sheet of white paper. Make it such a size that the enlarged negative will be convenient to handle in your printer or enlarger.

2. With the enlarger light and all room lights off, replace the white paper with a sheet of low-contrast panchromatic film such as Kodak Plus-X Film Pack, or Super-XX sheet film. Make a test exposure. Develop and fix the test. If the negative seems too thin, give more exposure; if too dark, decrease the exposure. But do not increase the development time. You will have to decrease development to lower your negative contrast.

3. From the correctly timed and enlarged black-and-white negative, either contact prints or enlargements can be made.

For special effects, color filters can be used over the enlarger lens, just as over the camera lens when making black-and-white negatives.

If you use a color negative process, such as Kodacolor or Ektacolor, you can make black-and-white prints directly from the color negatives by perfectly conventional methods, using Kodak Ektacolor BW paper in place of Azo, or whatever your favorite contact paper may be. Koda-bromide paper works well, too.

CHAPTER 13

What About Exposure Meters?

IN THE relatively simple photographic world of thirty years ago, the box camera was the common denominator of practically all amateurs. Because of its fixed focus, fixed aperture, and fixed single speed, there was no apparent exposure problem. Photographers made their pictures in full sunlight and averaged a high percentage of correctly exposed negatives.

Into this innocent situation crept technological progress, with faster, wide-aperture lenses which could be stopped down or opened up through a broad range of f-numbers; multiple speed shutters came along; and finally films of strange new speeds and color sensitivities were introduced. Camera users hailed each innovation with delight. As picture possibilities broadened, they became more adventurous, photographically speaking, and their batting averages sometimes slumped. Exposure, it was discovered, was no simple thing to be taken for granted. Some few wise ones remembered that the good old box cameras operated at about $f/16$ and $1/25$; they held to that formula in good light, and all was well.

But the rank and file felt that they had to make use of the extreme abilities of those fast lenses, high-speed shutters, and ultra-ultra films. In so doing, they often floundered around, making exposures with their fingers crossed.

Under these circumstances it was perfectly natural that a demand should arise for some device which would give an immediate and impersonal answer to the question, "What's the exposure?"

Well, Yankee fashion, let's ask another—and pretty important—question. *What constitutes correct exposure?* The answer is—it's the exposure that will give adequate detail in both the highlight and shadow parts of the picture. With black-and-white films there's a fairly broad range of exposures through which the desired end can be attained, assuming we have the means and skill for the appropriate printing compensations. (With color materials, the latitude is very much less.)

So, with a range of possible exposures, which shall be picked as the right one? In general you'll want to use the least exposure that will yield good results. In so doing, with the smallest practicable lens aperture and the most rapid shutter, you gain the utmost (under the specific circumstances) depth of field and maximum freedom from camera and subject motion.

Rather than to go 'way down to the minimum exposure, however, play it a little safe. The difference between a "reasonable" exposure and the absolute minimum is your safety factor; use it when you can. In so doing you are simply applying the old rule for black-and-white photography: if in doubt, up the exposure a bit.

In color work, as we have indicated, we have no such fielder's choice. We need, and have to find, the *one* best exposure.

Fortunately, there is plenty of sound guidance available. And, as you will see, the several sources of exposure guidance agree pretty well.

There are two basic types of exposure calculators; printed instructions and photoelectric meters.

In the hands of most un-specialized picture makers, printed exposure instructions serve excellently; for average conditions they lead to a higher percentage of good exposures than do photoelectric meters. While printed instructions also deal with other than average light conditions, such as outdoors without sunlight, the recommendations are intended primarily as helps and not as specific solutions to such exposure problems.

Printed instructions, of course, are relatively easy to come by. With many films the manufacturer packs adequate exposure information, along with recommended processing technicalities. Then there are the inexpensive card calculators, such as the Kodaguides, the Kodak Master Photoguide, and finally, the American Standards Association (ASA) Computer, which is remarkably specific.

Photoguides and Kodaguides

Photoguides and Kodaguides represent the sum of a vast amount of general and technical experience. They come up with exposure recommendations based on what has worked out well for many people. They require of you the ability to identify and distinguish between four basic light conditions. Here they are:

1. *Clear sky—bright sun.* That's easy.
2. *Hazy sun.* Not difficult at all.

3. *Cloudy bright.* If you can locate where the sun is, you're in business.

4. *Cloudy dull.* Frankly, it's not always easy to say how dull is dull. Generally we tend to over-correct, especially if we are conscious of our eyes' capacity for adapting easily to varying degrees of brightness. Actually, on an over-cast day shadow areas in a scene do not fall off as rapidly as the highlights. Hence we do not need as great an increase in exposure (for black-and-white) as might be indicated by our judgment of the sky's brightness, or darkness (and degrees of darkness are tricky to estimate). In color work, with highlight detail governing exposure, the needed increase is greater. So, the fourth light condition specified in the Kodaguides calls for considerable supplementary judgment on your part.

But the Kodaguides incorporate so large a safety factor that (in black-and-white) you can be fairly faulty in your estimates and still come off well. By the way, the Kodak Master Photoguide covers so many situations, involving both color and black-and-white film, by day and by artificial light, that it is a practically indispensable accessory.

The ASA Computer

In its work in photography, the American Standards Association has been effective in clarifying terminology and bringing together the manufacturers of film and of meters in matters of measurements and specifications. And the ASA has given us a very useful tool in what is called the Exposure Index. The Index is a number, which is derived from the sensitivity or speed of the material (the film), the light transmittance of camera lenses, the degree of reflectance within a camera, and all the other known factors influencing light as it arrives at a camera and travels through it to the focal plane where it is recorded. Thus the Index is of more practical value than a number which merely indicates the film speed.

While an Index is intended primarily for use with meters or guides, it can be used independently. Suppose, for example, you know only the Index number of your film—a black-and-white film. Well, one divided by that number (1/number) gives you your shutter setting with the lens at $f/16$ in bright sunlight. That gives a basic exposure with a safety factor of 2. Shift the lens to $f/11$ and you have a safety factor of 4. This, you'll find, checks with your Kodaguide; like the Kodaguide, too, it assumes a near-by scene.

For color work, one divided by the Index number, gives you your basic exposure in bright sunlight at $f/16$. Here the safety factor is small (about

155

1.5) because of color film's far more limited latitude.

Let's put the Index to work. Kodak Plus-X Film has an Index of 50. Very well, your basic exposure in sunlight is 1/50 at $f/16$. (Safety factor, 2) For a greater safety factor, about 4, the exposure becomes 1/50 at $f/11$.

With Kodachrome Film you use its Index, 10. Thus you have 1/10 at $f/16$ or, to translate it to a more usable exposure, 1/50 at $f/6.3$ for bright sunlight.

The ASA Computer was created to meet a specific need of the U. S. Navy during World War II. Because the use of a meter under combat conditions was sometimes impractical, the Navy asked for a computer which could be used in pre-setting cameras to meet anticipated conditions. And those conditions varied vastly.

The ASA Computer was designed to take into account not only the Index but the altitude of the sun and scene types, with particular reference to the importance and brightness of the shadows. Thus, when conditions make exposure guidance of real importance and we have no meter, we may place our problem in the Computer's lap. We can do so with confidence, but also with the reservation that the precision of any printed guide tends to drop off as the conditions under which it is used depart from normal—or clear sunlight.

In collecting the data on which the Computer is based, many points affecting exposures were revealed. For example, the difference between summer and winter exposures with black-and-white films (in the general neighborhood of 40° latitude) is only about 25 percent.

Then there is the matter of how much less exposure is needed in the tropics, or in Mexico. Actually, it was discovered that the difference is attributable to the fact that, generally, the buildings, the colors, of Mexico are brighter and visitors have a tendency to make more distance shots, for which less exposure is needed, anyway. True, tropical exposures can be cut finer, but the sun-angle factor in the ASA Computer takes the problem in stride.

Photocell Meters

It is the apparent power of decision which is one of the top assets of the photoelectric exposure meter. Think of it. You point one of these meters at a subject or scene to be photographed. Instantly a needle (activated by the minute current generated in the photoelectric cell by the impact of the light) swings over on a calibrated scale and comes to a halt under some specific number. With that number as a basis, figuring the exposure is but an instant's work—work involving consideration of the meter rating for the film you're using, and the aperture or the shutter speed you wish to use. The result is specific, businesslike, impersonal. Thus, these meters appear to have licked the exposure problem. But wait a minute—that's not the whole story; it just can't be as simple as that.

In common with most other modern precision tools, there is always the factor of skill in use. The operator must understand how to use the meter before it can be of maximum practical value. It is not a cure-all for carelessness, and is not intended to be.

The usefulness of a meter obviously depends upon the availability of a number which represents the speed of the photographic film. As we have noted, in talking about the ASA Computer, the ASA Indexes give us such numbers, modified by certain other factors than film speed. At any rate, the ASA Indexes are used in most photocell meters (notably the G.E.); Weston meters are based on other ratings, but work out well in practice.

To be sure, the meter settings serve as guides but, since not all photographers are accustomed to exposing for the same effects nor in the same manner, the variation in their demands and techniques makes it impossible to issue any single set of meter settings for films which will satisfy everyone's requirements without alteration or modification. This is perhaps more serious in black-and-white work than in color photography, for in color the goal of all workers is limited to just about a single effect. If you wish to determine the speed of a specific film in terms of a system for which no ratings are available, here is a possible procedure.

Make a series of exposures arbitrarily applying a wide range of meter setting numbers to the film. Select a scene you feel is typical of those you are likely to encounter later on, and use your meter according to your customary habits. After development, pick out the correctly exposed one.   157

The ASA Computer . . . . . The Kodak Master Photoguide . . . . . and three photoelectric meters

By referring to the setting used to make that negative, you'll discover the number you should use for future picture making.

If you plan to use your meter to determine color film exposures, use color film for the calibration. So calibrated your meter can be used for both color and black-and-white work; a calibration based on black-and-white film will not be sufficiently precise for color work.

As you make more and more pictures you probably will want to modify the meter setting to improve its validity under your own working conditions. Numbers arrived at in this manner are superior even to published data, for they apply not only to the film, but to your particular meter and to your way of using it.

Reading by Reflected Light

Originally, the use of photocell meters was exclusively in terms of reflected light. You observed your subject, and photographed it, in terms of reflected light. So you took readings that way. And the technique is still perfectly sound, if you observe a few precautions. Here are two basic procedures for the use of meters in terms of reflected light.

1. *Meter reading from the camera position.* This is the conventional procedure. It involves aiming the meter at the scene to be pictured. The exposure is figured directly from the resulting meter reading. In practice, however, difficulties arise, for the meter can only strike an average of the various light intensities in the scene, whereas the camera *images* them individually. Thus a brilliant sky, a strong but unimportant shadow, or an overbright foreground area may upset the average as interpreted by the meter. If you are aware of such disturbing factors, it's wise to compensate for them by aiming the meter so as to discount them. Experience alone can tell you how much meter deflection should be used. In general, the camera-position reading of the meter is useful but not universally successful and should not become an iron-clad habit.

2. *Close-up meter readings.* Close-up readings will often avoid the disturbing factors mentioned above, in picture situations which permit you to measure the important individual elements. Such meter readings should be made from the camera angle you plan to use and at a distance from the object roughly equal to its diameter (as seen from the camera angle). An adult face should be meter-read at a distance of about ten inches, whereas a horse should be read at six or seven feet. If the close-up meter reading concentrates on one of the brightest objects in the camera's ken,

such as a white face, give twice as much exposure as the meter indicates. Take care lest you cast a shadow on any object you read, for the shadow will lead to a false reading.

A. *Middle tone reading.* For more or less flat scenes, involving a relatively small range of brightnesses, you can sometimes make direct readings of one or several of the important individual elements. Strike an average if necessary, and you have a workable index.

B. *Shadow detail reading.* In more contrasty scenes the darkest shadow or object in which you desire to show detail can be used as a means of establishing the correct exposure. Assuming that your dark object is not below the sensitivity range of your meter, take a close-up reading from it. The result, if applied to the whole scene, might easily produce heavy over-exposure in the brighter portions. For this reason, one of the meter manufacturers has included a multiplying factor of 16 times on its calculator to make allowances. Using this arbitrary factor, you arrive at an index which will place the resulting negative high enough in the characteristic curve to preserve the shadow detail and, at the same time, give the higher lights a break. But you must be careful. If you get too close to the shadow, you will shade it still more with your meter or body. If you're too far away, you'll no longer measure the shadow.

C. *Highlight detail reading.* By reversing the procedure of B, the meter manufacturers advise that you can use the brightest object in which you wish to preserve detail and *divide* the reading by 8 to achieve an index which will assure a good degree of shadow detail. For this technique to be successful, the distribution of lighting over the scene area must be normal. If the subject is flatly lighted, for example, highlight readings will lead to overexposure. However, the technique is well suited to color exposure where highlight brightness is the criterion.

D. The procedures B and C can be used, in effect, in combination; this is the *brightness range method.* The least bright and most bright objects are both individually read. Multiply the one by the other and take the square root of the product to arrive at a working reading for the scene. For example, suppose that the low reading is 4 and the high is 400. 4 x 400 = 1600. The square root of 1600 is 40, which is your brightness reading.

Differences between the calibrations of several meters of the same manufacture sometimes reach troublesome proportions. Similarly, age and operating conditions, such as extreme cold, sometimes cause variations in

159

shutter speeds. The variations in meters and cameras may tend to cancel each other. At other times they may be cumulative and increase the chance for trouble. The principle of the meter is the evaluation of average brightness, not single parts of the picture. The user should learn by experience to compromise between reading "close-up" and from the camera position for best results.

On days when the sky is free from clouds and when all objects are flooded with sunshine, the wide angle included by the meter makes very little difference for an average scene. However, with clouds in the sky or with spotty lighting, the wide angle is far more likely to produce erroneous results, particularly if one continues to use the meter at the camera position. Any accidental highlight or deep shadow just outside the picture area will produce an erroneous reading on meters taking in a wide angle.

To utilize the full capability of a meter, it is wise to keep in mind the relative color sensitivity of the eye, film emulsion, and photocell. In general the photocell exposure meter has its *maximum* sensitivity in the same region as the eye, but has greater relative sensitivity to both blue and red. This more nearly matches the color response of *panchromatic* emulsions now in use than it does the eye. There are other types of emulsion—infrared, for example—to which the cell has no comparable sensitivity.

Reading by Incident Light

In theory, the incident light method gives you an index of exposure in terms of the intensity of light falling on a scene. For specialized photography—as in Hollywood—it is now the almost universally accepted technique, but it involves serious difficulties for the amateur. Direct sunlight, for example, is far beyond the brightness recording range of the average meter; to compensate for this excessive brilliance some photographers have evolved baffles or shields to place over the meter, thereby reducing the light's intensity to such an extent that proportional readings can be made. Each such device involves a tailor-made series of calibrations, adapted to the light-absorbing factor of the baffle used.

A somewhat simpler application of the incident light method involves the translating of incident into reflected light by means of some arbitrarily selected medium, such as a gray card, a sheet of newspaper, or the palm of your hand. A definite guide to the potency of the light can be obtained by taking readings from this single intermediary. If it reads half as bright today as it did yesterday, doubled exposure is obviously called for.

The procedure to be followed in working out this method goes something like this. Decide, first, what intermediary you want to use. It should be something to which you can handily refer at any time, something not easily lost, something stable in color, matte in texture, and unchanging in shape. Want ad pages of newspapers the country over are much the same. Fold such a page in half, read it from about 15 inches and you have a type of standard as readily obtained in San Diego as Syracuse. Go out in the street, for example, on a good picture making day and, in direct sunlight, take a reading, in approved close-up manner, from your selected intermediary. Record the reading or memorize it. Then, in the same light, make a series of pictures, all of the same scene. Begin with an exposure that's likely to be on the *under* side and work up to overexposure. Keep a record of the exposure for each shot. Then develop the films by your favorite method. When they are all finished, inspect them carefully and select the one which has the quality you'd like to have in all your pictures. Consulting your records, you find it was made at, say $f/11$ and $1/200$. And the meter reading from your intermediary was, for example, 500. Now, the next time you go out to make pictures, all you need do is to take another reading in full light from your faithful intermediary. If, again, it reads 500, you can rely on $f/11$ and $1/200$; but, if it reads only 250, you know you have to double your exposure, so you shoot at $f/11$ and $1/100$.

As you become familiar with this incident light method you will find that it is particularly useful in photographing interiors by artificial light. In fact, many photographers use it as a means of tailoring their light to meet their exposure desires. On the basis of such readings the lamps can be moved forward or back until the illumination is found to be right in terms of the film and exposure to be used.

But, always keep in mind the importance of the subject. With incident light readings allowances must be made for light and dark subject matter, just as with printed recommendations.

Several photocell meters have been designed expressly for use by incident light. The Norwood is possibly the best known; with adapter, both the G.E. and the Weston can be used for incident light readings.

• • •

There's no one explicit answer to the question of a meter's importance to the individual photographer. It's much like all other photographic accessories and niceties, $f/2$ lenses, flash guns, range finders and the like. You can make pictures—good pictures—without them as long as you confine

161

yourself to what might be called "average" subjects, those in good light or those for which exposures are specifically recommended by the Koda-guides. But when you attempt the unusual, that is, pictures in deep shade, interiors illuminated by a variety of lights, then the accessories and the meter can be definitely helpful.

Keep in mind that blind reliance on a meter is not the answer to any exposure problem; similarly, you are not guaranteed good pictures just because your lens is rated $f/2$. The more experience you have with a meter the less you will be forced to resort to its use, for you will acquire a more seasoned "exposure sense." At the same time the readings you do make should become more and more meaningful.

162

Meter Techniques

	General Landscapes Reading from camera position Tilt meter to avoid strong skylight	*Room Interiors* Incident light method	
	Beach or Snow Scenes Highlight reading	*Flat Lighted Portraits* Close-up reading	
	Back Lighted Subjects Shadow detail reading	*Contrasty Interiors* Brightness range method	
	Sports Events Camera position or incident light method. Take reading before action begins. Set aperture and shutter and be ready	*Copying Paintings* Incident light method Close-up reading	

CHAPTER 14

Pictures, Free Style

"I DON'T know much about art, but I know what I like."

You've heard—or made—that classic remark many times. It is classic because, although trite, it is the average man's bristling defense of his own taste against what he feels to be the mysterious and dogmatic rules of professional art. And the phrase, "I know what I like," indicates that the browbeaten average man makes a strong distinction between pictures he considers good and those he thinks are poor.

Simmered down, it implies that some pictures mean something to him, while others stutter, limp, and fall flat.

And the secret of a picture that does its job neatly is mainly a matter of arrangement. Call it composition if you like, but composition is essentially a matter of arranging the various elements in a picture so that, together, they make sense—the sense the artist wanted to convey.

It's arrangement that makes the difference between sense and nonsense in practically anything. You don't say to a friend, "Country how cameras about hike our a in the with?" To be sure, a long-suffering friend might spend a while trying to dope out what you had said, but you're on your way a lot sooner when you say, "How about a hike in the country with our cameras?" You've simply arranged the words so that they make sense. It's the same in music. There are 88 keys on a piano, but you don't get music by leaning on all of them at once. You select a few to produce a song, and a few others to provide harmony for it.

So it is with pictures. If you fail to arrange the various things in your picture so that they make sense, you can't have a successful picture, and no amount of darkroom magic can make it so.

Fortunately, there are a few basic rules of arrangement, rules which are not presented arbitrarily, because they were not drawn up arbitrarily. They grew, slowly, out of the accumulated experience of the race.

*Arrangement makes
the difference*

What's this picture supposed to say?   No question about this one

First, a picture must have *emphasis*. Some one thing or group of things must stand out unmistakably as the reason for the picture. In the rectangle of the picture area there must be one major feature, something which appears important, significant, or interesting. A picture without this one dominant element is like a sentence without a subject; it doesn't mean anything.

Practically all of the other "rules" of composition are concerned with the ways and means of producing pictorial emphasis. They may be grouped handily into two major classes, one dealing with what might be called the "plane geometry" of composition, and the other with the use of color or tone contrasts. And, of course, there's a good deal of overlapping and combination.

Probably the most useful of all the geometric systems is a simple matter called "the thirds." It works this way. Divide your picture area into thirds, vertically and horizontally. Any of the four points at which the lines cross, within the picture space, has been found to be a "natural" for the placement of a subject which is intended to be dominant. And secondary points of interest can be located at or near any of the other three intersections.

This, frankly, is a rule-of-thumb, not to be slavishly used. But you will find that it works, works particularly well when you're dealing with action and movement. A little further investigation will show that it is rather closely related to the principle of "dynamic symmetry" which is a fascinating affair, a little too specialized for discussion here. The picture and sketch, overpage, show the application of the "thirds" idea.

165

The "rule of the thirds" at work. Try it on some of your own pictures.

Among the other geometric schemes of arrangement there's a whole group based on the flow or direction of "lines" in a picture—lines which may be real and visible, or merely implied. A gesture, an extended arm, or the concentrated attention of several pairs of eyes can create definite lines, and the eye of the beholder will tend to follow those lines. The letters of the alphabet are sometimes arbitrarily used to describe types of linear arrangement. For example, the various elements of your picture may arrange themselves in an "A", or pyramid. Likewise you'll find picture possibilities in arrangements corresponding to "S", "C", "L", "O", "N", "T", "V", "Y", and "Z". In no case is it important to start out with the intention of making, for example, a picture arranged "T" fashion. The

166

important thing is to arrange the elements in your pictures so that they make sense. If you succeed they probably conform to one of the letter patterns.

Overlapping this set of rules-of-thumb is another which is concerned with the contrast of directional lines in your picture. In the "T" arrangement, for example, the horizontal and vertical lines come together at a stark right angle, much as a side road bangs into a highway. The point of contact is a danger point, a point where you expect things to happen. The same is true of "L" or "Z" shapes; the points where two directional lines come to a sudden contact are bound to get a good deal of the eyes' attention.

If you transform the sharp angles into soft curves, as in the "S" and "C" shapes, you eliminate the clash of lines and achieve, instead, a directional flow of action and interest.

When all is said and done, the function of composition is to interest the eye of the beholder. And, quite as important, the lines of flow or points of

167

You may detect the alphabetical influence on the compositional lines of these pictures

One involves a whole hillside, the other only a few square yards. Both prove the effectiveness of simplicity ture is made up of various tones or colors of light, ranging from the brightest lights, or highlights, to the deepest black. It is in your arrangement of these several tones that emphasis can be gained or lost.

The human eye has a special liking for highlights, for lustre. We like diamonds and silk and polished wood, because we like the gleam of light in and on them. So the successful photographer makes sure that his highlights fall where they do the most good, create the most emphasis. Like a smart jeweler who displays his gems on dark velvet, the photographer puts his most important highlights close to a dark area. Then those highlights really shine.

Carrying on, for a moment, with the jeweler, you will find that he seldom plunks down a whole bevy of gems for your inspection, all at once. No indeed. He gives each one a separate showing on the velvet. That way, each shines and sparkles without interference or competition. In other words, he is a canny user of the principles of emphasis and unity.

Emphasis was mentioned a few pages back; *unity* is closely akin to it, for it implies unmistakable emphasis, gained through the elimination of non-essentials. And both *emphasis* and *unity* combine to mean, essentially, *simplicity*. If there is any one word which has the magic secret of success in it, that word is *simplicity*. For in simplicity you gain efficiency by cutting out those things which are not important to the theme of your picture; in simplicity you tell your story without hazard of being misunderstood; and in simplicity it is far easier to approach that mysterious intangible called beauty.

Study Pictures—All Pictures

Form the habit of looking at all pictures carefully, to determine, first, whether or not they appeal to you and, if so, why. Then, second, try to analyze their compositional plans. Apply your study to your own camera work. Give it a critical going-over.

In studying pictures, there's a simple little device you should have. You can make it in two minutes from a generous sheet of white cardboard. Simply cut out two "L" shaped pieces and use them to frame any part of an average-sized picture. Vary the size of area included in the "frame;" move it around over the picture under scrutiny. There's no better nor more interesting way to discover how and why a picture succeeds or fails and how it can be improved.

In the course of your viewing of pictures, you will frequently find

Don't let the horizon split your picture in halves; make it work for you

his lot exclusively with either of these schools of thought. Indeed, it is definitely unwise to do so. However, the more attention you pay to planning, the better you equip yourself to take advantage of unexpected opportunities. The self-discipline imposed by planning tends to eliminate buck fever and ineffectualness when something fine but unexpected comes along. Almost automatically you select a vantage point, a camera angle, and a concentration of interest which give you not merely a pictorial record but a picture which makes capital of the opportunity.

After some practicing you may find that you, like many others, belong to a group of "middle men." Confronted with a picture possibility, you recognize that somewhere in the scene is a neat composition. Unable to pick it out definitely and lacking time to make a detail study in the camera finder, you make shots from several different angles that seem to have the wanted material in them. Then, after the negatives have been developed, you bring out the best arrangement, create pictorial emphasis by cropping, dodging, and shading while making enlargements. Purists may scorn composition in terms of the enlarging easel, but practical-minded souls are grateful for it and embrace it.

It is the ability to work both by plan and by "spontaneous combustion," to give the planned picture animation and to make the unplanned picture appear to have happened for his own special benefit, that distinguishes the well-rounded photographer.

A FEW DON'TS AND DO'S

While the "laws" of composition are sometimes successfully violated, those laws are so valid from a common sense point of view that they

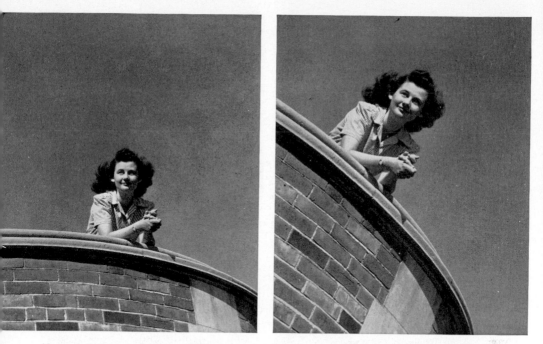

Above, left, is a perfectly good little snapshot. The quality is good and the composition, while very ordinary, does not offend. The same subject is given enhanced interest and vitality by slightly raising and tilting the camera to produce a more dynamic compositional scheme

Below, left, an example of camera "sprouts." To avoid such unfortunate results, keep an eye on what lies beyond your subject. Usually, the sky will afford your most convenient and flattering background

Let your subject move into—not out of—the picture space

should be part of every camera user's subconscious background. Here are some of them.

1. Avoid halving of your picture, either vertically or horizontally. A picture that "splits in the middle" tends to lack strength and interest. So keep horizon lines above or below the "equator" of your picture area.

2. Try to keep your major interest out of the dead center of your picture. It's a static spot. If there's action indicated, let it lead *into* the picture, not out of it.

3. Avoid confusing backgrounds. Many an informal portrait has been marred by a background which, for no good reason, demands the lion's share of interest. Unsightly buildings, the monotonous siding of a house, a background tree or post which appears to sprout from a person's head or shoulders; these are things to watch and to avoid. The sky is about the finest of all backgrounds, because it is unobtrusive and infinitely varied, and because it usually forces you to use a fairly low camera angle, an angle that gives your subjects a psychological advantage, thereby giving *you* a better picture.

4. Allow more space for your subjects to look and move *into* than out of. Think of the side of your print as a wall. People usually prefer to stand with their backs to a wall.

Any list of *do's* and *don'ts* must obviously be incomplete. Your concern is more with *do's*, anyway.

The first, the basic rule for the aspiring photographer is, *keep your camera busy*. In your pictures, whether they are successes or failures, you'll find information that is twice as convincing as anything you may merely be told. For in photography, as in every other human activity, it's practice that counts. Learning without doing is generally unsatisfactory.

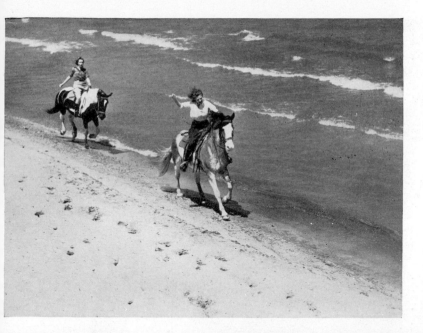

Action and composition combine to produce rhythm and strength

Compositional lines dominate, yet they are kept from running away with the picture by the relatively small figures

CHAPTER 15

Land, Sea, and Sky

THERE IS SCENERY—and scenery. Some of it is so obvious that it practically knocks you down. The Grand Canyon, Niagara Falls, Natural Bridge, Half Dome Mountain—these and dozens of other similar phenomena carry a wallop that none can avoid. Picture postcards by the million proclaim their glories; a fair week-end at any well-publicized scenic center leaves a trail of empty film cartons, ample evidence that snapshooters have been seeing the sights in more ways than one.

But photographing such "naturals" is a little too easy, too obvious for a steady diet. The true photographer knows that his greatest pleasure comes in picturing scenes that others have overlooked, in finding and glorifying unexploited beauties.

Mr. Maeterlinck's play, "The Blue Bird," is built on the thesis that one may search far and wide for the blue bird of happiness only to find it, at last, in one's own back yard. Similarly, one may travel to all sorts of famous beauty spots only to discover that the most deeply satisfying scenic pictures can be made within a few miles of home. Any such discovery, however, depends solely on the relish and intelligence with which you use your eyes.

The picturing of any scenery, be it world-famous or your own personal "find," can be humdrum or exciting. It's up to you. Forthwith, then, consider some of the means by which natural beauties can be immortalized on film.

THE GRAND VIEW

First, the spectacular, far-flung panorama of grandeur. In this classification fall the majority of mountain scenes. The problem, in the face of such lavish scenery, is where to stop, or what not to include. And the answer lies in getting right back to the first principles of composition.

Despite the apparent richness of the available material, the wise photographer doesn't try to get it all in one picture. He knows, in fact, that he shouldn't even try to get it all in. Too much detail is apt to dwarf the principal points of interest.

The picturing of any such view is best approached in terms of your camera's view finder. The view finder's definite limits give you a better notion of picture possibilities in any scene than your unrestricted eyes can do; for it takes a sedulously trained pair of eyes to "frame" individual shots in a widespread landscape, all of which may seem to be pictorial. When, by constant reference to the view finder, you discover something that really holds together as a picture, with limiting sides, top and bottom, and gives you something specific to look at, then you're ready to consider making an exposure.

There's another advantage in concentrating on your view finder; it forces you to disregard, for the moment, the total effect of any scene—

and the total effect may be a composite of brilliant coloring, a holiday mood, charming company, a good dinner, and the excitement of seeing something new. This is said without any intention to belittle the emotional or spiritual values of scenic beauty. But unless you take the time and trouble to scan the view critically, your ultimate picture may easily miss fulfilling its purpose—which is to give you, every time you look at it, an encore of your original thrill. We have all, unfortunately, seen travelers' snapshots which so far missed their purpose that they had to be accompanied by something like—"This really doesn't give you any idea of the place. You simply can't get it in a picture. It's wonderful, honestly it is."

Unless your pictures are designed to serve only as springboards for conversational high dives, try hard to avoid the need for such drab apologies. They do not become the true photographer.

And so back to photographic ways and means.

The grand view contains, as does any long shot, a good deal of haze.

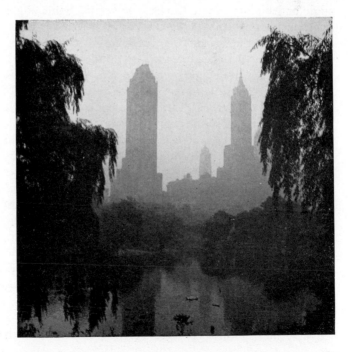

Mist can be just as effective in town as in the mountains

It may be imperceptible, but it's there just the same and may show up in your prints. When using black-and-white film, a yellow or orange filter will eliminate most of this haze and enable you to show details on the far horizons. This may be desirable in some kinds of documentary photography, but pictorially the photograph is better if the haze shows as a part of the view. It adds to the illusion of distance and depth by separating the various receding planes in the picture.

When color film is used, haze not only obscures distant detail, but reflects a great deal of blue light from the sky, which in the photograph affects the color of all parts of the scene covered by the haze. Hence, when using Kodachrome Film, you really gain by also using a haze filter.

Possibly the most important content of the scenic shot, especially in the mountains, is a great deal of very powerful light. *Actinic* is the word for it. Because of it you can cut your basic exposures somewhat; up in the mountains, a mile high or thereabouts, the reduction may be a half stop, that is, 50% or even a bit more.

But the intensity of the light isn't as significant to your picture as the angle at which the light reaches the scene. Some angles, you'll discover, belittle; others glorify. Obviously, you'll wait for the moment of glorification. Note the word "wait," for good scenics are not made casually. They deserve patience; if they're good, they are usually the fruit of patience. Full, front light, with the sun at your back is seldom the right lighting for large-scale shots. A bit of cross light, you'll find, reveals more interesting contours and variations. Back lighting, of course, gives you shapes and outlines, with relatively little detail.

Another factor to watch is that of distance. You may be tempted to stand on the brink of Inspiration Point (there's at least one of these at every well-regulated beauty spot) and aim out over miles of valley toward the distant peaks. The result may be fairly good, but it seldom has the "feel" of vast distance—and that feeling is one of the emotional considerations which should not be ignored. To get the veritable sense of distance, find some significant bit of foreground which will give your picture a jumping-off place, for *distance* depends on its relationship to *nearness* to be at all significant. Show that relationship and capitalize on it. The old trick of showing a member of your party in the foreground, his back to the camera, is not at all to be scorned. Sometimes it may offer you your only foreground interest.

All scenics of this type are made, of course, with the lens focused at infinity. In order to get maximum depth, the diaphragm is usually stopped down as far as the exigencies of exposure will permit.

THE INTIMATE VIEW

Related to the grand view type of scenic is another which can be called the Intimate View. It differs from the grand view primarily in scale and in subject matter. Where your grand view may deal with a vista of many miles and a mountain, the intimate view is concerned with a few hundred yards and, for example, a rural church steeple.

Obviously a little different treatment is needed. You want a good bit of significant foreground detail, such as a tree branch which frames your view. And you're dealing with individual shapes of trees, fences, roads and buildings, rather than with masses of forests, rocky slopes, and cloud shadows. It is in this type of scenic that you are most likely to discover your "blue bird" pictures—the home scenes which you and your friends have overlooked because they are so familiar.

From the standpoint of composition, little more can be added to the rules already outlined. Just be certain your picture holds together and that the wandering eye of the observer will always be led by your arrange-

Left, intimate views generally benefit when natural "frames" are used.

Below, pictorial interest can be found in the most commonplace subjects—even mail boxes

183

ment to the center of interest. A pathway, roadway, or foreground people leading or pointing to this center are effective tools.

Pictures of mirror-like reflections from water deserve special mention; those are the pictures you make from alongside the mill pond or quiet lake. Since the water absorbs about half the light from the scene, you will need at least a full stop more exposure than is required by the direct view. And make sure that no one can ever question which way is right-side-up in any reflection picture of yours. Break the perfect reflection with ripples from a tossed stone, or use a strong foreground feature to establish right-side-upness.

For all landscapes, in black-and-white work, you're practically lost without a filter. It's true, as was said in talking of filters, that it is possible to achieve relatively successful results solely in terms of controlled exposure—provided the light conditions are in your favor. But it's risky to work that way, especially when filters are so inexpensive and so easy to use. For average scenes, a simple, light yellow filter—such as the Wratten K2—should give you sufficient correction. It will help preserve sky-cloud contrast and will tend to keep foliage from going too dark.

If you're concentrating on clouds, with the landscape serving only as a base for your picture, the Wratten A filter (red) with panchromatic film will give you high cloud-and-sky contrast, together with all there is to be had in the way of cloud texture.

Scenics with Infrared and Pan Films

While infrared film, used with a red filter, is not suggested for the general run of scenics, there are times when it serves interestingly and well. It unveils distance as no other medium does, and the results may be of interest both scientifically and artistically.

Full development of infrared film negatives produces strikingly dramatic "posterish" effects. Clear skies reproduce as black, green grass and trees as snowy white. Faces appear chalky.

With less development, very pleasing and unusual, somewhat "ethereal" results can be obtained. Try a few infrared landscape exposures. Develop some fully; develop others only about ¾ of the time recommended in the instructions packed with the film. There has been some controversy on focusing for infrared shots. While the infrared rays do converge slightly behind the focal plane of the other rays, the correction required is so slight (¼%) that it can be accomplished more practically by simply

184

A vivid example of the power of infrared to change and to "reveal" a scene

stopping the lens down to $f/16$ or thereabouts. This requires a tripod which, incidentally, is always worth-while in serious pictorial shots.

In black-and-white scenic photography, there's no point in using the ultra-high-speed films. Usually a good, standard speed, fine-grain film, such as Kodak Plus-X, will do all that you need. For work with a variety of filters you'll need a panchromatic emulsion, but if you're using only the blue-restraining filters you'll find that such a film as Kodak Verichrome works out admirably. Not long ago, a perplexed camera user complained that he got no image at all, "not a darn thing," when he tried to photograph Old Faithful, in Yellowstone, using ortho film and a red filter. A puzzling phenomenon, indeed, until the nice relationship between filter and film color sensitivity is remembered.

Sunsets

Sooner or later, everyone tries a sunset. And the result is frequently disappointing. The reason, therefore, is found in the fact that the visual appeal of a sunset is largely a matter of *color*—of subtle, shifting color. With color film you can capture such beauty easily. If, perchance, you underexpose slightly, the colors will be deepened and you'll get a more vivid effect. Slight overexposure will soften the colors and make them

A flaming, red-and-gold sunset, pictured with ortho film

more delicate. You can't miss. But in black-and-white you'll encounter more difficulty. And it's hard to prescribe a definite sunset technique—again because of the unpredictable quality and color of the light. In some cases an ortho film will work well, especially when you've a lot of orange, red, and yellow to deal with; again, your dominant colors may be on the cool or blue end of the spectrum, and you'll naturally have to change to pan, plus a filter, to get what you want. By all means try a sunset or two; whether or not you're entirely successful, you'll be garnering some useful experience.

Before leaving landscapes, there's one other subject to consider, because it's bound to come up.

Panoramas

From a strictly pictorial point of view, panoramas do not make sense. The human eye doesn't embrace the far-flung horizon in full panoramic fashion. For the sake of a record, however, a panorama can be justified.

Unless you own one of those trick, clockwork panorama cameras—and the chances are easily a million to one that you don't—you will have to make a panorama by overlapping a series of shots, all made from the same point. In theory, the camera should be pivoted, for the successive shots, on a point exactly under the lens; in practice, pivoting on the tripod socket works fairly well. Overlap each exposure about one-third. And if the complete arc involves you in considerable variation in lighting, make progressive exposure adjustment. When your prints are finished, experiment will show you the best possible points at which to join one to   187

Two stages in the completion of a composite panorama. After the individual units are matched and mounted together, a copy negative is made of the whole thing and either contact printed or enlarged

For moods, nothing compares with the sea

another. Usually, strong vertical lines in the panoramic scene will give you good joining places. Mount the joined series on a card, and make a copy negative of the complete paste-up. And there's your panorama, complete in one negative.

SEASCAPES

Marine scenes are in some ways more difficult than landscapes, especially if you try to picture a broad expanse composed exclusively of water and sky. With such material, it is obviously a problem to establish a main center of interest or to utilize any of the tried-and-true compositional schemes. The most famous marine painters have solved this problem in two categorical ways; they have either used large foreground waves and a lot of detailed texture as the interest-nubbins of their paintings, or they have introduced boats, birds, or some very impressive clouds to break up the monotony of sky and water.

Of course, the minute you start bringing in birds, boats, bathers, or what-not, you simplify the whole thing, for your interest centers can then be nicely organized. Frequently, in photographing landscapes and marine views, you find that distant but important features are reduced in size to mere specks. These are clear-cut cases calling for the use of a lens of longer focal length. Its narrow angle of view eliminates the unwanted surrounding detail and affords larger images of the more important and desired distant subjects.

In one aspect, marine views differ drastically from landscapes. Back lighting can be, and frequently is, used to excellent effect. With the light coming toward you over the water, you pick up a multitude of glinting waves, and these glints, dapples, and sparkles of light give your picture a very special kind of animation. Under such circumstances, of course, foreground objects—boats and such—are rendered as silhouetted shapes, and the pictorial photographer finds ample reason for rejoicing in this state of affairs.

For back and strongly cross-lighted subjects anywhere, beware lest the sun's rays reach your camera lens directly. The result of that may be the setting up of reflections and flares within the lens. Hold your hand or hat out to cast a shadow on the lens. Otherwise, you'll find a shadowy image of the iris diaphragm on your negative. The use of a lens hood to shade your lens from direct rays in cross lighting will be a big help. Of course, if you really want the sun in the picture, you'll have to cut down the diaphragm almost to the extreme, and speed up your shutter. The resulting picture will be one of those pseudo-moonlight jobs, and may be very attractive, too.

Speaking of moonlight, you may be tempted to make some pictures in the full of the moon. Try it. It's an interesting experience. But remember, bright moonlight is really very dim light; a time exposure is certain to be your only recourse in picturing moonlit scenes. There is, however, an interesting exception to this. If you want to picture the moon itself, then your problem becomes one of shooting a subject in direct sunlight; hence, you can use a snapshot exposure. Sounds absurd, doesn't it? But a recent experiment, made with a home movie camera, proved it to be fact.

Take Time Out for Beauty

In the old days, long before anyone thought of speaking "candid" and "photography" in the same breath, amateur photographers concerned themselves almost exclusively with "views." Those were leisurely, unsophisticated days, and pastoral scenes were part of them. Today, the mood of the world in general and of photography in particular has changed. The tempo is swift, our emotions are brittle, and we lean naturally toward irony and satire. Hence, it is good for us to take time out, once in a while, and to prowl with our cameras, seeking out a little of natural beauty and serenity. We can use all we can find.

CHAPTER 16

Action

PRIMITIVE PHOTOGRAPHY was a cumbersome thing, dependent on long time-exposures. Subjects were propped up with head rests and arm rests; they were stiff and unnatural. Even so, the camera was much faster than the swiftest artist in creating a detailed, factual record. Ever since that time, photography has been increasing in speed. New films, better lenses, fleeter shutters, and special lights have all helped to knife time into thinner and thinner slices. Today, pictures are made quite casually at a millionth of a second. And greater speeds are not improbable.

Naturally, speeds of the astronomical sort are primarily for laboratory use; most of us will get along—and very well, too—if our cameras are capable of speeds up to 1/200 second. Camera shutters with rated speeds up to 1/400 are fairly common. Shutter speeds of 1/1000 are, for the most part, luxuries, just as a 150 H. P. motor car is a luxury. A clever driver of a 75 H. P. car can outmaneuver an eager but uncertain driver of a 150 H. P. job; just so, a canny photographer whose camera's top speed is 1/200 can bring home better action pictures than those made by an enthusiast equipped with a higher speed outfit and less good judgment.

Speed, as Mr. Einstein is said to have indicated, is relative. And, as a corollary to that profundity, be it added that there are more ways than one to skin a cat.

The fascination of picturing speed is a real thing. No small boy with a Brownie can resist the temptation to photograph a plane, or a racing car, or a track race, or the Overland Limited. And, almost as often as not, he gets a fair picture, despite the fact that a Brownie's shutter works at a speed somewhere between 1/25 and 1/50. Theoretically the thing's impossible. But remember Mr. Einstein.

It is in the field of straight-line action—a plane, a train, a race—that relativity is photographically most important. Stand close beside a highway

191

and watch the cars come along steadily at the legal limit. While they're still a hundred yards up the road, they give you no real sense of speed; they merely grow larger. Closer, they grow larger fast. Then, as they pass, you have to swing your head swiftly to follow them. The "growing" goes into reverse and the cars diminish in size, swiftly, then slowly.

Camera-wise, this simple phenomenon means merely that it takes much more shutter speed to "stop" action as it crosses the camera's axis than when that action is approaching or receding.

Back to the highway for a moment, only this time stand at least 100 feet away from the traffic. The angle between yourself and the oncoming cars is greater; their speed, at a distance, is a little more apparent but, oddly enough, the speed at which they pass directly in front of you seems less than when you were standing close-by. At any rate, you don't have to swivel your head as fast to follow the action. Translate that into photography. It means that you need a little more shutter speed to catch the approaching or receding cars, and not quite as much speed to stop the cross-axis movement as when you were close to the traffic.

Calculating Exposures for Speed Work

Here's a tabulation which puts the whole situation into compact form. It rates a bit of study. It is, frankly, conservative, in that it indicates shutter speeds which will certainly give you sharp, enlargeable negatives. Johnny with his Brownie may be well satisfied with his results made at, say, 1/40 when the table indicates 1/100 as the right speed; but try enlarging those Brownie negatives a few diameters, and you'll find them plenty blurred. But don't chide Johnny; he'll learn.

ACTION-STOPPING GUIDE

FOR SUBJECTS SUCH AS	DISTANCE FROM CAMERA	SHUTTER SPEEDS FOR SUBJECTS MOVING		
		DIRECTLY HEAD-ON	AT ABOUT 45°	AT ABOUT 90°
Pedestrians, construction work, most ordinary activities	25 feet	1/100	1/200	1/400
	50 feet	1/50	1/100	1/200
	100 feet	1/25	1/50	1/100
Most sports and more energetic activities	25 feet	1/200	1/400	1/1000
	50 feet	1/100	1/200	1/400
	100 feet	1/50	1/100	1/200
Fast cars, trains, planes, and other swift motion	25 feet	1/400	1/1000	....
	50 feet	1/200	1/400	1/1000
	100 feet	1/100	1/200	1/400

There's a mathematical formula by means of which you can work out your own tabulation, suited specifically to your lens and shutter. It runs this way:

Shutter speed calculation for motion at right angles to the camera axis

$$\text{Shutter Speed} = \frac{\text{Distance in feet x circle of confusion in inches}}{\text{Focal length of lens in inches x speed in feet per second}}$$

or

$$\text{S.S.} = \frac{D \text{ x c.c.}}{F \text{ x } S}$$

For motion at 45° angle, S.S. (as above) x 3/2
For motion head on, S.S. (as above) x 3/1

Sample Situation

You wish to photograph a city street scene involving ordinary traffic running at say 20 miles per hour. When photographing at 50 feet from the action, as the cars run across in front of the camera, what shutter speed would be required? Assume the lens being used has a focal length of 4 inches and the tolerable circle of confusion is 1/200 inch.

Answer

15 m.p.h. equals approximately 30 feet per second

$$\text{Shutter speed} = \frac{50 \text{ x } 1/200}{4 \text{ x } 30} = \frac{\frac{1}{4}}{120} = \frac{.25}{120} = \frac{1}{480} \text{ sec.}$$

Since this is beyond the capabilities of the fastest conventional shutter, you may take the cars as they approach at an angle—say 45°. In that case

$$\text{Shutter speed} = \frac{1}{480} \text{ x } \frac{3}{2} = \frac{3}{960} = \frac{1}{320} \text{ sec.}$$

This is within reason for some cameras, but not for the majority. Consider, then, the possibilities of shooting head on. The equation works out this way:

$$\text{Shutter speed} = \frac{1}{480} \text{ x } \frac{3}{1} = \frac{3}{480} = \frac{1}{160} \text{ sec.}$$

If that is still too much shutter speed for your equipment, you can always back farther away—and re-figure.

The only purpose in mentioning this formula is to suggest that you work out one or two equations based on situations you have already experienced—or on a setup you may encounter, any day now. If you are going out to photograph races of any sort, a little of this figuring beforehand may save a lot of explaining afterwards. Then, having thereby nailed down a fact or two, go on about your action photography on the basis of your own good judgment and common sense—the two most important of all photographic "accessories."

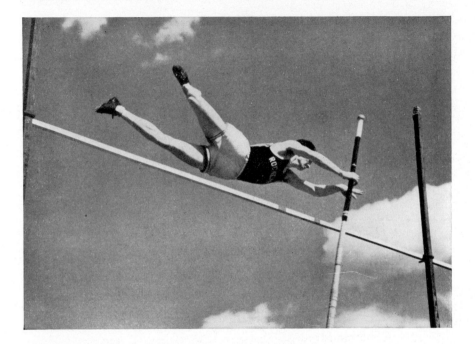

Poised Action

In many sports, particularly in races, movement is constant enough to permit picture making in terms of calculated speeds. But there are other sports in which the action is spasmodic, defying calculation. In those sports, the instants when action is poised are, pictorially, just as vivid and interesting as the moments when action is wildest. Take pole vaulting, for instance. At the very top of the vault, with the vaulter's body flung out horizontally over the bar, action is relatively quiet—yet it's the best pictorial moment in this field event. This peak instant can be "stopped" with much less shutter speed than either the rise or fall.

194

These look like top speed, but . . .

Baseball has a number of moments which are full of poised action. The pitcher winds up and then unwinds to throw his speed-ball. In that instant, between winding and unwinding, action is suspended, yet a picture of it tells a story of speed and power. An instant later, having released the ball, the pitcher is again poised—all his energy having gone into the delivery. There's another pictorial moment. To picture either of these moments you need to work swiftly, but a high shutter speed is less important to your success than an understanding of the sport and of the personal style of the athlete before your lens.

Check over other sports, other activities which seem, off-hand to call for top speed. Rowing, basketball, fancy diving, tennis, hunting—in all of these the best picture moments are not necessarily those in which action is most frenzied. It takes practice to learn exactly what and when those moments are; reading about them is just a start. Keep your eyes peeled for pictures when you read the sports page of the newspaper. Analyze the pictures. There are real lessons to be learned from them.

Or watch a veteran sports photographer at work. He knows sports so well that he can predict the next most likely developments during play—and moves over to take advantage of them.

Even in boxing, a good photographer gets his pictures as the blows land, not as they travel. There was that famous instance at the Louis-Nova fight in '41. Two photographers, on directly opposite sides of the ring, saw a heavy punch coming and shot just as it landed. Both used Photoflashes, of course, but—one of the lamps failed to work. The Photographer whose light had failed discovered, on developing the film, that he had a picture—a most unusual and vivid silhouette—*made by the light of his competitor's flash.* The fighters hid the other man's flash bulb, so the silhouette effect was perfect—and dramatic. The only moral to this yarn is that experience teaches pressmen and other pro's that there are right instants for any shots. The photographers on opposite sides of the ring were right—and right together, within the same hundredth of a second.

Another factor in action photography is a purely personal one—the speed and precision of your own nervous and muscular reactions. How long after your mind says, "Shoot!" does it take your shutter finger to respond? If your reaction time is slow—and that's nothing to be ashamed

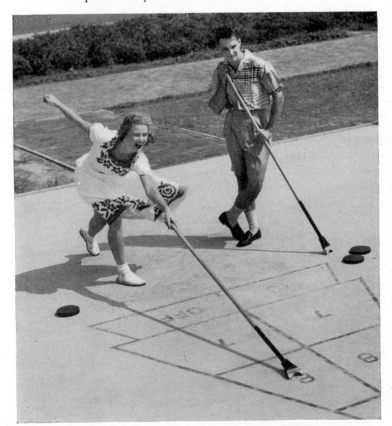

A poised instant comes at the end of the "follow-through" in many sports. Such instants need more alertness than shutter speed, yet they are full of a sense of action

196

of—you simply have to train yourself to work a little farther ahead of the action. Those two photographers at the fight didn't wait to see that blow land; they saw it coming and, each according to his own reaction time, sent the shooting order down to his trigger finger.

Poise vs. Pose

There's a world of difference between pictures of real action and those of posed action. We have all seen posed pictures, ostensibly showing people involved in some such simple business as walking. But those pictures didn't fool us for a second; for the balance wasn't the real dynamic balance of honest motion.

You may possibly be called upon to make some action pictures of individual athletes. The first thought is posing—but don't do it. Focus your camera and then let the basketball player pass or bounce the ball as you make the pictures. He doesn't have to do it with fury, but he shouldn't "pretend." Remember, too, that some attention should be paid to lighting in these pictures. The flat single flash may be the only answer on a rush

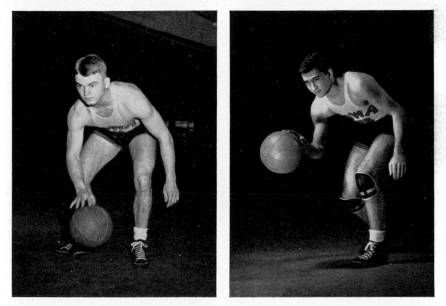

There's a middle ground between intensely active and posed pictures of athletes. With some care in lighting, such pictures are more than mere "records."

197

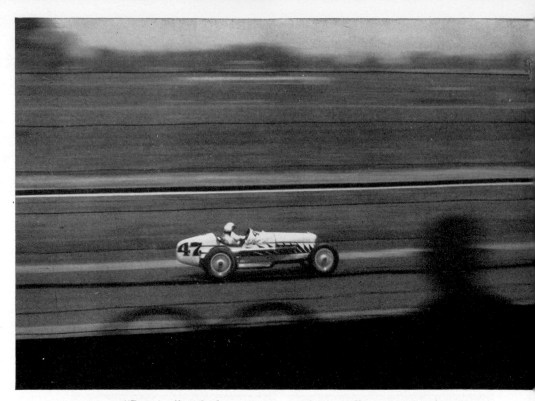

"Panning" with the action can produce excellent pictures of
high-speed action—with a low speed shutter

picture but, if time permits, set up a couple of Photofloods or add an
extension flash and shoot for a modeled lighting. You'll be well rewarded
for your added effort.

Panoraming

Panoraming is a good trick to know, especially if you're trying to photograph a passing car or train and you are using a relatively slow-speed
shutter. Follow the action with your camera, shooting as you follow. It
takes a little care, but it is certainly not difficult. Eye glued to your
camera's viewfinder, you spot your subject as it comes along; pivot your
head and shoulders so that you keep that subject in the finder. At the
right instant, without interrupting your smooth pivoting, you click the
shutter and follow through, as in golf.

The result will show the car, or whatever it may be, clearly—but the
fore- and backgrounds will be a mass of horizontal blurs or streaks. The
sense of speed will be nicely registered and you will have made a picture

198

at say, 1/50 that would have required 1/1000 without that "panning" technique. It's fun to do, too.

Before tackling any speed or swift action photography, it's a good idea to know what to expect of your shutter. The better between-the-lens shutters generally have maximum speeds of 1/400 to 1/800. And, as has been indicated, that's fairly ample. Focal plane shutters can work faster, but they have a strange quirk that should be understood.

Focal Plane Phenomenon

The slot in the focal plane shutter usually works from top to bottom; in other words it uncovers the top of the film first. The image it admits is, of course, inverted; hence the wheels of a car are registered on the film before the body. In the split second of the shutter movement down across the film, a passing car moves forward considerably. The resulting negative shows a beautifully exaggerated sense of speed, with the wheels rendered almost as ovals and the whole car canted rakishly forward in what appears to be a passionate lust for miles-per-hour. Naturally, the slower the shutter speed, and the smaller the slit in the shutter curtain, the greater this "italic" effect. If the camera is turned so that the shutter slot travels *with* the motion of the image, the subject will look stretched out; if the slot moves in the opposite direction from the motion, the subject will appear pushed in, or shortened.

Speed, as was said a while back, is inescapably fascinating. But the ability to stop swift movement should not obscure the fact that we are making—or hope to make—pictures. And pictures, to be successful, have to have some sort of composition and meaning. Otherwise they're the merest snap-shots. So watch your backgrounds; be sure they will be backgrounds and not protective or confusing camouflage. Try to get your action to lead into the picture, not out of it. In short, make pictures. 199

Both pictures were made with a focal plane shutter at 1/500. Left, curtain traveled in same direction as car image; right, in opposite direction.

Subject Motion Experiment

Object:

To determine the shutter speeds necessary to stop the motion of a person walking (A) across in front of a camera and (B) toward the camera.

Equipment:

A camera with a range of shutter speeds. A tripod will be helpful.

Procedure:

Set up the camera and focus it on a point fifteen feet distant. Mark the point focused on by dropping a small piece of paper or a handkerchief. Now, have the subject walk across in front of the camera at military pace,* passing directly over your marker. When he is over the marker, make an exposure using the fastest shutter speed your camera permits. As your subject repeats his pacing, make exposures at successively slower shutter speeds until you have

*Military cadence is 128 steps to the minute—30 inches to the step.

employed all the speeds available on your camera. Shoot in the middle of the stride and you'll catch the action at its fastest.

Don't forget to adjust the diaphragm (*f*-number) to balance each speed.

Repeat the series of speed exposures as the subject walks *toward* the camera, snapping the shutter as he crosses the marker at the same pace used in the first set.

After the films are developed and printed, mount the pictures in sequence and mark the ones showing no apparent motion. Verify your findings by applying the formula for determining appropriate shutter speeds, suggested in the preceding chapter.

Interesting variations on this experiment can be worked out by photographing an automobile traveling at a constant and known rate of speed at a known distance from the camera in a series of shutter speed tests.

¼₅ sec.   ⅟₅₀ sec.   ⅟₁₀₀ sec.   ⅟₂₀₀ sec.

⅟₁₀ sec.   ⅟₂₅ sec.   ⅟₅₀ sec.   ⅟₁₀₀ sec.

CHAPTER 17

By Flood and Flash

PHOTOGRAPHICALLY speaking, neither flood nor flash belongs in the catastrophe column. Fact is, two of the most fortunate things that have ever happened to photography have been the "flood" and the "flash" lamps.

Both introduced a new and badly needed tool for the specific use of those who couldn't support a whole battery of high-powered lights, Hollywood fashion. And their use has not been limited to the amateur. They are "musts" for commercial and news photographers as well.

The Flood Lamp

The "flood" lamp is simply an incandescent lamp burning under an overload of electricity. There are various legends surrounding its introduction into photography, but they are all based on the fact that someone took a 100-watt bulb of the type used on railway trains, where the voltage runs at about 64, and subjected it to the full impact of ordinary domestic current—110 volts, more or less. The surprised railway train bulb lighted up furiously, delivering an intensity of light approximately equal to that of an ordinary but expensive 500-watt lamp. Naturally, it burned out in an hour or two but during its life it gave "a lovely light," much in the manner of the abused candle in Edna St. Vincent Millay's famous poem.

The advent of this overloaded but very useful lamp in 1931 coincided with the arrival of panchromatic film. The new lamp and the new, fast films worked together beautifully.

In no time at all, relatively speaking, a new era in photography arrived. Hitherto, photography by artificial light had been almost exclusively the province of professionals with well and expensively equipped studios. With the new lamp and the new film, indoor photography came within the ken of anyone with a few dollars to spend.

Both still and movie amateurs began, with enthusiasm, to explore the possibilities of work by artificial light. It was fun. And the results were interesting.

Naturally, the lamp makers soon appreciated the vast appeal and value of these lamps and began to develop them. Presently the No. 2 Photoflood appeared. Like the No. 1, it could be used in any standard light socket, but its special appeal lay in the fact that it delivered twice as much light and lasted three times as long.

Later, came the R-2 Photoflood, a wide, flat bulb which contains its own reflector lining. The bulb is about as bright as the regular No. 2 bulb, and provides its own reflector. It's handy where portability is a desirable feature. Then there is the No. 4 Photoflood—1,000 watts for a ten-hour life—but this is, and should be, specifically a studio unit.

Since most household electrical circuits are fused for 15 ampere maximum loads, it is not safe to use more than 6 No. 1 Photofloods or 3 No. 2 Photofloods altogether on the same circuit. If the maximum number of bulbs are burned simultaneously, other loads, such as ordinary room lights and the radio, should be shut off.

The Flash Bulb

The flash bulb is the modern version of that ancient pyrotechnical display, the powder flash. Up to about 1930, the flashlights used by intrepid photographers were actually fireworks—magnesium powder touched off by a spark, to the accompaniment of noise, confusion, smoke and, frequently, a hurry-up call for an ambulance; for many a photographer was seriously injured by those old flashes.

The flash bulb of today is also a matter of fireworks, but now it's a "bonfire in a bulb," all nicely under control. The first such flash bulbs contained a small, easily fused wire, a quantity of aluminum foil and oxygen. When the wire was fused by an electrical current it instantly ignited the foil which burned swiftly and brilliantly in the oxygen. Later, a tangled length of shredded aluminum foil was substituted for the crumpled foil.

A newer type of flash bulb, called the Speed Midget or SM, was introduced about ten years after the first of these modern flashes. It is a small, walnut-sized lamp in which the "bonfire" is the burning of a chemical paste coated around the two small lead-in wires. The bulb is filled with oxygen, as were its predecessors, but the resulting flash is shorter, about 1/200 second. One of the big advantages of this type bulb is that it permits

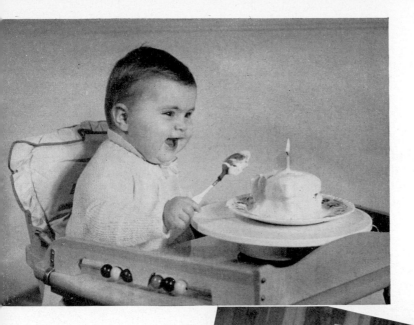

*Photography
by Photoflood*

Whenever time and electrical connections are available, photography by photoflood has much to offer. With two or more such lights and fast film, snapshot exposures are easily possible, yet arrangement or composition need not be at all snapshotesque.

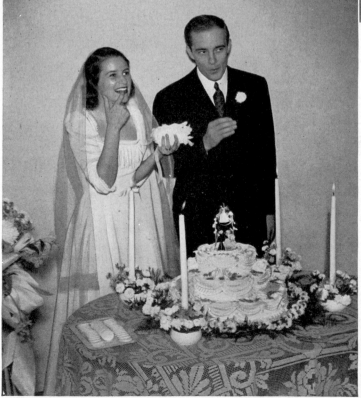

With compact flash equipment mounted directly on his camera, the photographer can shoot from places and at angles which would be difficult or impossible if floods were the only lights available.

With flash and synchronizer it is easy to get fully lighted candid, or unposed, shots — shots such as this, which make a beautiful supplement for formal, conventional wedding pictures.

greatly simplified synchronization with the camera shutter. Mechanisms for synchronizing the slow burning, older style bulb had to hold back the shutter until the bulb began to burn. This required intricate mechanisms and adjustments. Because of the speed with which it burns, the Speed Midget can be fired and the shutter opened simultaneously. The simple contacts it requires are easily incorporated in the shutter itself.

All the new flash bulbs provide a high intensity of light—an intensity so great that even the relatively slow ortho films can be relied on for successful work. The little flash lamps, used with small synchro-flash cameras and, by means of adapters, with many press cameras, have a bayonet base; the larger bulbs are about the size of an ordinary 60-watt lamp and have standard screw bases. All flash bulbs of this type are coated with a plastic-like lacquer which prevents the scattering of glass in case the glass fractures with the flash. These bulbs are, of course, dead after a single flash.

FLASHES AT WORK

Today, with Brownies and other very simple cameras equipped to utilize flash, flash photography is by no means limited to enthusiasts or experts. It was not always so simple. Early synchronizers, whose job was to make sure that the flash occurred as the shutter reached its full opening, sometimes were temperamental. And, too, many cameras simply were not designed to use flash. Under these circumstances a technique known as the "open flash method" was evolved — and is still a useful trick to have in your bag. It cannot be used in any situation where the general light level is high or in action shots. All it amounts to is this. With focus and aperture determined and the camera firmly positioned, open the shutter on Time or Bulb, fire the flash bulb to cover your subject, close the shutter —and that's that. The advantage of open flash, aside from its simplicity,

Left, synchronized flash outfit

Below, a line-up of flash lamps

205

lies in the fact that the flash is fired independent of the camera, possibly by an assistant, and at any angle or distance circumstances may suggest. This system requires some sort of gadget for holding and firing the flash. Such devices can be purchased or you can enlist the aid of someone with a very simple flash camera. There need be no film in the assisting camera; it needs only fresh batteries, a flash lamp, and a compliant operator.

Synchronized Flash

Obviously, the standard and classic use of flash is in an outfit attached to the taking camera, with flash and shutter so synchronized that the peak of the flash light occurs while the shutter is fully opened in an exposure of, possibly, 1/200 second. Synchronization, in such a case, must be positive, with nothing left to chance.

One of the persistent "bugs" affecting flash synchronization has been the unpredictable quality and potency of the small batteries used in most synchronizers. Even fresh batteries have been known to let their users down, amid uncouth comment and lamentation. To eliminate this hazard the battery-condenser system was devised. Essentially, it consists of a miniature $22\frac{1}{2}$ volt battery (of the sort used in hearing aids or other compact electronic devices), a condenser in which the charge is stored, and a means of releasing the charge at full power. The value of this B-C setup is, of course, its sure-for-certain supply of power to the flash lamp (and to extension outfits) and its much longer life. Kodak's B-C Flashpack is so designed and made that it slips into the battery case of the average synchronizer outfit, replacing the usual two end-to-end "C" batteries. And it's very inexpensive.

Whether you use a B-C or a conventional flash synchronizer, it needs to be adjusted for use with the kind of flash used. For slow lamps (Class M, such as the No. 5 Photoflash) an integral delay of a few milliseconds must be used to let the flash get really started; for fast lamps (Class F, with the SM as typical) no delay is necessary. If you use the electronic speedlamp, your camera will require an appropriate adjustment.

Exposures with Flashes

A neat system is now in use in making flash exposure recommendations. For each shutter setting, film and lamp combination, a *guide number* is issued. To find the aperture required, one merely divides the guide number by the distance from the lamp to the subject—the answer is the

f/number. Or you can divide the guide number by the f/value and find the appropriate distance.

Color Temperature

Physicists have long used a scale for measuring the color of light given off by burning matter. Just as we say that we like our living room to be kept at 70°F, physicists speak of the color-temperature of a standard domestic electric light as, on the average, 2600°K. The "K" stands for Lord Kelvin, who evolved the system and the theory back of it—a theory based on the type of light which a wholly black, inert body emits when heated. "Red hot," we all know, is not as hot as "white hot." Photographically speaking, then, a lamp rated at 3400°K emits a whiter light than one rated at 2600°K. The Photoflood is rated at about 3380°K; the Photoflash at 3600-3900°K.

To the casual photographer, this color-temperature business is of relatively little importance in black-and-white work; to all serious workers in color photography, it is a factor of great importance.

For example, there are 3200°K lamps for use when making color shots (using Ektachrome Type B—an emulsion specifically color balanced for studio work). The movie studios use 3380°K lamps in shooting Technicolor; other lamps, such as the Daylight Photoflood are not too far from the color of natural daylight. This means that the "blue" lamps can be mixed with daylight when using daylight type color film.

Few of these specialized lights are practical for the amateur whose principal concern it is to use the proper Photoflood lamps for Type A Kodachrome Film. But it is sobering to realize that lighting is an exact science—one of the several sciences with which the practicing photographer must have more than a nodding acquaintance.

Two other forms of photographic lighting equipment should be mentioned because they are destined to become important.

The Electronic Discharge Lamp

The first is the electronic discharge lamp, invented by Dr. Harold E. Edgerton and his associates, of the Massachusetts Institute of Technology. Its first and most obvious point of difference from other flash outfits is that it can be used over and over, for thousands of flash shots. Its second distinction is the extreme speed of the flash. Far faster than any camera shutter; it is so fast that, regardless of the camera's shutter setting, it "stops" hitherto "unstoppable" action. If you blink your eyes at the right moment you will miss seeing the flash. And in the third place, this kind of light can be designed to deliver a terrific intensity of light. Obviously with so much light, exposures can be made at otherwise impossible apertures and distances.

Its functioning depends on a supply of 60-cycle, 110-volt alternating current which, by means of a special transformer, is stepped up to 2000 volts. A rectifier tube changes the A.C. into D.C. which is used to charge a condenser. When the flash trip is released, the energy stored in the condenser is discharged by a Strobotron Tube through the flash tube in about 1/10,000 of a second. This sounds a little like a Rube Goldberg cartoon, but the end result is no joke. This lamp has already proved its capacity for handling a lot of studio work successfully. A smaller, readily portable model, of special interest to press photographers is available in several types and potencies.

By the way, there is a clever system by which several of these lamps can be fired in unison. They can, of coures, be wired together, but that sometimes is cumbersome. They can be especially fitted with neat little photoelectric cell trippers, which keep an eye peeled for the signal from the lamp nearest the camera. When it flashes, the several little electric eyes catch its first glimmer and, responding, set off their own lamps. Quite a trick, too, when you're slicing time into such thin sections.

Fluorescent Light

The second of the newer photographic illuminants is fluorescent lighting. Certainly the wild-fire spread of fluorescent lighting in shops, factories, restaurants, and offices all over the country has forced most of us to admit that here, indeed, is really Something. There is plenty to indicate that today's fluorescent tubes are but the first signs of a major development.

The white fluorescent light—cool to the touch but with an extremely high color temperature—is excellent, when used with Kodak Ortho-X Film, for much photographic work. It is highly actinic and it casts soft shadows. It is economical in operation.

Reflectors

In photography there are two kinds of reflectors, (1) those which are fitted directly to the lights, to concentrate and direct the flow of light, and (2) those which are placed, well away from the light source, to bounce light back on to the shadow side of the subject. For the sake of clarity, let's call them, respectively, lamp reflectors and subject reflectors.

To make a photograph with artificial lights which are not equipped with lamp reflectors is sheer waste. A well-designed reflector concentrates the light where it can do the most good and vastly increases its efficiency. Some reflectors are mirror-like in their polish, and produce hard, sharply defined shadows; others have a rough or granular surface, and, as a result, yield a more diffuse light. Some produce a wide cone of light— a "flood"—while others are virtual spotlights.

A subject reflector can be anything that will reflect light into the shadows. Obviously, a big sheet of gray cardboard will reflect less light than a white card of the same size. A mirror will reflect practically all of its incident light; a concave, mirror-like surface will produce a hot spot of intense illumination by reflection. And so on.

Watch a veteran studio man work. He pays as much attention to the type and placement of his subject reflectors as to the source reflectors. For he knows that "empty" shadows can, in some cases, ruin his picture.

LIGHTS AT WORK

Lighting is exacting work, but intensely interesting. And you needn't have a whole battery of floods and banks of spots and half a dozen varieties of subject reflectors to experience the peculiar pleasures of the art of lighting. One or two Photofloods or even a few ordinary Mazda lamps

209

in some sort of reflectors and a few sheets of white cardboard for subject reflectors—some such simple equipment will give you ample material for study, and for achievement.

Of all lighting problems, the one which is most frequently encountered is that of the informal group in the living room at home.

"Family" Pictures

The word family is quoted, above, merely because it's a generously embracing term, amply wide enough to include the intimate friends who belong in such pictures. Theoretically, at least, there's no need for haste in making these pictures. You can proceed more or less at leisure. So you *plan* the picture, working toward a specific composition. It may be some such simple matter as mother or dad reading to the youngsters.

As unobtrusively as possible, set up your lights. Make your lighting friendly and "homey;" don't give it an unnatural over-all harshness. Use Photofloods, capitalizing their economy, their flexibility, and their ability to "double" reasonably as ordinary lamps in bridge lamps and other such fixtures. Use a good, fast pan film—Kodak Super-XX or Plus-X—which gives you good skin tones and a generally normal black-and-white interpretation of colors.

Watch out for reflections of the bright lights in windows, in polished furniture, and in mirrors. Such reflections have an annoying habit of appearing less disturbing "on the set" than in the finished negative.

Take advantage of the softness of diffused light reflected from white cards, light walls, light-colored clothing, etc. In other words, get the full value of your lights. In so doing you are almost sure to get a pleasanter, more intimate total effect.

210

Flat lighting plus confusing
reflections

"Portrait" lighting, better arrangement,
and less confusion

Party Pictures

For capturing the cheerful mood of a party, the synchronized Photoflash is well suited. It is best used with an ortho film.

Naturally, a good many party shots can only be made—on the wing—with a single flash at the camera. But you'll be wise to rig up an extension for a second flash, well removed from the camera, by means of which you can encompass a larger area—and also obtain a little less ruthless lighting.

Here, again, watch out for those troublesome reflections in windows and mirrors. In using Photofloods you can, at leisure, make sure that the reflections are avoided, but in flash work you have no such opportunity. However, a good eye, backed by common sense, will usually see you through.

Groups—More or Less Formal

The fine art of lighting individuals for portraiture is a special subject, which rates—and gets—a chapter to itself. But the problem of lighting a group of people, indoors, is a little less specific and can properly be outlined here.

A group cannot be considered as an individual, with a highlight here and a shadow there; no indeed, for the purpose of a group shot is to reveal a number of people, each well and recognizably presented. One way out is to use strong frontal lighting, as with a strong flash bulb at the camera. That way, you will get a picture, but not as interesting a picture as one which is made with unbalanced light, so that each face in the group gets the benefit of a little modulation. Use two flashes on the same circuit—or two Photofloods, if you prefer—with one light a little above and to the right of the camera and the other about level with the camera, a little to the left and slightly back. Vary such a scheme as much as you wish, but try to avoid the straight front light; it's uninteresting.

Check Your Outlets

Before you undertake anything at all ambitious in the way of indoor shots, with or without people, make sure (1) that there are sufficient electrical outlets for your purposes, (2) that they can be conveniently reached by the wires with which your lamps are connected and, (3) that the wall outlets and your plugs are of the same type. Given time, you can correct all such circumstances; to try to adapt yourself to them at the last minute is an invitation to panic.

Interiors—Day and Night

There's a constant demand for pictures of interiors of your own home or of those of friends. An "interior" is not an easy assignment. By day, the first question to be settled is, "How about the light outdoors?" If it's a brilliant, sunny day, with direct sunlight streaming in the windows, your problem is really tough. For those sunny windows are bound to be areas of overexposure. Ditto for patches of sun on the floor or on a polished piece of furniture. You can, with a battery of brilliant lights or discreetly used Photoflashes, build up an over-all intensity of light to reduce the relative hotness of the sunny spots; an exceedingly "fine" (high shutter speed—small aperture) exposure will then give you a good result. But, lacking a big battery of lights, the best solution is to wait for dusk, when the light outdoors will be about the same as that which can be created within. After dark, the windows themselves will lose interest. This does not mean that such interior pictures should not be made after dark—for less window interest will mean more interest elsewhere, which may be quite desirable.

An old solution of the sunny day problem was a double exposure—a very short one with the window shades up, followed by a longer one with the shades pulled down. But this trick was never sure-fire; today, with draperies used more frequently than blinds, the double-shot technique increases in difficulty and uncertainty.

If the room is, as indicated, relatively small, and with light-colored walls, the problem of photographing solely with artificial light is not difficult. Two or three No. 2 Photofloods should suffice. Here are some points to watch:

1. Multiple—and hard—shadows, cast by table legs, bridge lamps and such. Put some cheesecloth diffusers in front of your lamps (far enough from the bulbs to prevent scorching); your hard shadows will fade away.

2. Take care lest direct reflections from the lights appear in the picture.

3. Beware of spotty illumination. If you want to put emphasis on one particular area, that's perfectly justifiable; unintentional emphasis from improper or accidental direction of light is the villain to watch.

In picturing most small rooms, you'll find that your lights will have to be arranged, usually, fairly close to the camera. If you can introduce some cross lighting to relieve the flatness of full frontal lighting, the picture will achieve a pleasant sense of depth.

Armed with a fast-lens camera loaded with fast, low-contrast film, you will find such scenes as this fairly easy

A daylight interior—and a rule-proving exception. The patches of sun and shadow serve, in this case, to add interest

If you're working with a minimum number of lights, plan for a long exposure at a small lens opening; then, during the exposure, wig-wag one of your lights gently over the whole scene, thereby throwing light into darker corners. This *painting* with light is fascinating; the only teacher thereof is Old Man Experience himself. Keep in mind that this recommendation applies only to rooms without people in them.

When you're faced with the job of picturing larger rooms—club rooms, chapels, auditoriums, and so on—you really have your hands full. You can no longer rely on a bevy of lights grouped near the camera, for the intensity of light has a distressing habit of falling off "inversely as the square of the distance."* You simply *have* to get lights into the distant reaches of the room.

Usually, you'll be able to plant lights behind doors or pillars so that, hidden from the camera, they will illuminate those far areas. Lights placed in this manner will also afford cross lighting, which gives furniture shape and relief from the background.

In this talk of room lighting, so far, the use of photoflood lamps has been assumed, primarily because they permit you to build up, visibly and definitely, your lighting scheme. If you need greater brilliance, you can substitute photoflash bulbs at the last minute. With all the lamps on one circuit—using the open flash technique, you can blaze away on a most impressive scale. (Only photoflash lamps suitable for operation on standard domestic current and fitting conventional lamp sockets should be used. Otherwise, you'll have a lot of trouble on your hands.) Many "pro" photographers use up dozens of flashes on a single shot. It's all very showy and impressive—and expensive.

To go to the other extreme in lighting—suppose you cannot obtain sufficient photoflood or photoflash lamps to meet your requirements. Then what? Well, ordinary 100-watt lamps can be substituted for specialized photo lamps. Obviously, you will need either many more lights or very much longer exposures. If 100-watt lamps are substituted for No. 1 Photofloods, multiply your exposure time by a general factor of *six*. To be entirely safe, make the factor *seven*; in rare cases a factor of *five* will suffice.

It is also a very simple matter to photograph a room by its usual lighting. The result is generally pleasing—if the room's lighting itself is pleasant. In fact, it is sometimes difficult to improve on a room's ordinary

*If objects A and B receive light from the same source and B is *twice* as far from the light as A, B receives only ¼ as much light, etc.

An interior, pictured by
its own, ordinary lighting

One 100-watt, one 150-watt lamp, both at
6 feet, 1/2 at f/8, Kodak Super-XX Film

lighting by using photographic lights. The Home Lighting Kodaguide
covers this situation explicitly.

Outdoors with Lights

Flash can be—and often is—used to fill in shadows in close-ups made against
the sun. So used, the flash should balance the natural light; *over*-balance
looks artificial. Supplementary flash is particularly useful in color work;
it eliminates troublesome, over-contrasty shadows and permits color
values to be . . . color values.

For pictures of people, of close-up action at night, there's no substitute
for the photoflash lamp. For the flash is wholly independent of other
lights and works perfectly when the subjects are fairly close to the camera.
Beyond 50 feet even the best flash is somewhat inadequate, but at ordinary
snapshot range, it is just right. In all cases, try to avoid "foreground flare"
—strong reflections of the flash from nearby objects, such as the side of a
car, a doorway, or even the ground in front of the camera.

Opportunities for any but conventional, full-front synchronized flash
shots are neither obvious nor rich when you're working out of doors.
But an effort to get away from that flatness can pay dividends.

215

For example, if you are able to extend the flash so that it is away, to the side of the camera, by as little as a yard or so, you will instantly gain in the modeling of your close-ups. Flash extension outfits permit you to work by the light of a flash which may be a considerable distance from the camera. Of course, if you have an accomplice to operate a flash, independent of the camera, you can use the open-flash method with success and profit in terms of better pictures.

Variation of the outdoor flash theme, of course, can be worked out to produce sure-fire camp fire scenes. Ordinarily, a camp fire doesn't produce a lot of light—not enough, at any rate, for a fast shot. So, the open-flash method again comes in handy. The flash should be flat on the ground near the fire, facing up, and so placed that it doesn't flare directly at the camera. With a little care, the flash will illumine the whole circle about the fire; naturally those whose backs are toward the camera will be rendered in silhouette. With flash, of course, ortho film is indicated.

City Lights

Of all after-dark pictures, many of the most interesting are those made on city streets or wherever there are massed lights and flood-lighted buildings. You need no special lights; your only necessities—beyond camera and film—are a tripod and a bit of patience.

The "rules" of such night photography are few.

For example:

1. Avoid strong foreground lights if you're interested in picturing what lies beyond them.
2. If automobile headlights aim your way, cover the camera lens until the danger is past.
3. Compose your picture as carefully as for a daytime scenic. Remember that every visible light will register, during the long exposure.
4. Remember that passing cars or lighted boats will show only as streaks of light; passing pedestrians will not show at all.

The exposure, of course, will depend on the intensity of the lights in your scene, and on the film and lens aperture you use. For most city scenes, an exposure of from 20 seconds to two minutes at $f/11$ should work; longer exposure seldom does more than "burn" the highlights deeper. Kodak Verichrome Film is a favorite for night photographs because of its pronounced "anti-halo" characteristics and its remarkable toleration for exposure variations.

Because night photography is, itself, unusual you may find yourself under suspicious scrutiny. Hence, be discreet in your choice of subject matter. If in doubt, get permission.

If you want to picture a house at night, there is a simple trick that, with practice, produces pleasant results. Beg or borrow a car equipped with a movable spotlight. When your camera is all set up, ready, and open, use the spotlight to "paint" the house with light. Go over it several times with the light, moving the beam slowly and evenly. The result can be charming.

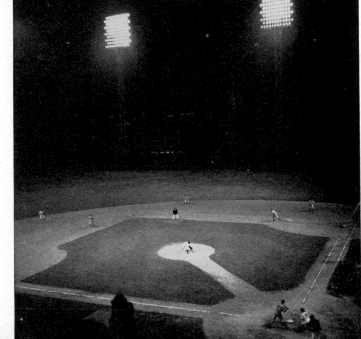

Cameras enjoy their night life, too. The baseball shot—1/50 at ƒ/3.5, Kodak Super-XX Film, and a good eye for action. The other two were simply time or "tripod" exposures

CHAPTER 18

Pictures of People

By FAR the most interesting thing to the human race is—the human race. That's why pictures of people constitute such a huge proportion of all the pictures in the world.

The cycle through which most photo enthusiasts go is revealing. At first, they concentrate almost exclusively on people—schoolmates, playmates, the gang. Then they discover that the world at large is pictorial, so they add landscapes and scenic views to their picture making. They may reach a stage where, for the moment, both people and scenery seem a bit commonplace—and they shy off on a tangent, looking for unconventionality. Eventually, they tire of the strain, for unconventionality must become more and more unconventional to keep its punch—and back they come to picturing people. And they do it better because of their richer experience and the perspective and understanding gained in the course of the cycle.

Of course, this cycle is not airtight. There are exceptions. But it is as true as any generality can be. Let the most hard-boiled "abstractionist" —one whose pictures are concerned with brittle patterns or abstract forms —become a parent, and he will promptly go in for an orgy of picturing a certain young person. It's perfectly right that this should happen, so don't let your temptation to be human bother you.

But be reasonable about it. Don't succumb to the notion that all you need do to get a picture of a person is to aim your camera at him and push the shutter button. Pleasing personality pictures sometimes happen that way, but they are accidents.

There are, of course, two schools of thought about pictures of people. On one side is the idea that a portrait should idealize the subject. The other insists that a realistic portrayal is the only proper thing, no matter how it hurts. Extremists in both camps produce some remarkable results

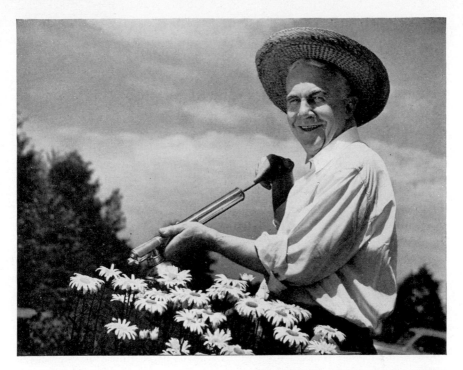

A happy subject is a busy subject

—slicked-up masks on one side and brutalizations on the other. But the most successful portraitists avoid the extremes; they idealize without falsifying and are candid in retaining the lines, the irregularities which reveal the subject. In short, they remember that the prime function of a portrait is to "look like him."

Theoretically, our literal-minded cameras should never fail in producing faithful portraits; for the camera, legend has it, never lies. Maybe not, but light and shade and angles of vision and accidents of attitude, background, and posture can combine to do a baleful lot of falsifying.

Our concern, then, is the procedure which, given reasonable support in technique, will produce valid portraits.

OUTDOOR PORTRAITS

The informal outdoor portrait, despite the ease with which indoor work can now be done, remains the type of portrait with which most of us will have most to do. The trick in it is to lift it out of the "lucky snapshot" class. Fortunately, there's nothing difficult about it.

The first rule in such work is again *simplicity*—simplicity in composi-

219

tion and simplicity in idea. Otherwise your subject will be lost. Except as a stunt, you would never try to make a portrait of your favorite aunt as she struggled to keep her feet, her purse, and her poise in a subway at the rush hour. Any inappropriate background, any hodge-podge of lights and shadows, tends to defeat the purposes of portraiture.

The second rule is—unless you are dealing with a professional model—don't get your subject primarily concerned with "having his picture took." Give him something to do. Most of us have a fearsome, "lost" feeling when we are being photographed. It is because we are, for the moment, forced into a kind of suspended animation, deprived of all the comforting small activities of living. That's not right, for it doesn't lead to good pictures. Let your subject talk, or fondle a dog, or do any of a thousand and one things which are natural and appropriate for him to do. Action, or implied action, helps to give your picture interest and animation.

The third rule is to use close-ups. If you are going to portray somebody, do it; don't make a long shot of it. (This assumes, of course, that your camera can be focused for work at close range or that it is equipped with a simple supplementary lens which permits close-ups.) By "close-ups" it is not intended to imply the kind of monstrosity which makes every pore of the skin look like a moon crater as seen through the Yerkes

220

Soft, feminine lighting	Strong, masculine lighting

telescope. A simple rule is to shoot at a comfortable "conversational" distance. You rarely carry on a conversation at a range of six inches, nor do you back off twenty feet.

Fourth, use your lighting to help portray the character of your subject. Thus, cross lighting, with its sharply defined shadows, is appropriate for portraits of strong, vigorous, forthright subjects, while soft shadows achieved by softer, diffused light, definitely set the key for portraits of little girls and for femininity in general. Over-harsh shadows, usually accompanying brilliant sunlight, can be softened by using a reflector on the shadow side. Most such reflectors are merely large sheets of white cardboard, but there are photographers who use parabolic metal reflectors; these devices are easily misused, as they give a "hot spot" of reflected light in a very definite area, with results that are sometimes excellent and, just as often, crude and laughable.

This is as good a point as any to mention the business of using synchronized flash bulbs for outdoor portraits. You have doubtless seen examples of this technique. The result is that subjects which, under the obvious natural light conditions, would be rendered in semi-silhouette become brilliant on the shadow side, when flash-lit. Sometimes the result is pleasing; more often it looks like plain fakery and therefore becomes uncomfortable. In other words, it is all a matter of taste; if you like such shots, go ahead.

Another point about light. Avoid the midday sun for portraiture; it produces deep, unpleasant shadows under the brows, nose, and mouth. The slanting sun of morning or afternoon gives more pleasant results. Never force a subject to look directly at the sun; squints are sinful. It's far better to have shadows than squints.

The fifth point is one of the most important. It concerns backgrounds. Modern miniature cameras, with their short-focus lenses and great depth of field, emphasize the necessity for care in selecting backgrounds. A telephone pole, a garage, or a billboard so far away that you neglect it as you use your view finder may, in the finished print, loom up importantly — and impertinently — in the background and demoralize your portrait.

It is disheartening to see—as we do—so many pictures of people in which the backgrounds are distracting, inappropriate, intrusive. It is simply because the camera users (they aren't photographers) do not use their eyes, either in or out of the view finders. They spot their primary subject

Always watch your backgrounds. They can make or break your pictures

and *assume* that all is well beyond. It is not a safe assumption.

By far the best background is sky, with or without clouds. With black-and-white film, use a yellow filter to be sure of ample sky tone; the same filter will give you good skin tone. Red filters are out; they render your subjects pallid and unreal-looking.

Finally, beware of stunt angles. In most cases they produce nothing but unreasonable distortion. There are good and bad angles for portraiture, varying with individuals, but extremes are practically never justified.

It is never safe to be completely dogmatic about rules in photography. After writing an article which stated that the best pictures of black dogs were made against light backgrounds, a writer on photography received from a correspondent a magnificent shot of a black Scottie against an equally black background. Still, it was such an exceptional picture that it proved the writer's rule. Hence, the following recommendations for lighting, film, and paper appropriate for black-and-white pictures of various subjects are offered without hesitation.

222

Pictures of People

Subject	Suggested Action	Lighting	Film	Paper
BABIES	Playing peek-a-boo in basket. — The first steps. — Sitting on blanket. — Playing with rattle.	*Back light with reflector.* If outdoors avoid strong sun in their eyes.	Fast Pan. For fast shutter speeds and soft contrast.	Smooth Semi-Matte
YOUNGSTERS	With toys and playthings in costumes and baseball outfits.	Almost full front light.	Pan.	Smooth Semi-Matte
HIGH SCHOOL AND COLLEGE AGE	Sports participation with campus architecture as backgrounds. With books. — Hobbies.	Cross lighting. If it tends toward harshness try a reflector.	Pan. Make it a fine-grain Pan. if you use a miniature.	Almost any surface—depends upon subject. Use glossy paper for yearbook newspaper shots.
MIDDLE AGED	Hobby picture such as golf — on picnics — with road maps for travel pictures.	Cross light for men. Front light for women.	Ortho for men. Pan. for women.	Medium rough semi-matte.
OLDER PEOPLE	Action and expression to portray character.	Cross light for character studies. Diffuse light for women —this will soften skin texture.	Ortho for strength. Pan. for softness.	Texture papers either rough or med. rough.

223

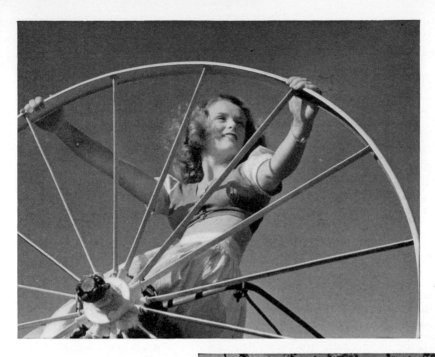

There's free style in outdoor portraits, too. Real freedom is frequently achieved by fashion photographers in their constant search for novelty

Portraits Outdoors in Color

Looking back over these rules, let's see how they apply to outdoor portraits on Kodachrome or Kodacolor Film. Simplicity is of course paramount, not only in composition and idea, but in color itself. Combine a few colors wisely, not gaudily, so they do not detract from the personality of your subject. Don't feel that you need all the colors of the rainbow for a good color picture.

When it comes to lighting outdoors for color, be on the look out for dense shadows. It will probably be necessary to use the reflector a little closer to the subject than you do in black-and-white work. The softer lighting afforded by hazy days often permits the most pleasing results, since the shadows aren't as black and sharply defined. Kodachrome pictures made on dull or cloudy days are apt to be bluish in color unless a haze filter is used over the lens. It is undesirable to try to use Kodacolor under this condition.

Just before sunset the color of the light is markedly red; it is only natural that pictures made at that time sometimes appear abnormally colored. Avoid this difficulty by making your color pictures of people earlier than two hours before sunset.

When it comes to backgrounds for color portraits outdoors, you might try these: plain blue sky (one of nature's finest gifts to photographers), the blended colors of autumn foliage, or the shade of trees for very dark effects if your subject is in sunlight.

INDOOR PORTRAITS

The primary difference between indoor and outdoor portraiture lies in the far greater control of light possible in indoor work. Even with a brace of Photoflood lamps in simple reflectors you can work wonders right in your own living room; add a cardboard subject reflector and an improvised spotlight and you have a home setup capable of considerable versatility. Play around with such simple, inexpensive equipment for a while. Then you may discover the need for more specialized lighting tools, but don't let it fret you. As has been said before and shall doubtless be said here again, an ounce or two of perception and imagination, coupled with a little ingenuity, is worth tons of expensive gadgetry.

To prove the point, overpage is a group of portraits made with one light only, plus the suggested reflector. Some are good, some bad. But they show what to expect when the light comes from those angles.

225

One light, close to the camera ... raised, and moved to the left ... then to the back, with a reflecto to lighten the face

In indoor work the basic considerations of simplicity in composition and background hold just as true as in outdoor portraiture. Action, real or implied, is necessarily a bit more limited; and the inevitable nearness of the background may make you more aware of it and hence more careful. You will undoubtedly want to work with the camera on a tripod, despite the fact that snapshots indoors are easily possible. But you are after more than snaps; so don't use snap methods.

The use of lights is, in itself, an art, and not an art which can be standardized to fit all cases and conditions. There is, however, a kind of A-B-C of lighting, and it goes like this.

"A" is the over-all light, placed so that it comes in on the subject's face at about a 45° angle. The side of the face nearest the light is fully revealed, while the off side goes considerably into the shade, excepting a triangular patch under the eye. That patch is often used as a kind of key to the whole problem of facial lighting. This single "A" light, unsupplemented, results in a contrasty, generally unsatisfactory portrait.

So, the "B" light is brought into play. This is the "fill-in" light, the light that fills in those empty shadows. It can be either a reflector or a second light; at any rate, it is lower in intensity than the "A" light. Flat, equalized light is uninteresting; hence the "B" light is either of lower wattage or is used at a greater distance.

Now, with the subject's face well lighted, how about something to give it relief—to make it stand out clearly from the background? Very well, use light "C" to create some interesting highlights along the side and top of the head. "C" can be aimed in at any angle which seems desirable, as long as it doesn't upset the frontal lighting. Sometimes "C" is a carefully handled spotlight; sometimes it is guarded by screens to delimit its scope.

226

| With the "A" light only | The "B" is added . . . | and then the "C" |

And there's the A-B-C of lighting. It is rudimentary, yet capable of such infinite variation that its possibilities are practically inexhaustible. Try it and see.

For black-and-white pictures, the particular bulbs used for this lighting are relatively unimportant as long as the amount of light used is properly balanced. However, when making indoor pictures with Kodachrome Film, make sure your bulbs are appropriate for your film; any of the white Photofloods are suitable for Kodachrome Type A and 3200°K Mazda lamps are correct for Kodak Ektachrome Film Type B. Again, when arranging the lights for the color photographs, balance the illumination to avoid excessive contrast. A ratio of 4:1 between highlight and shadow brightness is considered a maximum by some workers and while not an absolute limit will serve as a good basic guide.

Of course, it is possible to elaborate lighting, to add the effects of spots, baby spots, highlight reflectors, and so on until you are all tangled with wires and diffusers and reflectors. It may seem pretty impressive, too, but it doesn't mean a thing unless each light and each reflector and diffuser has a specific and calculated function, just as the many "voices" of an orchestra play their parts in creating the full beauty of a symphony.

As far as camera equipment for portraiture is concerned, it is likely that your regular outfit will serve nicely. However, the use of a lens with longer than usual focal length will be found advantageous; its narrow angle of view permits the making of full-frame close-ups at greater than your usual close-up distance—a factor in your subject's peace of mind and your own convenience in posing and direction. With a longer focal length you have another advantage—less depth of field—hence less chance of sharp background intrusions.

227

In portraiture it is easily possible to become obsessed with technique, with systems and devices. It is therefore a good idea to stop, every so often, and contemplate the fact that the end of portraiture is to depict a person, not to display your cleverness. It's the old business about ends and means; the experienced photographer commands his means, driving them expertly to an explicit end.

Home Portrait Lighting Experiment

Object:

To show the variety of very pleasing and successful portrait lightings possible with limited home lighting equipment.

Equipment:

Three lamps in reflectors. A camera for making close-ups, that is, one focusing as close as 3½ or 4 feet or one with a portrait attachment.

Procedure:

Make one photograph according to each of the following suggested patterns, arranging the lights to conform with the illustrations.

Print or enlarge the developed negatives on a texture surface paper. Mount them on cards and rule neat lines around the prints for the finishing touch.

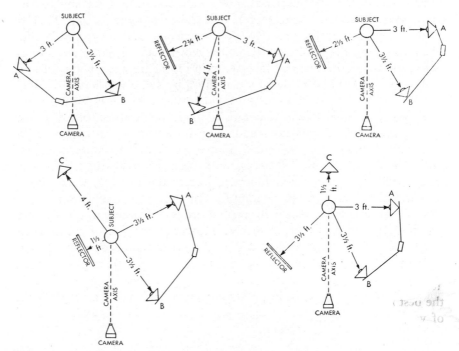

CHAPTER 19

There are Tricks in all Trades

EVERY DAY and in every job that comes to hand, an expert photographer utilizes many a deft little trick to gain a particular effect, to save time, to eliminate or forestall trouble, or to make amends for a mistake. Some of these tricks involve only the photographer's way of handling his equipment and include variations on the theme of the chapter "Be Camera Wise." Other tricks are more directly concerned with the means of producing unusual pictures. Both are learned only through long, practical experience. If you persevere in photography, you will learn them—and you will create a new set suited to your own equipment, working conditions, and your own temper.

In these pages there is no attempt to offer a short-cut substitute for experience, but a few of the well-established techniques by which specific ends can be gained are herewith outlined.

Spotting and Retouching

First, a note or two on eliminating the tiny white and black specks on finished prints and negatives. These may result from dust that settles on the film in the camera before exposure, dirt accumulated on the negative while drying, dust on the enlarger glass, and so on. Dirt has a demoralizing affinity for both prints and negatives.

The really careful worker keeps his camera, darkroom, and enlarger clean; it is just common sense to work that way. But dust *is* elusive stuff. In spite of the utmost care, it finds its way into places where it causes photographic trouble in varying degrees. But almost every print, enlargements in particular, can be improved by some "touching up." "Touch up" is the best name for this kind of spotting, since the technique involved is one of very lightly touching the white spot with a pencil lead until the accumulation of touch marks blends perfectly with the surrounding tones. Soft pencils should be used to blend spots with dark surroundings, harder ones to blend with lighter tones.

For your first experience with spotting and retouching, go to work on some prints. Any print will do. You'll find some spots to be touched up even on a clean-looking print. If, perchance, you do a better job of learning than spotting, don't worry; the prints can be discarded and others made. Start with the small spots, then tackle the larger ones as you gain a little more confidence in your own ability. Special retouching pencils, available at low cost at most photographic and stationery stores, have leads that mark without leaving shiny or glossy lines. It is in this respect that ordinary pencils are not satisfactory—the lines and dots made with them have a sheen that makes the spotting job too easily noticeable. These pencil lines will not "take" on glossy ferrotyped paper but will work nicely on most other surfaces.

Some workers prefer spotting inks or paints to pencils; they are a bit more difficult to handle, but once you get the knack of them, you'll turn out considerably neater work. They can be used on glossy as well as matte-surfaced paper. A tiny brush is wetted, twisted between the fingers to an extremely fine point, and the water-soluble paint picked up off a card on which it is supplied, and spotted or stroked lightly onto the print. In this same manner, dark spots may be lightened simply by the application of a little white over the black specks. The white and black paints, if carefully mixed, can be used to match any required shade of gray.

It is a mistake to pass off a spotting job as something that can be done in a hurry. Speed almost inevitably winds up in the application of too much paint, or in spreading or smearing of the applications. Good spotting is slow and exacting. You will be safe if you will only remember that it's easy to add *more* "touch up" and almost impossible to "untouch."

When you have acquired reasonable proficiency in print spotting, you will be interested in trying your hand on negatives. Start on waste negatives. You'll not want to take the chance of spoiling good ones. Negative retouching is really an expert, precision craft in itself, one which takes a great deal of patience and practice.

On the light or transparent parts of negatives, retouching is much like print spotting, except that the negative emulsion must be treated or "doped" with an oil-like retouching fluid, so the touch marks of the pencil lead will "take." Professionals say it gives the negative a "tooth." With cotton a drop of this fluid is spread evenly over the area to be retouched.

Where there is an excess of silver, it must be etched away with a very small, delicate, razor-sharp knife. Good etching is not as easy as spotting, for the silver must not only be evenly scraped away, but must be shaded and blended with surrounding parts of the picture, so as not to be detectable in the print.

One big difficulty in negative retouching arises from the fact that you may subsequently want to enlarge the negative. In doing so, you magnify all the touch-up marks, which, unless expertly done, may be worse than the original blemishes.

So, with these points in mind, get some pencils, retouching fluid, an etching knife, and some fine sandpaper for sharpening your pencils. The total cost will probably not exceed $1.50. Rig up an illuminator on which you can see the negative blemishes and comfortably work on them. Use a magnifying glass to watch your work; it's easier on your eyes and you'll do better retouching.

Paper Negatives

From the pictorialist comes a specialized photographic process, the paper negative, considered by its exponents too dignified to be called a trick.

The paper negative process has several variations, but they all allow for extremes in retouching and doctoring before the final print.

1. Make a straight enlargement the same size as the final print is to be, but considerably darker than usual. This is necessary because the print will subsequently be used as a transparency. Use single-weight, smooth paper.
2. Place the dried print face down on an illuminator where all parts of the picture needing further darkening can be so treated. Darken large masses or areas with a dab of lampblack on a cotton tuft, small areas or lines with a regular soft pencil. After a little practice you can even put in clouds and take out trees or barns. You can, that is, if you're really very good. The curse of the paper negative is enthusiastic but inept workmanship.
3. Make a contact print from the retouched paper print. When developed, this gives a negative on paper with a slightly granular texture from the paper fibre. This should also be darker than a usual print. Use single-weight paper, of course.
4. Touch up the paper negative, using lampblack and pencil to darken the negative areas. This will mean the lightening of final print areas.

The evolution of a paper negative print

Left, above, is a straight print from the original negative. The sky is a monotone, the falling water lacks sparkle, part of the foreground is too heavy, and a few windows in the old mill are needlessly conspicuous. The center picture is the front of paper negative. It is on the back of this that the corrective work is done, as indicated in the right hand illustration above. Finally, having created a "fortified" negative, a new print is produced, as shown at the right.

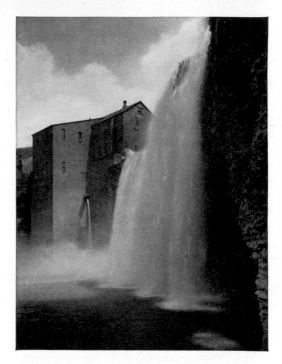

5. Make the final print by contact from the paper negative on any surface or contrast desired.

Many workers project the original negative onto a sheet of film, so the only paper part of the process is the paper negative. This has the advantage of assisting in the retention of greater detail in the final picture, but does not afford the beginner the wide retouching range of the straight paper positive-negative process.

Multiple Exposures

Just about the most common photographic boner is the double exposure, the miserable, unhappy result of forgetting to turn the film to the next number between exposures. But there is a special kind of double, or triple or quadruple exposure than can be fun; it can provide some very interesting pictures, too.

Commercial photographers use this multiple exposure plan to make a series of story-telling pictures all on one film, often for advertising purposes. They are sometimes called *montage* effects. Similarly Hollywood cameramen make ghost pictures, shooting the background scene first and then, with a second exposure on the same film, superimpose the ghost on the scene. With the same general plan you can make such trick pictures as these:

Dad playing checkers with himself.

The baby as her own tea party guest.

Sister waving a salute from inside a milk bottle.

This is the way it's done. The essential parts of the picture are exposed separately on the same piece of film. The only requisite is a black background, for only the main part of the subject must be allowed to affect the film. For example, to picture Dad beating himself at checkers, seat him at the checkerboard making a play; the background is black, and there is no chair at the opposite side of the table. One exposure is made. Dad and his chair are then moved to the other side of the board, where he sits in contemplation. On the same piece of film, the second exposure is made, and since the black background did not affect the film on the original exposure, there is a picture of Dad on that side, too. The checkerboard will be double exposed but it makes no difference, if it's not moved between times. The camera, of course, must be on a tripod, and unmoved between shots.

The quartet, presented on the following page, is an elaboration of this multiple exposure idea—and executed with great gusto. As with most really successful jobs, simplicity is its keynote. "Props" are almost eliminated, so that our attention has a chance to rest on and relish the variations in expression, and in "voice" achieved by the singer. Such a picture as this is would make an excellent, a memorable Christmas card.

The milk bottle trick is somewhat complicated by the differences in scale involved—the bottle is a close-up shot and the girl to be shown in it

One-man quartet—an excellent multiple exposure

must be about 20 feet away. Too, placement on the film area must be accurate. For such work, ground glass focusing is almost necessary.

Multiple exposure need not be limited to camera exposures. They work for enlargements, too. It's a good way to superimpose titles over prints, to make posters, etc. The enlargement is made in the usual way; then, with the paper still in place, a negative copy of the lettering is substituted for the picture negative and exposed across a light portion of the print.

One other method of combining many pictures on one film consists of simple cutouts. The pictures for assembly are cut according to the desired pattern or in jig-saw puzzle fashion, pasted onto cardboard and a picture made of the combination on a copy film.

There are, of course, a good many variations on the multiple image theme. Some of them, especially those involving several projected negatives on one piece of paper, become pretty complex.

Toning

A really good black-and-white enlargement is an accomplishment. But, once in a while, a bit of color toning will make it even better, more

234

realistic, more natural, or more fantastic. Toning involves changing the customary silver grays and blacks to colored tones—blue, brown, red, yellow, or green. The toning, of course, should be appropriate to the subject. For example:

Subject	*Tone*
Indoor portraits	brown
Snow scenes	blue
Fall landscapes	brown
Sunlighted summer landscapes	green
Marine views	blue

Toning techniques may be divided into two classes.

1. The gray or black silver forming the image may be wholly or partially replaced by other metals or their compounds, including sulphur, iron, gold, or selenium. These are brown, blue, etc. Some intensification of the photographic image takes place during the toning, and it is therefore advisable to begin with prints that are on the light side.

2. The silver image may be treated so as to attract colored dye from the toning solution and hold it in an insoluble form. This technique affords a wider range of tones, but the colors are not as stable as those in group one, and it is sometimes difficult to keep the highlights clear.

Toning of the first class is not a difficult process technically, but it does require skill gained from experience to know when to tone a print and how much. Overtoning can be more disastrous than no toning, naturally. Use browns for portraits and other pictures in which warmth is desirable, blues for cold tones, in snow scenes and for moonlight effects.

There are many toners in both classes, some listed in formula booklets, others sold in packaged form. Just as you find packaged developers convenient, so will you find toners. The Kodak Rapid Selenium Toner for brown tones and the Kodak Blue Toner, both packaged metallic-type toners, are outstanding for their respective colors.

Line Drawings from Prints by Tracing

While a properly made photograph is generally the most effective means of describing any object, there are occasions when a line drawing is better to show construction details, etc. You can make such drawings simply and easily. First photograph the object in question from the angle you wish to show. Clip a plain sheet of white paper over the face of the finished enlargement, put the sheets on an illuminator and trace the important features in ink.

Some workers draw directly on the print, then bleach the photographic image out, but it's difficult to see just what kind of a job you're doing; it involves a chemical bleaching operation—and if you make a mistake you must start all over again.

Here's a sample of what can be done. In this case both the drawing and photograph served as illustrations for an article on building a boat trailer.

From a photograph   . . . a working drawing

Intensification

Someday, despite your complete and masterful command of all the factors of exposure and development, you may find yourself faced with the problem of getting a good print from a negative which is, to be blunt about it, *too thin.* Even No. 5 paper cannot save you. What to do? Retake the picture if at all possible. But if you can't take it again, you may be able to save the situation by chemical treatment to intensify the faint image you have.

If the lack of density comes from underexposure, there's not much that can be done. On the other hand, if it is flat or thin from underdevelopment, "intensification" will probably help. Intensification, remember, is an antidote for underdevelopment only; for underexposure there's no real hope or help.

Every formulary lists several intensifiers. Familiarize yourself with one —then hold it in your bag of tricks as a last resort.

Reduction

If, through some misfortune, your negatives are too dense, the remedies are many and the results varied. The "reduction" of silver is accomplished in a physical sense—there is simply less of it when the process is complete. The word as used here should not be confused with the chemical reduction of exposed silver bromide during the original development.

According to results, reduction and reducers may be classified as follows:

1. *Subtractive* reducers take equal amounts of silver from all densities. They are used principally to correct for overexposure and fog.
2. *Proportional* reducers take from each density an amount proportional to that density. They correct for excessive contrast.
3. *Super-proportional* reducers are simply proportional reducers of an extreme potency for the treatment of extreme cases of high contrast.

Formulas for reducers are as abundant as those for intensifiers and, like intensifiers, belong in the "life saver" class.

Toning Experiment

Object:

To illustrate the range of color tones obtained with Azo, Kodabromide, Medalist, and Opal papers and two brown toners; one a sulfide toner, the other selenium.

Equipment:

Printing and enlarging facilities.

Procedure:

From a good quality negative make three matched prints on each of the above papers. Develop fully in the appropriate developers, fix and wash thoroughly.

For the sulfide tones, bleach one set of prints in the following solution until only very faint images remain.

    Potassium ferricyanide..40 grams
    Potassium bromide .....10 grams
    Water................1000 cc

Wash all of the above yellow solution from the prints and then redevelop the images in this:

    Sodium sulfide ....10 grams
    Water................1000 cc

Develop until the mottle and spottiness

have left the prints, usually about 30 seconds. Wash in running water for 30 minutes and dry.

The selenium toner contains some hard-to-find ingredients so it's best to buy it in prepared form. Kodak Rapid Selenium Toner need only be diluted with water for use. Immerse another set of prints in the diluted selenium toner for 3 minutes, wash 30 minutes and dry.

Mount the 3 prints on each paper on a display card or notebook sheet for study and comparison.

An expanded version of this project, including more papers and toners, will provide a ready reference in choosing just the right combination for special cases that arise.

Questions:

1. Which toner results in lighter prints? How much more than normal exposure must be used when prints are to be so toned?
2. Which combination would you prefer for portraits? For autumn scenes?
3. To which class of toners does this sulfide toner belong?

CHAPTER 20

Special Purpose Photography

MODERN PHOTOGRAPHY is as diverse as the interests and professions of men. It is the eye of the astronomer, in an almost literal sense; it is the guide and fact-finder for surgeons, dentists, and metallurgists; it is the scout and map-maker for armies—and the tool of cities in the administration of the present and in planning for the future. Photography, directly or indirectly, figures in the production of practically all advertising, as it does in all types of exposition. It is a growing medium for the illustration of fiction; it is basic in such matter-of-fact affairs as blueprints, Photostats, and bank records. The war-born Seventh Symphony of Shostakovich came overseas as a roll of film; and millions of soldier letters, each a tiny bit of film, have flown the seven seas. The development of new military aircraft has been immensely accelerated by the application of photography to the making of patterns and templates.

Photography, in some form or other, impinges on a far wider range of human activities than most of us realize. Obviously, the more we understand about it, and how it is used, the better we are equipped for our own special jobs.

It is, of course, quite impossible for the average amateur to equal the equipment—to say nothing of the hard-won experience—of the professional photographic specialist. It is, however, entirely possible for the amateur to undertake, for himself and on a limited scale, some forms of special-purpose photography. Indeed; the ability to carry out some of these photographic operations may make the difference between real distinction and mere competence in his chosen vocation or avocation.

The processes briefed here are those which are believed to be most useful to the average amateur in the extension of his photographic interests or as applied to his activities in any of scores of fields which may seem wholly unrelated to photography.

238

COPYING

To some, the most humdrum job in photography is that of making copies of drawings, paintings, or photographs. Yet there are experts who make good livings at it because they substitute imagination and skill for ordinary humdrum methods.

The basis setup for copying involves perfect symmetry. The camera is accurately centered on the material to be copied (the "copy") and the illumination is nicely balanced to provide smooth, glareless, shadowless lighting. The sketch shows the relationship between copy, camera, and lights. The strict centering of the camera on the copy and the precise paralleling of film and copy are not merely arbitrary rules; they are essential if the copying is to be free of distortion.

Because of variations in reflectors, it is a good idea to build up the lighting for each job methodically. Illuminate the copy with *one* of the lights as evenly as possible, retaining a 45° angle to the copy. Then turn that light off and repeat the process with the other one. Thus, when both are turned on, you can be sure of maximum uniformity. The technique of copying can be, and often is, thoroughly mechanized and automatic, for the goal of copying is seldom a "creative" photograph. It is, rather, the most slavish possible reproduction of something already created.

And that's why copying *is* humdrum, so long as it is concerned solely with black-and-white reproductions of clean black-and-white originals. But, let the copy be a painting, in water color or oil, let it be stained with 239

Perfect copying depends on accurate symmetry in setup and lighting

age or chemicals, faded, a page from a book which must be kept intact—let all these or a thousand other variations come along, and the humdrum business of copying becomes an art, worthy of and demanding a specialist in the selection of films and filters.

In all copying, whether it be simple or complex, accurate exposure is essential. In straight photography it is possible to fudge a bit, to exercise artistic license a little; but the result of your copying has to stand the acid test of direct comparison with the original. If your copy isn't extremely close to a true reproduction, it's a failure. Hence, exposure and development must be just as accurate as focus and lighting.

Copying Line Work

In copying drawings, wood cuts, music, blueprints, etc., your major concern is maximum contrast, to give strong, clean, black lines on white paper, crisp lettering, and so on. Eastman Contrast Process Ortho and Contrast Process Panchromatic Sheet Films are best for such work. Properly exposed and developed, they print easily and well on normal contrast paper. The recommended developers for these films produce high contrast because of their high hydroquinone content. Accurate exposure is a prerequisite to good copy work. Run a test exposure just to make certain your setup is perfectly arranged before attempting any mass copying.

Copies of blueprints benefit by the use of a red filter which, in conjunction with the process pan film, assures the reproduction of blue as black, with the white lines standing out clearly.

Filters, naturally, are also useful when you are dealing with other line work in color, if either the paper itself or the lines are colored. For example, to get a clear, sharp, black-and-white copy of a drawing or design involving blue, red, or black lines on green paper, you'd best use a green filter with the high-contrast pan film. The theory is to use a filter which transmits the color of the paper easily but does not transmit the color of the inked lines.

Copying Photographs

Under this head are included "continuous-tone" originals—such as wash drawings. Whereas all parts of the line copying process are designed to accentuate contrast, continuous-tone copying involves the use of moderate contrast methods all the way. A fine-grain film is indicated, with soft development. The color sensitivity of the film is unimportant.

Should rough surface texture or wrinkles in the original give you glinting reflections, experiment with a change in lighting angles, with diffusion frames over the lights or—if you are fortunate enough to have them—with Pola-Screens over both the lights and the camera lens.

Copying Color

The purpose of copying oil paintings, water colors, etc., is generally to achieve a black-and-white record. So, it's best to use a fine-grain, panchromatic film, with a filter to correct for the light used—a Wratten X1 (yellow green) for tungsten light and a K2 (light yellow) for daylight.

If you are interested in depicting texture, such as brush marks in painting or the weave of the cloth in a colored fabric, increase the light on one side or the other.

Naturally, the best copies of color are in color. The same general rules of balanced lighting apply. But make certain that the lamps are correct for the type of film used. You may expect to get excellent copies of water colors and oils. Experience indicates that there is usually a slight loss in saturation when copying most printing inks, and you may encounter occasional color changes in some unusual blues and greens.

With Ektachrome film you can check exposures in your own or a nearby processing lab; with Kodachrome make a series of exposures to bracket the one you feel is correct. If you do considerable copying you will soon establish your own standard setup and exposure conditions, and will be able to hit the right exposure almost automatically. This, of course, holds for black-and-white copying as well.

The technique of copying is no arbitrary thing; it must be flexible and adaptable despite its basic simplicity. The photographer with a sound understanding of color, films, and development will not find copying— or any other phase of photography—a bore.

Once more suggestion—not exactly photographic, but related. The law prohibits the copying of stamps, money, bonds, citizenship papers, and other Governmental documents, but for a few exceptions such as:

1. The copying of coins for the purpose of illustration in numismatic, historical, and educational publications.
2. The copying of foreign postage stamps for the purpose of illustrating philatelic or historical publications, provided the illustrations are in black and white only, are so defaced as to indicate that they can not be adapted for use as stamps, and are at least four times as large as the

original.

3. The copying, in black and white only, of United States stamps for the purpose of illustrating philatelic publications, provided the illustrations are either less than three-quarters or more than one and one-half times the size of the original.

In the interests of "safety first," get written permission from the copyright owner before copying any copyrighted material.

Making Black-and-White Slides for Projection

Whether you are a teacher, lecturer, salesman, photographer, or just interested in something, you will probably want to tell your story in slides. Chances are that you will have prints or book illustrations as your originals. Even if you have negatives, you may find it easier to work from prints, good ones that is.

Strangely enough the most practical way to make black-and-white slides from black-and-white prints is by the use of Kodachrome Film, Type A. No darkroom work is required and the quality is excellent. If you count your time as worth anything, the cost of producing slides this way is actually lower than it is by other methods.

The most appropriate equipment for the job is a miniature film adapter back on a bellows camera, such as an adapter on an enlarger head, or a miniature camera with a copying attachment. All of these setups make it simple to focus and frame accurately.

You must light the original for copying, as shown on page 239. Use photographic flood lamps, as they have the required color of light. If you have two RFL 2 lamps at 45° to the camera axis and 30 inches from the center of the subject, the exposure time will be about 1/25 second at $f/5.6$ or equivalent, preferably at a smaller aperture.

If the long dimension of the picture you are copying is shorter than about 12 inches, your camera bellows will be extended enough to change the effective aperture of the camera lens, regardless of its focal length. You must correct for this, or the slide will be underexposed.

To allow for the loss in aperture, open your lens diaphragm in accordance with the long side of the area being copied thus:

Long side	12 inches	6	3½	2½	2	1½
Lens opening wider by	⅓ stop	⅔	1	1⅓	1⅔	2

This correction applies only to focusing by extending the lens. If you use Portra Lenses, with little or no lens extension, no correction is needed.

If you need the older size of slide, that is 3¼ x 4 inches, then you can print from negatives on lantern-slide plates which are meant for the purpose. After processing you add a picture mask, cover glass, then bind the whole thing.

There are loads of other ways of making slides starting from either negatives or prints. If you have a special problem, consult the Kodak Data Book, "Slides," published by Eastman Kodak Company.

Good slides, properly presented, steal the show on any lecture, educational, or entertainment program. Better be prepared.

PHOTOGRAPHY BY POLARIZED LIGHT

Also falling under the general heading of "Special Purpose Photography," is the use of polarized light in making pictures.

Normal light rays consist of waves—waves vibrating in all planes and at right angles to the direction of travel. Light, which has, by nature or by optical means, been reduced to vibrations only in one plane is said to be *polarized*. To our eyes, polarized light looks quite like any other kind, but photographed through a Pola-Screen, there's all the difference in the world.

Nature Polarizes Light

1. Light coming from a clear blue sky at an angle of 90° from the sun is polarized. If the sun is directly overhead, light from the sky near the horizon in any direction is polarized. When the sun is low in the west, light from an arc from the northern horizon extending overhead and to the southern horizon is polarized. In all cases only a *clear sky* favors polarization.
2. Light reflected from non-metallic surfaces at an angle of from 32 degrees to 37 degrees is polarized. This includes reflections at those angles from pavement, store windows, the enamelled parts of automobiles, polished table tops, etc.

All other light which vibrates in all directions is said to be unpolarized. Light can be optically polarized, too, for photographic purposes by passing it through a filter-like Pola-Screen. A Pola-Screen is made by laminating Polaroid sheeting between two pieces of thin glass. It may be regarded as an optical picket fence. As light passes through the "pickets," all but one direction of vibration is eliminated.

In most cases, Pola-Screens are used over the lens, as filters are. When "crossed" with the rays of light already polarized by nature, the light is withheld and just doesn't get through to the film.

Uses for Pola-Screens

1. In making a landscape which includes sky light coming from an angle of 90° to the sun. The sky will reproduce darker, for the light coming from it is polarized and can be cut out by the Pola-Screen. The color balance of the remainder of the picture will not be disturbed. In fact, the use of a Pola-Screen is the only way you can get darker than usual blue skies and accentuated sky-cloud contrast in color photography.

2. When photographing store windows during the daytime, reflections from buildings across the street may obscure detail from within the window. If the camera is placed so that the reflection seen is a "35° angle" reflection, and a Pola-Screen placed over the lens in a position to cut out the naturally polarized reflection, full detail beyond the glass is photographed.

3. You can eliminate glaring surface reflections which visually and photographically obscure surface detail, such as those from the top of a highly polished table. Get your camera into a position so the reflection

Troublesome reflections . . . eliminated by a Pola-Screen

244

rays are polarized; then cut them out with a Pola-Screen.

Obviously, Pola-Screens eliminate a considerable portion of the light waves, since they pass only those vibrating in one general direction. Thus when a Pola-Screen is used over the lens, filter-fashion, it has a factor of from 2 to 4 times, depending upon the particular type used.

Pola-Screens are supplied in larger sizes for use over studio lights. With them, the commercial photographer can avoid objectionable surface reflections by polarizing his light at the source, and controlling it with another Pola-Screen over the lens.

While Pola-Screens cost more than conventional filters, and their uses are special and limited, there are pictures that simply cannot be made any other way. If your picture making necessitates such photographs, a Pola-Screen will be a real investment.

STILL LIFE AND TABLE TOPPERY

Many of us get our first intimations of special purpose photography from our experience with some sort of still life photography. The important factors are all there—a picture idea, props to pose and arrange, and lighting problems to be solved.

"Still life" photography is, in a sense, a misnomer. For it is the function of the photographer to make his subject—no matter how "still"—come alive. It must, to succeed, have pictorial vitality and interest.

The necessary equipment need not be elaborate. A simple camera, a camera support, and a few lights can, if necessary, achieve considerable still life success. But you're far better off if you have a camera which permits (1) accurate viewing and focusing on a ground-glass screen, without worry about parallax and, (2) close-up focus. A small view camera is ideal for this type of work; lacking one, be sure you make the proper allowances for parallax and equip yourself with an accessory lens of the Portra type.

The professional's aim, in still life work, is generally to produce the most attractive possible "portrait" of his subject, a portrait which, when reproduced in an advertisement, will arouse the acquisitive instincts of prospective purchasers. But the still life shots that most non-professionals make are "idea" pictures—pictures made with the purpose of revealing some combination of lines, curves, masses, and tones that the photographer finds interesting or exciting. Both the pro' and the amateur use much the same means to produce their slightly different ends. Both need a table or bench or stand on which to pose their subjects. Both need a variety of lights—floods, spots, back lights, and so on. And both need to be able to improvise backgrounds, supports, props, reflectors, and light shields.

Still life can be anything from a piano to a pill box. And it remains still life unless and until it includes a living figure. When a person or an animal

Still lifes and table tops take thought and skill, but they can be rewarding

246

is included, the basic problems change and, with them, some of the techniques. But there is no basic technical change involved when still life photography becomes the picturing of miniature models, toys, dolls, and other small scale objects. There is a change, but it is a subtle one.

Merely to place a doll on a table and to photograph it there is not "table-top" photography. The important thing is *an idea*. Let the doll assume any specific pose, so that the resulting picture conveys a bit of a story—then you have table toppery.

Because this kind of picture making usually involves miniatures—dolls, tin soldiers, toy cars, houses, etc.—the matter of scale or proportion has to be watched carefully. Some degree of grotesquery is, of course, permissible; but it is dangerous, for it can turn whimsy into whamsy—and whamsy is another word for failure.

Within photography's admitted limitations, table toppery offers a tremendous field for creative work. Some of the finest battle scenes ever published were table top shots, involving tiny models of ships, planes, and a few square yards of fabric "ocean." They were not only vivid but, because they had been carefully prepared on the basis of known naval data, they were given just about as much space as would have been accorded actual aerial views of the same action—if such views had been obtainable. Into the making of these pictures went much more than photographic ability; the tactics of naval warfare had to be known, and interpreted with imagination. Boners in such matters cannot lightly be laughed off.

As you experiment with table top pictures you will soon discover that they have outgrown their name. For a table top, as such, may never be used; you may find yourself making an "aerial" view of something on the floor, or shooting a model plane, suspended in space.

Because you're dealing, usually, with inanimate and "stable" objects, you seldom need short exposures; hence brilliant lighting is not required. Even ordinary domestic electric lights, in reflectors, in improvised "spots," or in baffles can be used successfully. Of course, should you be picturing materials which wilt or droop—cut flowers, for example—over-long exposures have to be avoided.

For backgrounds you can use enlargements, tapestries, framed pictures, or anything of the sort that is appropriate.

In short, the only limits on table toppery are those of your imagination, inventive ability, and good taste.

ARCHITECTURAL PHOTOGRAPHY

Architectural work is related more closely to outdoor portraiture than to any other kind of photography. It's a matter of selecting the most interestesting, most flattering angles. Sun angles have to be watched and the best one used. Cross lighting and extended shadows show shape and give the feeling of depth. Distortion has to be eliminated or used deliberately to achieve a dramatic effect. Sometimes the photographer must work under cramped conditions; for example, he may have to picture a tall building from an "across the street" vantage point. Therefore, he must know his wide-angle lenses. At other times, he may have to record a detail far up on the facade; long-focus lenses are then clearly in order.

For architectural photography a view camera, with a full complement of swings and distortion rectifiers is needed. Ground glass focusing and composing are essential. Small apertures are needed to assure maximum depth of field; so exposure times will probably be long. In view of all these, a tripod camera support is important. (Notice the series of architectural photos on the opposite page.) Architectural photographers are very keen about dark sky backgrounds which make buildings stand out in bold, shining relief. Hence, many of such pictures are heavily filtered. Sometimes, even so, the sky remains uninteresting; the resourceful photographer then "prints in" a suitable sky, using one of the several sky-and-cloud negatives he keeps on file expressly for such a purpose.

SCHOOL AND CLUB PHOTOGRAPHY

There are the hundreds of informal pictures needed for every high school and college yearbook. These include such matters as pep meetings, campus "atmosphere" shots, graduation sidelights, etc. Those who make such pictures must be equipped to work under conditions which parallel those encountered by press photographers. They need not merely cameras, flashguns, and such, but they must have the skill and timing and poise needed to take in their stride a basketball game in the afternoon and a P.T.A. meeting in the evening. Gathering informal photographs for a yearbook can be valuable training if it is undertaken seriously. Many a first-rate photographic career has started on the campus.

Garden Clubs

All such groups appreciate photographs taken to record the picture story of a season's achievements. Here, of course, the emphasis falls on color-

248

Successful architectural photography is nine-tenths
point-of-view—with a sense of significant details and
angles and the photographic "know how" taken for granted

color in terms of Kodachrome transparencies which can be shown by projection at club meetings or, perhaps, in terms of Kodacolor Prints that can be passed around for individual inspection.

The technique of flower photography is specialized; in the photographic journals are many articles dealing with its various phases. The major considerations, you will find, are (a) diffuse lighting, to minimize harsh, black shadows and (b) various means by which single flowers or plants can be isolated from confusing or distracting surroundings. A word of warning —don't use half-way measures on flowers. Either make clean-cut recognizable close-ups or show the whole garden. Midway shots tend to be confusing.

PHOTOGRAPHY CAN'T DO EVERYTHING

One of the natural temptations of the enthusiastic amateur is to assume that photography can do anything that any other form of graphic art can do. Photographs are made which try to be etchings, paintings, posters, cartoons, or low-relief sculpture. Sometimes they succeed. But photography is at its best when it is being frankly itself.

The field in which photography has the greatest difficulty is humor— the natural province of the cartoon. For photography and humor do not mix naturally. Photography is realistic; humor is not.

Cameras, of course, can record cuteness, the pranks of youngsters, and animals, or situations which evoke a chuckle. But, a photograph is bound to reality by the literalness of the camera; it is extremely difficult for it to achieve the unfettered freedom of a cartoon. Our leading magazines of humor recognize this fact. There is nothing to worry about in this situation. Photography is an upstanding, tremendously capable and vivid medium; the fact that it has limitations only endears it to its devotees.

Table-Top Lighting Experiment

Object:
To illustrate the three basic lighting effects (front, back, and side lighting) on objects that are spherical and cubical.

Equipment:
A camera capable of making close-ups, a Photoflood lamp in a reflector and a sheet of white cardboard.

Procedure:
Place some single-colored ball, such as a tennis ball, in front of your camera on a table. The camera-to-subject distance should be adjusted so the image nearly fills the available film area.

Make four pictures, one each with the light in these positions:

A. *As close to the camera as possible,* illuminating the ball from the *front.*

B. *Behind the ball.* The light should be raised or lowered slightly so as not to shine directly into the lens.

C. *At one side,* shining at right angles to the direction in which the camera is pointed.

D. *As in C,* but with a white card held in a position to reflect some light onto the shadow side of the ball, plus the back light.

Repeat the exposures and lightings using a square box and cylinder as the subjects. The accompanying illustrations should give you some ideas.

If the light from the Photoflood bulb is too bright, the intensity can be cut down by arranging two cardboard masks in front of the light.

Mount the finished prints as a permanent record. Try variations of these lightings and notice the great number of effects obtainable.

251

Front light	Back light	Side light	Side and back lights, plus reflector

CHAPTER 21

Now That They're Finished

MILLIONS of snapshots are stowed forlornly away in curling packs in desk and dresser drawers. Hundreds of thousands of enlargements, mounted and unmounted, lie forgotten in dusty envelopes. And the negatives for all these prints are enduring the same or even a more dismal fate.

Like many another example of mass inertia, this situation affords a background against which any reasonably alert individual can rise and shine.

It is assumed that you are such a person. Very well, what do *you* do with *your* negatives and prints?

File Your Negatives

Prints can be replaced almost anytime; most negatives cannot. A system will make the location of negatives easy; obviously you will be more likely to get full benefit from your printing sessions if your negatives are readily and definitely at hand.

A file of some sort is indicated—a file in which negatives are (a) protected from dust and moisture and (b) arranged in some sort of useful classification. There is a variety of ready-made negative file systems on the market. Kodak Negative Albums are made in several sizes and afford excellent protection as well as easy accessibility. If you prefer to make a file of your own, you'll discover few difficulties—beyond the temptation to make it too elaborate.

Negatives should be filed individually in paper envelopes, on which pertinent data are recorded. Some photographers paste a contact print on the outside of the envelope to identify the negative within; such a system, while explicit, increases the bulk of the file considerably.

The classifying of the negatives will vary with the kind of photographic work you do. Anyone specializing in portraits, for example, will classify his negatives according to the names of his subjects; a traveler will use place names as the basis for his file; others, with diverse subjects to classify, will make some such alphabetical arrangement as this:

Animals	Gardens	Scenics
Architecture	Greeting Cards	School
Aviation	The House	Sports
Babies	Night Scenes	Table Toppery
Children	Portraits	Vacations (by year)

The important thing, of course, is not the filing system nor its details, but the fact that your negatives are all in one place, protected yet accessible.

If your file box is metal, so much the better; for films—like other valuables—deserve fire safety as well as protection from dust, excessive moisture, and handling. Given reasonable care, your negatives will last indefinitely.

Give Prints a Chance

And what about prints? There's no need for embarrassment even if all you do with a finished picture is to sit back and ponder it, comparing it with your memory of the original scene or with your hopes for the ultimate result. If this calm consideration is even faintly critical, it is well worth-while; for we can be our own best teachers.

If the picture is reasonably satisfactory, what do you do with it? Tack it up on the darkroom wall? Take it upstairs to show to the family? Enter it in a contest or exhibition? Send it to Uncle Bertram? Or what?

Undoubtedly the simplest, and one of the best means of getting enduring pleasure from a picture is by incorporating it in an album. Remember the stuffy, old-style album—the bulky, unattractive, pointless affair, with its clumsily mounted prints and its scratchy white ink captions? If so, forget it.

The modern photograph album has as much relation to the old-timers as the latest issue of a modern illustrated weekly has to a 1915 mail order catalog. The new album definitely is not a catch-all—or a "miscellaneous department."

In place of bigness, the new album emphasizes compactness. Instead of one or two big, bulky books, the modern picture collector maintains a number of smaller volumes, uniform in size and appearance but with relatively few pages. Each book is devoted to a specific subject—such as

253

any year's vacation, a trip, the building of the house, military or civilian defense duties, "Junior," "The Kids," the garden, family hobbies—and so on and on. Everyone, of course, compiles his own kind of album library. Enlargements are intermingled with contact prints or small projection prints from miniature negatives. Each double-spread of album pages is "laid out" or planned so that the best pictures have a chance and so that the total effect of all the pictures will be right.

The opportunities for individualism in a series of such albums are great; still, "cleverness" isn't at all necessary. If the pictures are logically, neatly presented, you can get along nicely without being clever in a self-conscious sort of way. You'll find that your friends are much impressed with your ship-shape collection; approbation of that sort is extremely easy and pleasant to take.

Some of your albums may be made up wholly of enlargements. The enlargements themselves, mounted back-to-back, will comprise the actual pages, and reinforced double-weight prints, can be the covers. If you use Kodak Dry Mounting Tissue, you can be sure of a permanent, non-cockling bond. Spiral wire bindings or the colorful and practical plastic bindings can be obtained from most modern printers or binderies. The cost, you'll find, is very reasonable.

To neglect contact prints entirely, in favor of big, impressive, enlargements is not sound sense or sound economy. Remember that change of pace, the shifting from slow to fast, from large to small, from whispering to shouting, is one of the most reliable tools of showmanship. So do not scorn small prints — and by small we mean prints down to some such dimension as 2 x 2 inches. Prints smaller than that are hard to see and to understand.

254   Contact prints, of course, have uses outside the covers of the albums.

Specialized albums are fun—and satisfying   **Photo-announcements, for a refreshing change**

They can be properly matted, mounted and framed to make attractive miniatures for use on desks or dressers. They can also be made especially for use as:

Book plates	Mosaic patterns for serving trays,
Place cards	screens, etc.
Greeting cards	Book marks
Birth announcements	Calendar decorations
Party invitations	Change-of-address announcements

This is, obviously, a sketchy listing. You will discover other uses; every new one will suggest others. Hence no such list can ever be complete.

All such quantity-production enterprises have much in common; the basic essential of each of them is a bright idea; and they all wind up as modified production line jobs in which your family or your friends can join.

Christmas Cards

Doubtless the most generally appealing of these contact specialties is the photographic Christmas card. Its appeal lies partly in the fact that it is photographic, but principally in its inescapable individuality. Because it utilizes a picture of your family, your house, or simply an appropriate picture taken by yourself, it is bound to be unlike any other. For better or worse, it bespeaks *you*. Under the circumstances, a good job, a job which does you credit, is in order.

Here are a few suggestions. Although they pertain to Christmas cards, the principles involved can be applied to most of the other specialities.

1. Start early to concoct your idea. If you wait until the Christmas rush is on, you'll be working against time and really good things are seldom produced in a panic. Work out your idea early in November and get it into production right away. If complications arise, you will then have time to work them out.

2. The simpler ideas are frequently the best. Remember, the purpose of your greeting card is not to display your cleverness; it is to convey a sincere and timely greeting to your friends. Your finished greeting may be a simple contact print mounted on a white card bearing a handwritten message, or it may be multiple-negative, French-fold creation. The important thing is to visualize its ultimate effect. Will it produce a spontaneous, "Hey, here's Bill's card! Just like him, too!" or something less

255

cheerful, such as, "Well, well, Bill must have worked nights for a month to produce this."

You may find that existing negatives will work out well for your greeting. Possibly some shots you made last Christmas of the house in its holiday dress, of the Christmas tree, or of the kids about the fireplace will work out nicely. Or you may want to create something brand new, especially appropriate for this year. Once you have the basic idea, it's up to you to decide how it is to be presented—as a straight photograph, with or without special "props," as a silhouette, as a table-top creation, as a multiple exposure, as a combination of photography and line copy, or in any other manner that appeals to you. But the total effect must be appropriate. In a sense, your greeting card must be like a good advertisement. It must "sell" your message, neatly and convincingly.

3. If yours is a family greeting, enlist the help of the family in producing it, not merely in making the original pictures, but in printing and finishing the cards. Once you have the darkroom procedure established, with correct exposure and development times, set up a production line so that your total output of cards can be printed quickly and well. One person is at the printer, another does the developing, another takes care of the rinsing and fixing, while still another supervises the final washing and drying. Some such organization will not only produce results but, more importantly, it will give the entire family a sense of participation in the finished products.

Later on, if you feel inspired to make photographic book plates or any other specialty involving considerable quantities, you will be able to count on a "gang" procedure that will be effective as well as fun.

256

Two examples of photographic greeting cards

Whee! MERRY CHRISTMAS
From the Hendricks Family
HOWARD, JR. - LORRAINE - HOWARD, SR.

A Full house of Boltes sends Christmas Greetings

Through the years the photographic magazines have been telling and re-telling the story of how to make all sorts of photographic novelties. In most cases, you'll need no help, but there's no harm in seeing how others have proceeded; hence it is suggested that you keep in touch with what others are doing through one or more of the photographic journals.

Enlargements at Work

A "wasted" enlargement is a waste indeed; the time, money, skill, and hope involved certainly justify some use beyond the confines of the darkroom.

The most obvious of uses, of course, is as a framed picture for the wall of some room. Very fine indeed—but be careful. There's an art to the matting, mounting, and framing of a picture; if it is well done, the picture benefits; but if it is done clumsily or without regard for the decorative style of the room where it is to be hung—well, it might better not be done at all.

Kodacolor enlargements made from either Kodacolor or Kodachrome originals, mounted and framed, will add infinitely to the decoration of your home; too, they add a personal touch that is attractive and satisfying. Pictorial shots of your hobby or your family interests again fill the bill. Hunting, fishing, sailing, gardening, skiing—these and many others provide magnificent opportunities for color photographs which can ultimately mean much to your home's decoration.

There is, obviously, a limit to the number of walls on which one is free to hang enlargements. But enlargements have multiple uses. Their use in books has already been mentioned; here are a few other possibilities:

Lamp shades	Screens	Backgrounds for
Book covers	Cut-out statuettes	table-top pictures

And, of course, if you go in for enlarging in a really big way, there's the specialized enlargement known as the photomural. Because of its size and because of the necessity of harmonizing it with existing decorative schemes, there are few amateurs who are tempted to play with murals.

There is, however, one very practical variation of the photomural theme. It consists of a band of adjoining photographs, perhaps 20 inches high, running in series. Suppose, for example, you have a recreation room to be so decorated, and you'd like to use the candid pictures you've taken of your best friends over a period of years.

257

Photomurals don't need to be big and costly. A panel of enlargements can achieve a true mural effect

Enlarge all your negatives to the same size, in this case 20 inches high and 16 inches wide. Dry mount them on heavy cardboard or Masonite and trim uniformly. The pressed wood board is best, for it won't buckle or curl with normal changes in temperature and humidity. Frame the entire series as a unit, using strips of molding appropriate to your room, and there's your "mural."

Series of pictures of a hobby, such as model airplane building, skeet shooting, hunting, or any sport, will be ideal for your recreation room, while pictorial series are better suited for mural type decoration in your living room or front hallway.

Enlargements make excellent gifts too, but they can be embarrassing. Consider the sad case of the astonished gentleman to whom a friend sent two dozen 11 x 14 enlargements mounted on 16 x 20 cards. Beyond building a special gallery wherein to exhibit them, there was nothing whatever to do with them. Be discreet about your giving. A little is much better than too much.

An important use for enlargements is offered in the exhibits or salons of camera clubs. Competition is the life blood of photography to many; if you feel that you do your best work under the urge of competition, by all means join a camera club. Your association with others with similar interests is stimulating and certain to increase your photographic knowledge.

Mountings for Enlargements

Wherever or whenever enlargements are displayed, they should be suitably mounted. "Suitably" is, of course, another relative word; it is all things to all people. But, usually a simple mount serves best because it does not detract from the picture it bears. The simplest mount is a sheet of mounting board somewhat larger than the print, which is placed thereon so that top and side margins are equal and the lower margin a little greater. A neat black line is drawn around the print—and there you are. In general, the mount should be about half again as large as the print; thus an 8 x 10 print displays well on a 12 x 15 mount and an 11 x 14 looks right on a 16 x 20 board.

Variations on the simple mount include intermediate layers of black or toned paper between the print and the mount. These underlays show as bands around the print and tend to project the picture toward the observer. Another variant attains exactly the reverse effect, that of presenting the picture as seen through an opening or window. This is achieved through the use of a cut-out overlay.

THIS, THEN, IS PHOTOGRAPHY

If, perchance, you have been reading between the lines, you will have sensed the fact that the title of this book, despite its good intentions, is somewhat ambitious. No one book, no matter how inclusive and fact-laden, can hope to embrace all of photography.

For photography is one thing to you—and a totally different thing to your next door neighbor. It is a hobby, a science, a craft, an art, a tool, a casual pastime, or a basic interest—the sort of thing to which you respond, spontaneously, in some such gladsome terms as, "That's for me!"

As a career, photography is exactly like riveting, black-smithing, dancing, music, cost-accounting, preaching, or running a lathe. If you're good at it—really good—it is an ideal vocation. It is not an easy profession, nor does it often lead to great wealth. But a good photographer can carve out a reasonably happy, prosperous life.

What does it take? It depends, naturally, on whether you plan to run a commercial studio, a portrait studio, or an assignment job. But, fundamentally, the requirements are:

1. A sound, basic understanding of photography. Books such as this can help in gaining such an understanding, but actual practical training is

vital. Courses in photography are given in some schools; and intensive training is offered by specialized schools of photography. In photography, as in music or any other field of high skill, theory is important only if it is supplemented by lots of practice.

2. A background of artistic appreciation and, best of all, artistic achievement. A sculptor or painter is not automatically a good photographer, but a photographer who knows something of sculpture and painting has a real advantage.

3. An understanding of the simpler electrical hook-ups.

4. A handy-man's knack of improvising "props" or special studio equipment. There's a lot of Rube Goldberg carpentry back of some of the best pictures.

5. A willingness to get your hands dirty and to live on a slightly erratic schedule. If someone needs to get a picture to the engraver tomorrow morning, the photographer on the job must pass up dinner, the movies, bridge, or even sleep to get that picture out.

6. Adaptability to changing methods and styles in pictures. For photography is not static; it progresses—and progresses, sometimes, with bewildering speed.

7. Finally, a sound sense of business is handy. Competition is stiff and the photographer who expects to eat regularly must operate on a strictly business basis.

It All Depends On You

Photography may be, for you, only a casual pastime. Or it may be a hobby. Or it may be an important adjunct to your hobby. Or it may be the thing on which you focus your whole active life.

Whatever it may be, photography has in it the capacity to produce satisfactions far more deep and real than you may now suspect. But to discover and to realize those satisfactions, you have to do your part. You have to know what you want to do, and how to do it. For satisfaction is never an accident.

Back of every good picture is an idea; and back of every picture idea is an eye that sees and understands. So here we are, back where we started, with our theme song—you are the most important part of any camera you will ever own.